The Compassion-Based Workbook for Christian Clients

The Compassion-Based Workbook for Christian Clients integrates contemporary research in clinical psychology on compassion-based approaches to shame with a Christian worldview, offering a wide variety of strategies for Christians to better understand and combat shame and negative self-judgments. Chapters lay out a four-step process to help clients let go of unhelpful thinking patterns that lead to shame, experience God's compassion on a deeper level, and extend this compassion to themselves and others. Readers will find a wealth of Christian-sensitive experiential exercises, journaling assignments, biblical examples, and case examples throughout the workbook. Audio recordings for several guided meditations are also provided to help Christians practice the strategies offered in the workbook.

Joshua J. Knabb, PsyD, ABPP, is director of the Doctor of Psychology (PsyD) in Clinical Psychology Program and associate professor of psychology in the College of Behavioral and Social Sciences at California Baptist University. He is also author/coauthor of three previous books for Christian clients: *Contemplative Prayer for Christians with Chronic Worry* (with Thomas Frederick), *Acceptance and Commitment Therapy for Christian Clients*, and *Faith-Based ACT for Christian Clients.*

I0894593

The Compassion-Based Workbook for Christian Clients

Finding Freedom from Shame and Negative Self-Judgments

Joshua J. Knabb

Routledge
Taylor & Francis Group
NEW YORK AND LONDON

First published 2019
by Routledge
711 Third Avenue, New York, NY 10017

and by Routledge
2 Park Square, Milton Park, Abingdon, Oxon, OX14 4RN

Routledge is an imprint of the Taylor & Francis Group, an informa business

Library of Congress Cataloging-in-Publication Data
Names: Knabb, Joshua J., author.
Title: The compassion-based workbook for Christian clients: finding freedom from shame and negative self-judgments / Joshua J. Knabb.
Description: First edition. | New York, NY: Routledge, 2019. | Includes bibliographical references and index.
Identifiers: LCCN 2018022564| ISBN 9780815394358 (hardcover) | ISBN 9780815394365 (pbk.) | ISBN 9781351123549 (e-book)
Subjects: LCSH: Compassion–Religious aspects–Christianity–Textbooks. | Self-esteem–Religious aspects–Christianity–Textbooks. | Shame–Religious aspects–Christianity–Textbooks. | Psychotherapy patients–Religious life–Textbooks.
Classification: LCC BV4647.S9 K53 2019 | DDC 241/.4–dc23
LC record available at https://lccn.loc.gov/2018022564

ISBN: 978-0-8153-9435-8 (hbk)
ISBN: 978-0-8153-9436-5 (pbk)
ISBN: 978-1-351-12354-9 (ebk)

Typeset in ITC Stone Serif
by Sunrise Setting Ltd., Brixham, UK

Visit the eResources: www.routledge.com/9780815394365

Dedication

This workbook is dedicated to my compassionate wife, Adrienne, who welcomes me home with outstretched arms whenever I wander too far away.

Contents

Foreword

It is indeed an honor to write a foreword for this important, groundbreaking book. It offers Christian readers access to the latest scientific understanding of compassion and provides an intimate look into the "why" and "how" of compassion training contained in Christian Scripture and practice. I was moved by the author's devotional attitude, scholarship, and his commitment to alleviating the pain of shame and self-criticism in his clients. With a crystal-clear writing style and refreshing candor about his sources and intentions, Joshua Knabb shows Christian clients and their therapists how to tap the transformative power of compassion through an in-depth exploration of their own mental and emotional habits in the context of Christian values and beliefs.

Compassion can be inner or outer—directed toward oneself or others. When compassion is in full bloom, it's omnidirectional. Unfortunately, most people tend to exclude themselves from the circle of their compassion, believing that it is selfish or sinful to give themselves compassion, too. This tendency comes at a price. One look at the science of self-compassion shows that common misgivings about self-compassion—such as the concern that it is associated with selfishness, narcissism, self-pity, weakness, low motivation, or self-indulgence—are actually mis*conceptions*. Burgeoning research demonstrates that self-compassion is strongly associated with mental and physical health and well-being, emotional strength and resilience, lower levels of anxiety and depression, enhanced motivation to achieve, healthy habits such and diet and exercise, compassion for others, and more satisfying personal relationships.

So how do we come by the idea that we should love ourselves *less* than our neighbor? Are we less worthy? Will it lead to arrogance and pride? The research suggests otherwise, but our beliefs are sticky, probably based on cultural messages we have received most of our lives. Therefore, we need *permission* to include ourselves in the circle of our compassion. For Christians, the permission comes from Scripture—from the unconditional love of God.

Unfortunately, our capacity to see God as unconditionally loving is tainted by our personal relationship history. For example, if a person had a distant or anxious relationship with his or her own father, that experience would impact how close and safe the person feels with a heavenly father. If we felt loved and accepted as children, even when we made mistakes, we are more likely to expect the same from God. Our image of God is partially shaped by our personal history, and our sense of worthiness and capacity for self-compassion is reciprocally impacted by our image of God.

Joshua Knabb also makes the important distinction between the God *concept*—a compassionate God as described in Christian Scripture—and our *image* of God, mediated by how we were treated by others, especially during childhood. The bulk of this book is about reducing the gap between our God image and our God concept by examining the patterns of attachment we had toward caregivers, and then creating a new, secure base in God as the source of compassion and contentment. The fruit of this journey—and this book is a faithful companion on that journey—is learning to gently love ourselves as God loves us and then loving *others* because we feel safe and precious in the eyes of God. Self-compassion is the process by which we internalize the love of God.

Learning to love ourselves as God loves us is the shift from insecure to secure attachment to God. However, a major obstacle to secure attachment is shame, especially the debilitating sort of shame that drives us to self-criticism, makes us want to isolate ourselves, triggers useless rumination, and generally dismantles our sense of self and makes it difficult to function. This type of shame has many sources, often based on how we were treated as children (i.e., criticism, abuse, or neglect), cultural prejudice, and sometimes even genetics. As such, shame is not necessarily our fault, but it is our responsibility to do something about it.

There is also a healthier form of shame that inspires us to stop harming others and to become a better person. This kind of shame can be a reminder of our distance from God. As Joshua Knabb points out, shame has a unique role in Christian Scripture, beginning with the Adam and Eve story. Although God cast Adam and Eve out of the Garden of Eden because of their disobedience, God was also compassionate and clothed Adam and Eve. The grand narrative of Jesus' life is about reconciling humanity with this compassionate God. The author eloquently describes God's compassion as the "glue" that holds our broken pieces together and also spans the gap between humankind and God. The promise, "I will be with you," is the Christian antidote to shame.

It requires conscientious effort to move from insecure attachment based on shame, or separateness from God, to feeling safely enveloped in God's love. This skills-based workbook is a valuable guide along the way. The author begins by helping readers to identify destructive patterns of thought and feeling that lead to shame. He then invites readers to practice a variety of *apophatic* (wordless and imageless) and *kataphatic* (relying on words or images) Christian meditations that focus attention on God's benevolence, as well as offering his own Christian-sensitive adaptations of mind training practices from scientific psychology. The author brilliantly applies our modern understanding of the "contentment" and "danger" subsystems of the nervous system to help readers learn to feel safe in the presence of God. After learning to focus on the care, contentment, and compassion of God, then the healing practice of self-compassion can flow more easily and lead to genuine safety and trust, even to an attitude of surrender.

For better or worse, secular, evidence-based psychotherapy is the primary form of therapy taught today in universities and clinical training centers, and mindfulness-, acceptance- and compassion-based therapy is the leading edge of that approach. The author has delved deeply into this approach, discovered key principles already present in Christian sources, and integrated them seamlessly into the therapeutic endeavor. Even secular psychotherapists will find important insights in this book to help them support their Christian clients on the path to emotional wholeness and freedom. It was a joy to read this book and I hope it finds its way into the hands of anyone who wants to cast off the burden of shame and rest safely in the love of God. It is hard to imagine a journey more important than that.

Christopher Germer, PhD
Lecturer (part-time), Harvard Medical School
Author, *The Mindful Path to Self-Compassion*
Co-developer, the *Mindful Self-Compassion* program

Acknowledgments

To begin, I would like to thank God, the author of compassion, who perfectly displayed his mercy, grace, forgiveness, and love by providing a clear, illuminated path for traveling home. Also, thanks to my wife, Adrienne, and two children, Emory and Rowan, who regularly teach me that compassion is often the much-needed antidote for the ups and downs of life. In addition, thanks to Anna Moore at Routledge, who supported this project and helped to bring it to print. Furthermore, I appreciate the reviewers—William Hathaway and an anonymous reviewer—who helped me to strengthen the workbook with their thoughtful comments. Finally, I want to gratefully acknowledge Christopher Germer, a leading expert on the psychological benefits of compassion, who generously wrote the foreword and has engaged with me in a fruitful dialogue on secular and Christian approaches to compassion.

Introduction

"Man is born broken. He lives by mending. The grace of God is glue."

Eugene O'Neill (quoted in Dowling, 2009, p. 198)

Introduction[1]

Imagine you just bought a beautiful, expensive vase at your favorite store in town. This vase, which you have wanted for quite some time, will be the fanciest decoration in your house. As you drive home, you are excited to prominently display it on a table near the front window that looks out onto your street. Walking in the front door, you quickly set the newly purchased item in the location you have carefully selected. Yet, as you do so, the vase tragically falls to the ground, shattering into a dozen pieces. Devastated, you stand over the destroyed object, experiencing a range of painful emotions as you process what has just happened.

Struggling with a wide variety of feelings, you first accept the reality of the vase's fragmented state. Next, you realize a brand-new bottle of glue is close by in a kitchen drawer. Because you value the vase so much, you proceed to get the glue and put it back together. Slowly and steadily, you assemble the jagged clay pieces, gaining confidence, piece by piece, that the adhesive is working. After an extended period of carefully placing together each broken shard, you realize you have restored the vase to its prior form, although by no means resembling its original, pristine mint condition. Still, as the vase sits on the front table of your home, you experience a sense of gratitude, recognizing you can still enjoy its beauty, as the glue steadily holds together the chips of clay.

Like the introduction quote reveals, Christians believe that humans are born in a shattered condition, and struggle with our enduring brokenness (Psalm 51:5; Romans 3:23). Still, a mending process is available, in that God offers us his love, compassion, mercy, grace, and forgiveness within each passing moment. To be sure, God's responsiveness to humankind resembles the proverbial glue that binds a beautiful vase together. In the pages that follow, you will learn to reach for God in your experience of shame, who functions like a trustworthy, reliable bonding agent for your inner world.

The Human Experience of Shame

Shame is a common human experience, and involves a mixture of feelings (e.g., anger, fear), thoughts (e.g., "I'm bad"), and behaviors (e.g., hiding, avoiding, "covering up") (Gilbert, 1998). If you regularly struggle with shame, and this experience gets in the way of living the life you want, this workbook is for you. Because shame causes so much pain—and is even difficult to acknowledge by name—you may find that your life seems unmanageable, given your self-critical thoughts and avoidance behaviors are weighing you down. If so, my hope is that this workbook will assist you in relating differently to shame and negative self-judgments so you can once again pursue a meaningful, passionate life.

As a Christian, you may even find that shame gets in the way of your relationship with God. Because of this, you might withdraw even further in life, struggling to reach out to God in your moments of pain. Over time, you may find that hiding makes matters worse, in that you are *still* in pain, yet *also* experiencing the loneliness that comes from hiding and covering up. This initial reaction to shame—avoidance—is certainly understandable, given that, for Christians, it can be traced back to the Genesis account of creation. As this famous section of Scripture reveals, after eating the forbidden fruit, Adam and Eve quickly covered themselves up and hid from God (see Genesis 3).

Unfortunately, in reading this passage in the Bible, Christians can often miss one of the most important parts: God's *response* to Adam and Eve's regrettable behavior (Bonhoeffer, 1959). Although they had to permanently leave the Garden of Eden because of a unilateral decision they made, God, in his response, "made garments of skin for Adam and his wife and clothed them" (Genesis 3:21). In other words, God responded to them in their anxious, ashamed state with loving compassion, holding them together as their proverbial glue.

Building on this often-forgotten passage in the third chapter of Genesis, in the pages that follow, I present an organized strategy for turning to God in the midst of your shame, rather than hiding from him and covering up because of self-criticism. As you practice turning to God while you are in pain, my hope is that you will begin to cultivate self- and other-compassion, given that God wants to clothe you in response to your suffering. Even more, he wants to offer you grace and mercy from moment to moment, playing an active role in providing support and comfort as you struggle to regain your footing in life. Certainly, God has declared that "it is finished" (John 19:30), meaning Jesus Christ has already reconciled you with God through his atoning work on the cross; therefore, you can confidently walk towards (rather than away from) God's "throne of grace" in knowing he is welcoming you home whenever you wander away (Hebrews 4:16; Luke 15:11–32). Instead of "concealing" and covering up in shame, God wants you to reach for him, and is actively pursuing you in the midst of your pain (Luke 15:1–10).

To learn to boldly walk towards God's "throne of grace" (reminiscent of reaching for the proverbial glue to fix a shattered vase), you will be working on cultivating self- and other-compassion in response to shame and negative self-judgments, drawing from both the contemporary psychology literature and time-honored Christian faith. In balancing the two, my wish is that you will benefit from the best of both worlds: (a) psychologists have been researching compassion for some time now, and have developed evidence-based interventions that can help you in the midst of your shame; and (b) the Christian tradition has been offering a way to respond to shame for 2,000 years, rooted in the "grand narrative of Scripture" (Wolters, 2005).

For Christians, although God created humankind in his image, we turned away from him, leading to the fall; yet, Jesus' redemptive work on the cross means we are restored in our relationship with God if we believe in him (Romans 10:9), and can confidently walk with him, become more like him with his help, and wait patiently for his triumphant return (Wolters, 2005). The difference between a secular psychological and biblical response to shame, though, involves the ultimate source of compassion. From a secular psychological perspective, compassion comes from within (Desmond, 2016), whereas a Christian viewpoint emphasizes God's role in redemption and healing (Romans 5:8).

Ultimately, a workbook for *Christians* with shame and self-judgments is necessary so as to operate from *within* a Christian framework, drawing from the psychology literature to enhance a Christian understanding of the antidote to shame—*God's* loving compassion, mercy, and grace. By practicing the strategies in this workbook, my desire is that your healing will occur from the outside in, rather than the inside out, meaning that an awareness of God's active, loving presence will help you to recognize that his love has always been available.[2] Instead of striving, on your own, to think, feel, and behave differently in response to your shame, God is walking by your side in order to help you in your moment of need (see Psalm 25), functioning like the glue that holds together shattered pieces of clay to form a beautiful vase.

Getting Started

In the remaining pages of this introduction, I want to highlight a few key points to get us started, including (a) recent research on compassion in the psychology literature, (b) compassion in the Christian tradition, (c) some of the main sources I draw upon for this workbook, (d) the theoretical model I utilize as a guide for understanding the problem and solution, (e) the four-step approach I use in this workbook, (f) the main goals and techniques that you will be focusing on, (g) the intended audience for this workbook, and (h) my overarching strategy for organizing the material in this workbook. In doing so, I hope you will better understand the building blocks of this workbook, moving into the first chapter with a clear vision of what is in store for you as you steadily walk with God on the road to positive change.

A Psychological Viewpoint on Compassion and Shame

In the last decade, researchers in the field of psychology have increasingly focused on the role that compassion plays in mental health, often drawing from Buddhist psychology to conceptualize its ingredients and benefits. Although authors have yet to arrive at a unified definition of compassion, there seem to be several agreed-upon elements, which include being aware of (the cognitive ingredient), impacted by (the affective ingredient), and ready to respond to (the behavioral ingredient) suffering (Kirby, 2016). These components can be applied towards the self or others; in either case, though, there seems to be a heavy emphasis on finding effective ways to recognize, and relate differently to (with kindness, concern, sympathy, and non-judgment), suffering. Although typically influenced by Buddhist writings, many of the world religions, including the Christian faith, emphasize the role that compassion plays in daily living.

Recent research has revealed a negative link between compassion and psychopathology (MacBeth & Gumley, 2012), with compassion helping to explain the relationship between mental health and psychopathology (Trompetter, Kleine, & Bohlmeijer, 2017). With these types of studies in mind, researchers have started to develop interventions to help people with a range of psychological struggles, employing compassion to effectively respond to human suffering. Popular treatments that emphasize compassion (on at least some level) include compassion-focused therapy (Gilbert, 2010; Kolts, 2016), mindful self-compassion (Germer, 2009; Neff, 2011), compassion cultivation training (Jazaieri et al., 2013), and mindfulness-based stress reduction (Kabat-Zinn, 2013; Stahl & Goldstein, 2015). These approaches are sometimes influenced by Buddhism, as revealed by the use of mindfulness and loving-kindness meditations to cultivate compassion in response to suffering.

With mindfulness meditation, defined succinctly as "nonattached awareness" (Germer, 2009), practitioners learn to notice the inner world (including psychological pain) with non-judgment and compassion, relating differently to difficult intrapsychic experiences. In a similar vein, in loving-kindness meditation, a deeper connection to humankind is emphasized (Kristeller & Johnson, 2005), helping practitioners to generate compassion for themselves and others. These compassion-based approaches continue to gain research support (Kirby, 2016), with a host of self-help workbooks being published in the 21st century on compassion for mental health-related challenges.

One such mental health struggle within the compassion literature, shame, has received increased attention in recent years. Sometimes referred to in the clinical psychology literature as "shame-proneness," people who struggle with shame tend to be highly self-critical, viewing themselves as "bad" (versus the emotion of guilt, which focuses more on specific behaviors as "bad"), and may frequently "conceal" perceived shortcomings from others (Pineles, Street, & Koenen, 2006).

In addition to concealing psychological struggles, individuals who are shame-sensitive may tend to make sense of life occurrences by (a) employing self-blame to understand an event (e.g., "It's my fault"), overgeneralizing the event (e.g., "This always happens to me"), and (c) viewing the event as permanent (e.g., "This will never go away") (Pineles et al., 2006). Ultimately, shame-proneness is linked to a general experience of psychological distress (Pineles et al., 2006).

Beyond concealment, self-blame, overgeneralization, and psychological distress, shame is associated with repetitive negative thinking (McEvoy, Mahoney, & Moulds, 2010). This type of thinking usually involves ruminating about the past and worrying about the future, with ingrained, perseverative thinking patterns getting in the way of daily life. In the context of shame-proneness, this negative style of thinking may involve self-judgments, with people employing self-criticism in a repetitive manner. As a result, shame and self-judgments often work hand in hand, leading to inner struggles with both thoughts and feelings.

In the clinical psychology field, researchers have started to examine the role that compassion plays in buffering against the negative effects of shame. For example, recent research has suggested that shame-proneness is negatively linked to self-compassion, and meditation is positively linked to self-compassion (Woods & Proeve, 2014). This emerging research suggests that meditation may help to increase self-compassion, with self-compassion potentially protecting against shame-proneness. In fact, compassion-based programs are increasingly using mindfulness and loving-kindness meditations to combat shame, revealing the "potential benefits" of these types of intervention for clients suffering from shame and negative self-judgments (Kirby, 2016).

A Christian Viewpoint on Compassion and Shame

For Christians, shame is an inevitable human experience (Allender & Longman, 1993), quickly showing up in the first few chapters of the Bible. As noted previously, after eating the forbidden fruit in the Garden of Eden, Adam and Eve realized they were naked and exposed, concealing themselves by making clothing out of leaves, covering up, and hiding from God (Genesis 3:7–10). Some Christian theologians have suggested that a biblical view of shame has several ingredients, including an awareness of the chasm between God and humankind, a deep sense of loss of this vital, life-giving connection, and a "powerless longing" to repair this painful rupture (Bonhoeffer, 1955, p. 24). Shame, ultimately, is about "the loss of [humankind's] unity with God," and the far-reaching need to conceal this separate existence (Bonhoeffer, 1955, p. 24). Yet, the very act of concealing serves as a powerful reminder of our separateness, with the Christian solution to this shame-prone separation coming from a deeper, more intimate relationship with God (Bonhoeffer, 1955).

Interestingly, prior to Adam and Eve's "fall," they experienced no shame, despite the fact that they wore no clothes (Genesis 2:25). Although shame became a permanent human experience due to Adam and Eve's decision to turn away from God, in an act of compassion and mercy, "God made garments of skin for Adam and his wife and clothed them" (Genesis 3:21). This loving act suggests that God now "preserves" humankind, offering us a compassionate reply to the shame and vulnerability that naturally come from a separate existence (Bonhoeffer, 1959).

In the Bible, compassion, or "to enter sympathetically into one's sorrow and pain" (Stewart, 1998, p. 324), often comes from the Greek word, *eleos*, which refers to God's compassion, mercy, and sustained efforts to respond to human misery (Strong, 2001). From a Christian perspective, God is all-merciful, which means that Christians who believe in him are to pray for his mercy (Strong, 2001). Worth mentioning, the Greek word for olive oil, *elaion*, closely resembles *eleos* (Strong, 2001), with olive oil being used in Jesus' time as a source of healing for wounds (Mathewes-Green, 2009). As a result, asking Jesus for mercy involves asking Jesus for healing, requesting that he soothe your injuries in the midst of suffering. A Christian view of compassion as a response to shame is further developed throughout this workbook, including helpful strategies to deepen your awareness of God's love, compassion, mercy, and grace.

Workbook Sources

In this workbook, I draw from a wide range of writings in order to offer a specific set of skills for you to better manage your shame and negative self-judgments. In particular, I turn to the compassion (e.g., Germer, 2009; Gilbert, 2010; Jazaieri et al., 2013; Tirch, Schoendorff, & Silberstein, 2014) and shame-proneness literatures in clinical psychology in order to sensitively modify secular and/or Buddhist perspectives and exercises that have research support. Certainly, many of these exercises are already housed within your own rich Christian heritage; thus, rather than building this workbook with purely *secular* theory, research, and skills, I attempt to bridge the gap between science and faith, given that "what has been will be again, what has been done will be done again; there is nothing new under the sun" (Ecclesiastes 1:9). Stated differently, although the current vehicle through which compassion-based skills are presented in the 21st century is clinical psychology (typically influenced by Buddhist psychology), the other world religions (including Christianity) have been discussing the vital, life-giving role of compassion for millennia. Because of this, I want to be sensitive to your faith background, helping you to feel at home in your own tradition as you move through this workbook.

In closing this gap, I attempt to be considerate of your spiritual and psychological needs, as well as your Christian worldview, rather than primarily pulling from Buddhist psychology. I also want to help you make better sense of your relationship with God by reviewing recent research on "God concept," "God image," and "God attachment." Your God concept is what you learn from a local church, popular Christian writings, and the Bible, among other cognitive sources, whereas your God image is your deeper, affective, and experiential understanding of God that often forms based on some of your early relational experiences with caregivers. Finally, your attachment to God can be secure or insecure; with a secure attachment to God, you are more likely to utilize him as a source of soothing comfort in times of need, which can be helpful as you attempt to better manage shame and negative self-judgments.

As one more major source, I turn to the Christian tradition, including the Bible and popular Christian writings over the centuries. To offer one quick example, I utilize writings on *apophatic* meditation in place of mindfulness meditation (which originally emanates from Buddhism). *Apophatic* meditation began to develop within the Christian tradition roughly 1,500 years ago and is increasingly being employed as a Christian-sensitive alternative to mindfulness meditation for Christians with psychological problems (see, e.g., Knabb, 2016; Knabb & Frederick, 2017; Knabb & Vazquez, 2018; Knabb, Frederick, & Cumming, 2017).

Worth mentioning, in *The Mindful Path to Self-Compassion*, clinical psychologist Christopher Germer recently discussed *The Cloud of Unknowing*, recommending *apophatic* meditation to cultivate compassion (Germer, 2009). In this famous 14th-century Christian book, the *Cloud* author offered instructions for a deeper relationship with God, arguing for the use of love, rather than knowledge, during formal meditative practice. Also in *The Mindful Path to Self-Compassion*, Christopher Germer mentioned Christian spirituality several times, revealing that the Christian tradition (not just

Buddhist psychology) can offer healing practices on compassion as a coping skill to manage shame and negative self-judgments.

A Theoretical Model for Understanding the Problem and Solution

I have drawn upon several main sources to create a proverbial map—that is, a visual guide—for you to better understand the relationship between shame, compassion, and God's role in the process of healing. By doing so, my hope is that this map will capture both the problem and the solution when it comes to shame. On the psychology "side of the aisle," I have adapted British clinical psychologist Paul Gilbert's (Gilbert, 2010; Gilbert & Irons, 2009) theoretical model on the development of shame. Conversely, on the Christian "side of the aisle," I have integrated the writings of Lutheran theologian Dietrich Bonhoeffer (1955, 1959) so as to capture a Christian understanding of the link between shame and the human condition. Two other Christian sources include Allender and Longman's (1993) conceptualization of human and divine shame and Burroughs' (2010) work on contentment.

Although these concepts will be defined and expanded upon in subsequent areas of this workbook, for now, I would like to offer a quick overview of the interlocking parts. To start, humans are created in God's image to be in relationship with him and others. In particular, God has created humankind in such a way that, biologically, psychologically, socially, and spiritually speaking, we innately need security and closeness in our most intimate relationships. Yet, due to the fall of humankind, we end up experiencing human shame from family, cultural groups, society, and so on, resulting in what is called external shame (e.g., perceiving that we are judged by others). In turn, we may react to external human shame in several ways. As one possible response, we internalize the shame we perceive is coming from others, which may result in self-blame, self-judgment, chronic sympathetic nervous system activity (i.e., the "danger" system), anxiety and depression, and insecure relationships (i.e., insecure attachments) with others. As another potential reaction to external shame, we end up experiencing humiliation, leading to blaming others, judging others, chronic sympathetic nervous system activity (i.e., the "danger" system), struggling with anger and/or aggression, and experiencing insecure relationships (i.e., insecure attachments) with others. In either case, the end result can be a deep sense of rejection and isolation from the very community (i.e., the Body of Christ) we long to connect to, given God created us as relational beings (see Figure 0.1).

In that God is the author of creation, though, the solution must come directly from him. As a theoretical/theological pathway to healing, we are created in God's image to be in relationship with him and others, which means we have an inherent need for closeness and connection. Still, due to our fallen world, we inevitably experience ruptures (perceived and actual) in these fundamental relationships. Although painful, the experience of shame can serve as a signal—a reminder that we are separated from God and others. Stated differently, on its own, human shame can be paralyzing and painful, with no apparent benefit or reward; however, shame can actually help us to better understand our incompleteness without God, and our need to return to him over and over again. Rather than covering up and isolating when we experience the pain of separation, shame can allow us to identify our innate need for God, including his loving compassion, and serve as a catalyst for our return to him. Therefore, when we experience shame and the activation of the sympathetic nervous system (i.e., the "danger" system) due to external shame-based threats from a fallen world, we need to reach out to God for his perfect, compassionate reply. As we learn to rest in God's compassionate presence—activating the parasympathetic nervous system (i.e., the "contentment" system; Burroughs, 2010; Gilbert, 2010) in the process—we are better able to have

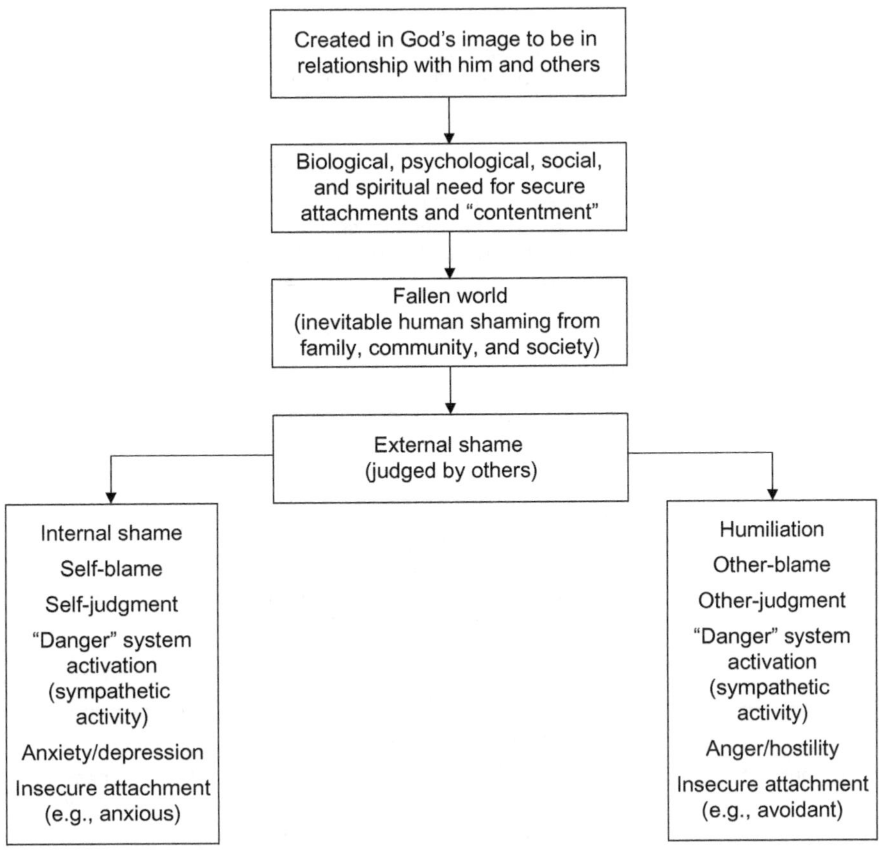

Figure 0.1 The problem. Adapted from Allender and Longman (1993), Bonhoeffer (1955, 1959), Burroughs (2010), and Gilbert and Irons (2009).

compassion for ourselves and others (see Figure 0.2). To do this, I will be teaching you a four-step approach to work towards resting in God's loving, compassionate presence.

Christian Meditation for Compassion: A Four-Step Approach[3]

In this workbook, I will be teaching you (among other skills and strategies) how to practice Christian meditation (both *apophatic* and *kataphatic* approaches) in place of Buddhist mindfulness meditation as a way to cultivate self- and other-compassion. With Christian meditation, you will be developing a deeper compassion for yourself and others: first, you will be practicing letting go of unhelpful thoughts and feelings; second, you will be developing a more focused, sustained attention on God, the source of love and contentment (Kristeller & Johnson, 2005). In these first two steps, you will be learning to spend time with God in solitude, first noticing your inner world (e.g., thoughts, feelings), followed by a gentle pivot towards an awareness of God's active, loving presence. As a third step, you will be developing self-compassion, given that God first had compassion for you in Jesus' loving, merciful responsiveness on the cross. As the fourth and final step, your newfound self-compassion can be extended to others. Above all else, you will be learning to notice your inner

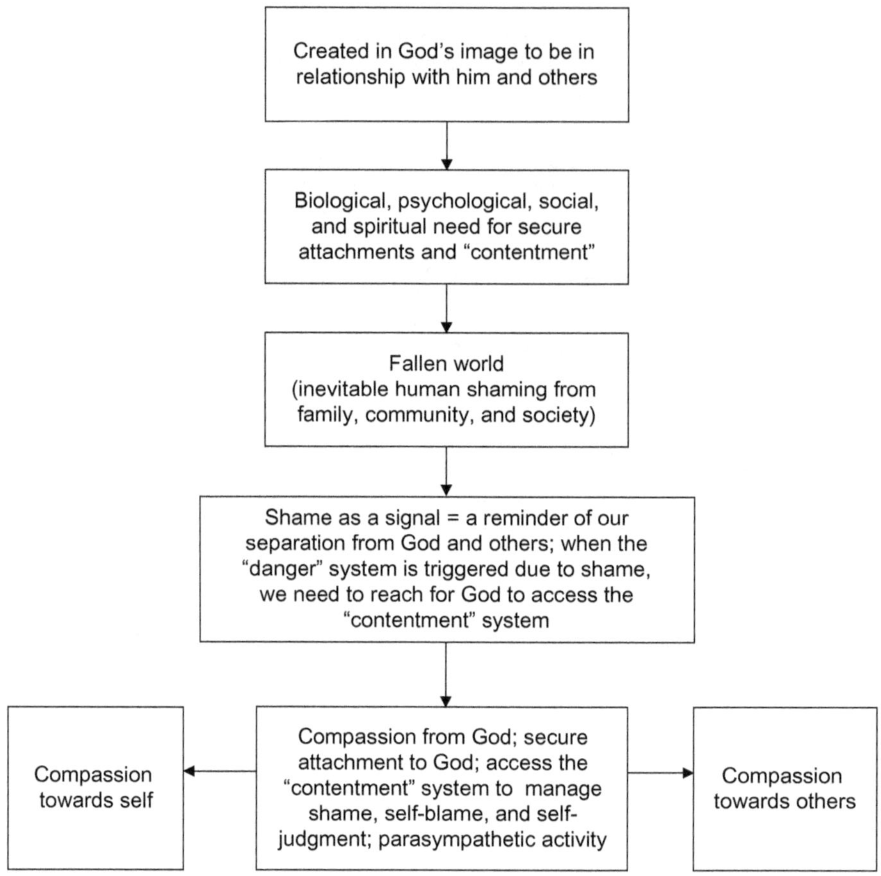

Figure 0.2 The solution. Adapted from Allender and Longman (1993), Bonhoeffer (1955, 1959), Burroughs (2010), and Gilbert and Irons (2009).

world, recognize God's unending compassion for you, and extend God's compassion to yourself and others.

In addition to serving as an alternative to mindfulness meditation, Christian meditation can function as a substitute for the loving-kindness meditations that are currently popular in the clinical psychology literature, usually involving (a) letting go of unhelpful thinking patterns that lead to shame, and (b) focusing on compassion and kindness to protect against shame and negative self-judgments (Desmond, 2016; Germer, 2009). Essentially, loving-kindness meditations consist of repeating phrases (e.g., "May I be safe and happy," "May others be safe and happy") to conjure up feelings of love and compassion for yourself and others. One of the major differences, though, between secular and Christian meditative practices involves the source of compassion. For Christians (such as yourself), self- and other-compassion is possible because God is *the* source of love (1 John 4:8)—God offers love, compassion, mercy, and grace because, by definition, he is infinitely merciful and good (Ephesians 2:4; Luke 6:36; Psalm 86:5, 145:9; Titus 3:5). In that these attributes of God are unwavering and never change (i.e., they are immutable), turning to him during instances of shame and negative self-judgments is key.

To review, the four-step process you will be practicing in this workbook focuses on (a) letting go of your unhelpful thinking patterns that lead to shame (*apophatic* and *kataphatic* meditative exercises are used from the Christian tradition, along with modified exercises in the psychology literature), (b) pivoting your attention towards God's love, mercy, and grace as *the* source of compassion and contentment, (c) gently loving yourself because God loves humankind (his ultimate act of love—the incarnation and atonement—is already completed), and (d) loving others because of God's love for you (1 John 4:19).

My hope is that this four-step process can help you to (a) relate differently to your negative self-judgments and shame, (b) shift towards an awareness of God's love, compassion, mercy, and grace, (c) begin to change your image of God and deepen your attachment to him in order to get in touch with a sense of safety, security, and contentment from God, and (d) extend God's compassion and mercy to both yourself and others. What is more, this Christian-sensitive four-step process combines the general psychological ingredients of mindfulness (which is about "attention," typically focusing on the senses or the breath) and loving-kindness (*metta*; which is about "connection," and usually emphasizes words) meditations (Germer, 2009). Certainly, Christian meditation employs both attention and connection—attention on, and connection to, God, who is the source of love, compassion, mercy, and grace.

The Goals and Techniques in this Workbook

In this skills-based workbook for Christians, you will focus on several main goals, including (a) learning to gently and compassionately notice your shame and negative self-judgments with a bit more distance, given God is loving you in each and every moment, (b) turning from the "danger" to "contentment" system (described in more detail in subsequent chapters; Gilbert, 2010) because God is with you, (c) cultivating a deeper awareness of God's compassion and mercy, and (d) practicing more compassion and mercy towards yourself and others (Desmond, 2016; Germer, 2009; Gilbert, 2010; Kristeller & Johnson, 2005; Knabb, 2016; Knabb et al., 2017).

You will be developing a range of skills (Germer, 2009; Gilbert, 2010; Knabb, 2016; Knabb et al., 2017; Kolts, 2016; Thomas, Moriarty, Davis, & Anderson, 2011) to cultivate compassion towards yourself and others—sometimes referred to as the "compassionate self" (Leahy, Tirch, & Napolitano, 2011) in clinical circles and the "new self" found in Christ (Colossians 3:1–17; Ephesians 4:24) in Christianity. The fourth through seventh chapters in the workbook focus on helping you to develop four skill domains, including "thinking," "feeling," "behaving," and "attending and imagining" (Germer, 2009; Gilbert, 2010; Kolts, 2016). Mapped onto these skill-based domains, I will be integrating five bodies of Christian spiritual writings: desert spirituality (drawing from the *Sayings of the Desert Fathers* and other sources); Protestant spirituality (emphasizing reformed theological writings and techniques, such as Puritan meditation and prayers in the *Valley of Vision*); Orthodox spirituality (turning to the *Philokalia*); medieval spirituality (utilizing *The Cloud of Unknowing* and *The Imitation of Christ*, among other writings); and Ignatian spirituality (influenced by *Spiritual Exercises*).

The Intended Audience

This workbook is for Christians who are (a) committed to the Christian faith, (b) looking for a Christian-sensitive workbook to help them with shame and negative self-judgments by developing a more intimate relationship with God, and (c) currently working with a psychotherapist or counselor in a professional capacity. Exercises, writing assignments (e.g., journaling), guided meditations (audio files), biblical examples, and case examples are integrated throughout the workbook, and material is presented in an easy-to-understand manner.

A Mixture of "Integration," "Christian Psychology," and Evangelical Perspectives

In the pages that follow, I will utilize both "integration" (Jones, 2010) and "Christian psychology" (Roberts & Watson, 2010) perspectives, meaning I will explore the ways in which the Christian faith and clinical psychology can work together to help you respond differently to shame and self-judgments. With "integration," secular psychology is often seen as a starting point, followed by an attempt to align secular theory and research with a Christian worldview. On the other hand, "Christian psychology" strives to utilize the Bible (and other Christian writings) as a beginning point, using the scientific method and secular psychology theory and research to enhance a biblical foundation.

In drawing from both approaches, I will, at times, start with the science of psychology, finding ways to enhance and enrich secular theory and research with a distinctly Christian viewpoint. At other times, I start from a Christian vantage point, exploring the ways in which secular theory and research can build upon a Christian base. In either case, I want you, as a Christian, to feel comfortable by working from *within* your own faith tradition, always circling back to a Christian understanding of shame and compassion to promote positive change.

From this Christian perspective, God has revealed himself to humankind in the form of (a) "general revelation," meaning researchers can better understand God by investigating both the natural world and human beings that he created (see Psalm 19:1; Romans 1:20), and (b) "special revelation," or God's Word, the Bible (2 Timothy 3:16) (Erickson, 2013; Grudem, 1994). Christians, therefore, can benefit from secular research on the relationship between compassion and shame, just as long as it is not inconsistent with a biblical perspective. Also, God offers "common grace" to all of humankind, meaning that God cares for us in such a way that we are able to pursue scientific advancements for healing, and "special grace" to Christians who put their faith in Jesus, revealing the redemptive work of Jesus on the cross that is available to those who believe in him (Elwell, 2001).

Finally, in this workbook, I write from an Evangelical perspective, given that an estimated quarter of the population in the United States identifies as such (Pew Forum, 2015). As Protestant Christians, Evangelicals believe the Bible is the Word of God, which guides daily living (Larsen, 2007). In addition, Evangelicals believe that Jesus is the Son of God, who died on a cross to reconcile a sinful and broken humankind with God (Larsen, 2007). Overall, Evangelicals believe in following Jesus Christ in a literal sense, based on his teachings in the Bible (e.g., Matthew 16:24).

To summarize with these points in mind, I draw from both theory and research in clinical psychology (i.e., general revelation, common grace) and a Christian worldview (i.e., special revelation, special grace). In doing so, my hope is that you are able to confidently move towards God's throne of grace (Hebrews 4:16) in order to find much-needed rest in his loving arms.

The Road Ahead

The workbook is organized into seven chapters, with the first three focusing on important background information, which is necessary to move on to the remaining chapters that offer a range of techniques to help you relate differently to your shame and negative self-judgments.

In the first chapter, you will further explore the definition of shame from both psychological and Christian perspectives, along with the characteristics of shame-proneness and repetitive negative thinking. Also in the first chapter, you will learn about your "danger," "drive," and "contentment" systems (Gilbert, 2010), including your possible overreliance on the "danger" and "drive" systems and underutilization of the "contentment" system in the midst of shame. To conclude the first chapter, you will explore the similarities and differences between mindfulness and *apophatic* meditation in order to begin to consider the role of Christian meditation in turning to God for self-compassion.

In the second chapter, you will learn about attachment theory, including the development of secure and insecure attachments. Attachment theory has been around for over 70 years and can help you better understand your relational functioning. You will also learn about several related concepts, including God concept (what you learn about God through cognitive means, such as church instruction and teachings in the Bible) and God image (your deeper, affective experience of God that often develops based on early relational experiences with caregivers). Furthermore, you will learn about the role that your attachments play in developing and maintaining compassion, which includes your attachment to God. Also in this chapter, you will have the opportunity to explore the role that your "contentment" system (Gilbert, 2010; Kolts, 2016) plays in a secure attachment to God. From a Christian viewpoint, God is the ultimate source of a sense of safety and contentment; therefore, learning to sit at Jesus' feet, like Mary in the gospels (Luke 10:38–42), is an important part of developing and maintaining self- and other-compassion.

In the third chapter, you will further explore secular and Christian definitions of compassion, including the role that your "contentment" system plays in maintaining psychological and spiritual health (Germer, 2009; Gilbert, 2010). From a Christian perspective, you will learn about compassion in the context of *eleos*, the Greek word for "mercy" that is frequently used in the New Testament. Moreover, you will begin to focus on the role that Christian meditation plays in helping you with shame and self-criticism. Before transitioning to the actual coping skills in the remaining workbook chapters, though, you will learn about the unified, integrative compassion-based approach that is presented in this workbook:

> By utilizing (a) modified exercises from the compassion literature in clinical psychology, and (b) *kataphatic* and *apophatic* forms of meditation in the Christian tradition, you will be working towards moving from shame, negative self-judgments, and repetitive negative thinking to an awareness of God's security, mercy, compassion, and grace, cultivating a secure attachment with God along the way.

In the fourth chapter, you will focus on the theme of "thinking with compassion and mercy towards yourself and others." You will practice several modified, Christian-sensitive, compassion-based exercises from the psychology literature (e.g., reciting a phrase to calm your mind, challenging distorted thoughts about God). From the Christian tradition, you will practice several exercises within Protestant, desert, and medieval spirituality, including thinking deeply about God's attributes, reciting the Psalms, and *lectio divina*.

In the fifth chapter, you will focus on the theme of "feeling with compassion and mercy towards yourself and others." You will practice several Christian-sensitive, compassion-based exercises from the psychology literature (e.g., relating differently to difficult feelings, developing positive emotions, loving-kindness meditations). From the Christian tradition, you will learn about medieval spirituality and *apophatic* meditation to help you reach out to God in love (rather than knowledge) during moments of shame and self-criticism. You will also draw from medieval spiritual writings to feel with compassion.

In the sixth chapter, you will focus on the theme of "behaving with compassion and mercy towards yourself and others." You will practice several modified, Christian-sensitive, compassion-based exercises in the psychology literature involving getting in touch with your values to practice compassion for yourself and others, as well as pivoting from a self- to other-focused orientation. You will also explore a range of Christian virtues, drawing from desert spirituality and the Bible. Finally, you will focus on strategies for living out a set of biblical virtues with compassion for yourself and others.

In the seventh and final chapter, you will focus on the theme of "attending and imagining with compassion and mercy towards yourself," drawing from the compassion literature to help you relate differently to difficult inner experiences. In this chapter, you will develop the ability to focus on God, and use your imagination to find rest and comfort in him. For example, you will learn about the role that breathing plays in focusing on Jesus' mercy and love, practicing meditation and the "body scan" to help you feel God's active, loving presence. Within the Christian tradition, you will focus on several different types of meditation, including exercises from Orthodox and Ignatian spirituality, so as to cultivate compassion and mercy for yourself and others.

A Brief Prayer

Before formally beginning this Christian workbook, I believe a simple prayer can help you to prepare yourself for being open to the possibility of change. Thomas Merton, the late Trappist monk and author of a range of books on Christian spirituality and contemplation, wrote the following prayer, which captures the importance of trusting God on this journey towards positive change:

> My Lord God, I have no idea where I am going. I do not see the road ahead of me. I cannot know for certain where it will end. Nor do I really know myself, and the fact that I think I am following your will does not mean that I am actually doing so. But I believe that the desire to please you does in fact please you. And I hope that I have that desire in all that I am doing. I hope that I never do anything apart from that desire. And I know that if I do this you will lead me by the right road, though I may know nothing about it. Therefore I will trust you always though I may seem to be lost and in the shadow of death. I will not fear for you are ever with me, and you will never leave me to face my perils alone.
>
> (Merton, 2007, p. 132)

Notes

1 This metaphor is inspired by biblical references to a potter and clay (e.g., Isaiah 64:8) and Eugene O'Neill's famous quote (Dowling, 2009, p. 198).

2 Worth mentioning, though, as you learn to become more aware of God's loving presence, my hope is that you will recognize that *God* is actually loving you from the inside out (C. Germer, personal communication, April 18, 2018). In other words, God is like the sun in the middle of your proverbial solar system (i.e., a heliocentric view), radiating from the center (Galatians 2:20), rather than revolving around you like some sort of distant sun (i.e., a geocentric view) (Laird, 2011).

3 The Christian tradition has typically used "meditation" to refer to the use of prayer with words and images, pondering God's attributes, actions, promises, and so forth (Finley, 2004). On the other hand, "contemplation" is commonly used to describe the process of cultivating a more intimate union with God by letting go of the use of words and images (Finley, 2004). Certainly, *lectio divina* ("divine reading," which you will learn more about in the fourth chapter) separates the two as distinct steps (Paintner, 2008; Talbot, 2002). In either case, in keeping with the current emphasis in the psychology literature on awareness and attention as central ingredients within meditation (Walsh & Shapiro, 2006), in this workbook, I use "Christian meditation" more generally to refer to both *apophatic* (e.g., the Jesus Prayer and the instructions in *The Cloud of Unknowing*, which de-emphasize the use of words and/or images) and *kataphatic* (e.g., Puritan and Ignatian meditation, which advocate for the use of words and/or images) approaches to meditation and prayer (Paintner, 2008). In doing so, I attempt to capture the importance of both practices in cultivating a deeper awareness of God's active, loving presence by focusing exclusively on him.

References

Allender, D., & Longman, T. (1993). *The cry of the soul: How our emotions reveal our deepest questions about God.* Colorado Springs, CO: NavPress.

Bonhoeffer, D. (1955). *Ethics*. New York: Touchstone.

Bonhoeffer, D. (1959). *Creation and fall*. New York: Touchstone.

Burroughs, J. (2010). *The rare jewel of Christian contentment*. Pensacola, FL: Chapel Library.

Desmond, T. (2016). *Self-compassion in psychotherapy: Mindfulness-based practices for healing and transformation*. New York: W. W. Norton & Company, Inc.

Dowling, R. (2009). *Critical companion to Eugene O'Neill: A literary reference to his life and work*. New York: Facts on File, Inc.

Elwell, W. (Ed.). (2001). *Evangelical dictionary of theology*. Grand Rapids, MI: Baker Book House Company.

Erickson, M. (2013). *Christian theology* (3rd ed.). Grand Rapids, MI: Baker Academic.

Finley, J. (2004). *Christian meditation: Experiencing the presence of God*. New York: HarperCollins Publishers Inc.

Germer, C. (2009). *The mindful path to self-compassion: Freeing yourself from destructive thoughts and emotions*. New York: The Guilford Press.

Gilbert, P. (1998). What is shame? Some core issues and controversies. In P. Gilbert & B. Andrews (Eds.), *Shame: Interpersonal behavior, psychopathology, and culture* (pp. 3–38). New York: Oxford University Press.

Gilbert, P. (2010). *Compassion focused therapy: Distinctive features*. New York: Routledge.

Gilbert, P., & Irons, C. (2009). Shame, self-criticism, and self-compassion in adolescence. In N. Allen & L. Sheeber (Eds.), *Adolescent emotional development and the emergence of depressive disorders* (pp. 195–214). Cambridge: Cambridge University Press.

Grudem, W. (1994). *Systematic theology: A introduction to biblical doctrine*. Grand Rapids, MI: Zondervan.

Jazaieri, H., Jinpa, G., McGonigal, K., Rosenberg, E., Finkelstein, J., Simon-Thomas, E., Cullen, M., Doty, J., Gross, J., & Goldin, P. (2013). Enhancing compassion: A randomized controlled trial of a compassion cultivation training program. *Journal of Happiness Studies, 14*(4), 1113–1126.

Jones, S. (2010). An integration view. In E. Johnson (Ed.), *Psychology & Christianity: Five views* (pp. 101–148). Downers Grove, IL: InterVarsity Press.

Kabat-Zinn, J. (2013). *Full catastrophe living: Using the wisdom of your body and mind to face stress, pain, and illness*. New York: Bantam Books.

Kirby, J. (2016). Compassion interventions: The programmes, the evidence, and implications for research and practice. *Psychology and Psychotherapy: Theory, Research and Practice, 90*(3), 432–455.

Knabb, J. (2016). *Acceptance and commitment therapy for Christian clients: A faith-based workbook*. New York: Routledge.

Knabb, J., & Frederick, T. (2017). *Contemplative prayer for Christians with chronic worry: An eight-week program*. New York: Routledge.

Knabb, J., Frederick, T., & Cumming, G. (2017). Surrendering to God's providence: A three-part study on providence-focused therapy for recurrent worry (PFT-RW). *Psychology of Religion and Spirituality, 9*(2), 180–196.

Knabb, J., & Vazquez, V. (2018). A randomized controlled trial of a two-week Internet-based contemplative prayer program for Christians with daily stress. *Spirituality in Clinical Practice, 5*(1), 37–53.

Kolts, R. (2016). *CFT made simple: A clinician's guide to practicing compassion-focused therapy*. Oakland, CA: New Harbinger Publications, Inc.

Kristeller, J., & Johnson, T. (2005). Cultivating loving kindness: A two-stage model of the effects of meditation on empathy, compassion, and altruism. *Zygon, 40*(2), 391–407.

Laird, M. (2011). *A sunlit absence: Silence, awareness, and contemplation*. New York: Oxford University Press.

Larsen, T. (2007). Defining and locating evangelicalism. In T. Larsen & D. Treier (Eds.), *The Cambridge companion to evangelical theology* (pp. 1–14). Cambridge: Cambridge University Press.

Leahy, R., Tirch, D., & Napolitano, L. (2011). *Emotion regulation in psychotherapy: A practitioner's guide*. New York: The Guilford Press.

MacBeth, A., & Gumley, A. (2012). Exploring compassion: A meta-analysis of the association between self-compassion and psychopathology. *Clinical Psychology Review, 32*(6), 545–552.

Mathewes-Green, F. (2009). *The Jesus prayer: The ancient desert prayer that tunes the heart of God*. Brewster, MA: Paraclete Press.

McEvoy, P., Mahoney, A., & Moulds, M. (2010). Are worry, rumination, and post-event processing one and the same?: Development of the repetitive thinking questionnaire. *Journal of Anxiety Disorders, 24*(5), 509–519.

Merton, T. (2007). *A book of hours*. Notre Dame, IN: Sorin Books.

Neff, K. (2011). *Self-compassion: The proven power of being kind to yourself*. New York: HarperCollins.

Paintner, C. (2008). *Lectio divina: Contemplative awakening and awareness*. New York: Paulist Press.

Pew Forum. (2015). *America's changing religious landscape*. Washington, DC: The Pew Forum on Religion & Public Life.

Pineles, S., Street, A., & Koenen, K. (2006). The differential relationships of shame-proneness and guilt-proneness to psychological and somatization symptoms. *Journal of Social and Clinical Psychology, 25*(6), 688–704.

Roberts, R., & Watson, P. (2010). A Christian psychology view. In E. Johnson (Ed.), *Psychology & Christianity: Five views* (pp. 149–198). Downers Grove, IL: InterVarsity Press.
Stahl, B., & Goldstein, E. (2015). *MBSR every day: Daily practices from the heart of mindfulness-based stress reduction*. Oakland, CA: New Harbinger Publications, Inc.
Stewart, D. (1998). Compassion. In C. Brand, C. Draper, & A. England (Eds.), *Holman illustrated Bible dictionary* (p. 324). Nashville, TN: Holman Reference.
Strong, J. (2001). *The Greek dictionary of the New Testament*. Nashville, TN: Thomas Nelson.
Talbot, J. (2002). *Come to the quiet: The principles of Christian meditation*. New York: Jeremy P. Tarcher/Putnam.
Thomas, M., Moriarty, G., Davis, E., & Anderson, E. (2011). The effects of a manualized group-psychotherapy intervention on client God images and attachment to God: A pilot study. *Journal of Psychology and Theology, 39*(1), 44–58.
Tirch, D., Schoendorff, B., & Silberstein, L. (2014). *The ACT practitioner's guide to the science of compassion*. Oakland, CA: New Harbinger Publications, Inc.
Trompetter, H., Kleine, E., & Bohlmeijer, E. (2017). Why does positive mental health buffer against psychopathology? An exploratory study on self-compassion as a resilience mechanism and adaptive emotion regulation strategy. *Cognitive Therapy Research, 41*(3), 459–468.
Walsh, R., & Shapiro, S. (2006). The meeting of meditative disciplines and Western psychology. *American Psychologist, 61*(3), 227–239.
Wolters, A. (2005). *Creation regained: Biblical basics for a reformational worldview* (2nd ed.). Grand Rapids, MI: William B. Eerdmans Publishing Company.
Woods, H., & Proeve, M. (2014). Relationships of mindfulness, self-compassion, and meditation experience with shame-proneness. *Journal of Cognitive Psychotherapy, 28*(1), 20–33.

CHAPTER 1

Shame, Negative Self-Judgments, and the Fall of Humankind

Introduction

In this chapter, you will explore the definitions and characteristics of shame from both psychological and Christian perspectives. In the field of psychology, shame typically involves global evaluations of personal "badness," along with a tendency to withdraw from others and "conceal" perceived shortcomings. From a Christian viewpoint, shame is a reminder of humankind's separation from God, coupled with a "powerless longing" to restore this rupture (Bonhoeffer, 1955, 1959). In other words, for Christians, shame is a signal that tells us we have a deeper need for God.

You will also learn about shame-proneness and repetitive negative thinking to help you better understand the symptoms of these shame-related experiences. With repetitive negative thinking, you may get entangled with either ruminations or worries. In either case, getting caught up in this form of negative thinking can lead to additional painful inner experiences, such as shame and self-criticism.

Furthermore, you will explore the "danger," "drive," and "contentment" systems (Gilbert, 2010); unfortunately, you may overly rely on your "danger" and "drive" systems, and underutilize your "contentment" system, during moments of shame and negative self-judgments. From a Christian perspective, although your "danger" and "drive" systems are necessary as a result of the fallen, broken world in which you interact and live, God has also provided the "contentment" system—including the neurotransmitter and hormone oxytocin to reinforce bonding, the parasympathetic nervous system, and a deeper relational connection during instances of distress and danger—to help you rest safely in his proverbial arms.

To conclude the chapter, you will compare and contrast mindfulness and Christian *apophatic* meditation, learning about how the latter can be used to simultaneously (a) relate differently to your difficult inner experiences of shame and negative self-judgments, and (b) turn to God to connect to your "contentment" system (Burroughs, 2010; Gilbert, 2010). Throughout the chapter, you will complete exercises and writing activities (e.g., journaling), as well as learn from biblical and case examples.

Defining Shame: Psychological and Christian Perspectives

Shame can be difficult to define, in that it is made up of cognitive, emotional, behavioral, and relational ingredients (Gilbert, 1998). In terms of cognition, shame often involves deeply entrenched views about yourself, such as "I'm worthless," "I'm unlovable," or "I'm bad." Your thoughts connected to shame may relate to globally rating yourself—in your totality—as bad, flawed, defective, and so forth. In other words, the focus is on your perceived flaws (Gilbert, 1998). Yet, these negative views of yourself, including self-blame as a central component, often develop based on beliefs about "missing the mark" or "coming up short" and are linked to some sort of external expectation or comparison to someone else (Gilbert, 1998). Therefore, your perception that you somehow lack worth or value develops based on comparing your behavior to the behavior of others.

Regarding your emotion of shame, it may involve an experience in its own right, or can be linked to anger, humiliation, anxiety, disgust, or a mixture of these affective states (among others) (Gilbert, 1998). Certainly, there is a wide range of emotional experiences that are attached to shame. As a result, shame can be a confusing, scary experience, leading to a struggle to fully understand just what you are feeling.

Behaviorally and relationally, shame often leads to the desire to cover up, hide, and so on. When you are experiencing shame, you may want to run away, isolating yourself from others because of the personal belief that you are inherently flawed, defective, or unworthy of others' love and esteem. Unfortunately, this desire to "conceal" can lead to added pain, in that you are now alone in your suffering, resisting the need to reach out to others for fear of further exposure.

Sensitivity to shame can develop based on a wide variety of early life experiences. For instance, abuse and neglect in childhood, or being bullied in adolescence, can lead to the conclusion that the world is a threatening place, given that people have mistreated you, criticized you, or questioned your worth or value; when this assumption is made, you may be especially vulnerable to turning on yourself via self-doubt, self-criticism, and so on (Gilbert, 2009). In other words, you may begin to treat yourself the way others have treated you. Without the sense of safety and support that come from close, trusting, and loving relationships, you can end up negatively judging yourself on a regular basis.

To state this differently, you may first experience external shame, which comes from being criticized or judged by others, rejected by a group, or neglected by friends and family; in turn, you may end up internalizing this shame (i.e., internal shame), devaluing and blaming yourself and experiencing depression and anxiety in the process (Gilbert & Irons, 2009). As an alternative response to external shame, you might begin to criticize and judge others, blaming them (rather than yourself) and experiencing anger along the way (Gilbert & Irons, 2009). In either case, shame is often experienced from the outside in, meaning it can originate in your environment, leading to turning on yourself or others as a way to defend against the pain.

To offer a quick example, Jonathan is especially sensitive to shame, and often struggles with shame-related experiences. On one particular occasion, he is told by his supervisor at work that he needs to increase his productivity when it comes to generating weekly reports within a sales company. When he is told to improve, Jonathan immediately thinks to himself, "My boss is saying this to me because I am a horrible employee. No one else is getting told to improve. This feedback must mean that I am worthless and am not valuable to the company." He also feels a mixture of anxiety about an unknown future and humiliation, in that his supervisor shared this information with him in front of several colleagues. Finally, Jonathan wants to go home and never come back. He also has a hard time talking to his supervisor for the rest of the day.

In the case of Jonathan, he is globally rating himself, which includes his behavior, as inherently flawed in some way, given he believes he has "missed the mark" when it comes to the standards of his job. These thoughts are accompanied by painful emotions—an amalgam of anxiousness and humiliation—leading to the desire to withdraw from work and his relationship with his boss. Over time, these difficult experiences of shame can certainly weigh people down, leading to heightened sensitivity to even the smallest of perceived criticisms and the ensuing downward spiral of self-doubt, emotional pain, isolation, and loneliness.

Transitioning from the psychology of shame to a Christian viewpoint, God created humankind in his image; yet, Adam and Eve turned away from him in their decision to eat the forbidden fruit, resulting in a sudden awareness that they were naked (Genesis 3:6–7). As the next step in this famous story reveals, Adam and Eve "hid from God among the trees of the Garden," with Adam expressing fear because of his newfound realization of being exposed (Genesis 3:8–9).

Although the two were tragically removed from the all-encompassing security of the Garden, God showed them compassion in his willingness to "clothe them" (Genesis 3:21; Bonhoeffer, 1955, 1959). For the Lutheran theologian Dietrich Bonhoeffer, the fall led to humans "seeing ourselves," rather than fixing our eyes upon God. In other words, we experience shame because we are aware there is a significant distance between ourselves and God (Bonhoeffer, 1955, 1959). Bonhoeffer described the Christian experience of shame more formally with the following:

> Shame is man's ineffaceable recollection of his estrangement from the origin; it is grief for this estrangement, and the powerless longing to return to unity with the origin. Man is ashamed because he has lost something which is essential to his original character, to himself as a whole; he is ashamed of his nakedness.
>
> (Bonhoeffer, 1955, p. 24)

Overall, a Christian understanding of shame tends to involve the following key elements (adapted from Bonhoeffer, 1955):

- With the fall, we erroneously turned from God to ourselves, which has led to our ongoing struggles with self-preoccupation.
- We now experience a deep awareness of our exposed, vulnerable, and separate existence, apart from God.
- We now struggle with a general feeling that something central to our existence is lacking/missing, which is a perfect union with God.
- We have a powerless yearning to return to a perfect relationship with God, reminiscent of Adam and Eve's original union with God in the Garden.
- After the fall, shame serves as a signal of our need for God, and our incompleteness without a perfect relationship with him.
- Shame points us to both the problem and solution—we are separate from the perfect love and intimacy offered by God; yet, the experience of shame functions as a reminder that we need to reach for God (not turn away from him), and that our very existence is incomplete without him.
- To overcome shame, we need to be "clothed with the forgiveness of God."

Ultimately, for Christians, shame is a signal that tells us we have a deeper need for God. What is more, the antidote to shame is the love, mercy, grace, and forgiveness of God, revealed in the grand narrative of Scripture. Although we chose to turn from God, he offers us redemption via his Son, and will eventually restore all things so Christians can live in perfect union with God. This workbook, therefore, will help you cultivate a deeper relationship with God as the Christian solution to shame, recognizing that God is offering you his perfect love, mercy, grace, and forgiveness from moment to moment.

Shame and "Missing the Mark" in the Christian Tradition

Before moving on to an exploration of shame-proneness, I would like to briefly review the notion of "sin" from a Christian perspective. In that this workbook is about your ongoing struggles with shame and negative self-evaluations, a Christian worldview inevitably acknowledges the role that "missing the mark" plays in human functioning. Interestingly, one of the Greek words for sin in the New Testament, *hamartano*, means "missing the mark," reminiscent of an archer missing his or her target (Erickson, 2013; Strong, 2001a). Commonly feeling like you have "missed the mark" when striving to meet God's standards is a ubiquitous human experience; still, it may lead to chronic self-criticism, which adds an additional layer of suffering in that you may struggle to truly experience God's love, grace, mercy, and forgiveness.

The Christian tradition teaches that, regrettably, sin is pervasive, impacting all of humankind on an ongoing basis and resulting in a chasm in our relationship with God (Bloesch, 2017). For Christians, one of the central ingredients of sin is "unbelief," which means we struggle with trusting in God's promises and infinite love, revealed throughout the pages of the Bible (Bloesch, 2017). Unfortunately, sin regularly impacts us on an individual, interpersonal, and societal level (Bloesch, 2017).

In the first half of the first millennium, Augustine of Hippo noted that we are like sick patients in a hospital because of sin, "fallen, wounded, and frail, standing in need of the healing and restoring grace of God" (McGrath, 2011, p. 381). This understanding is certainly a compassionate way of viewing the human condition. We need healing because of our ongoing struggles with "coming up short." God's grace, working through human relationships within the Christian church, can help us to deepen our relationship with him and others so as to ameliorate the shame that gets in the way of true intimacy and connection.

Returning to the original Garden account, because Adam and Eve wanted to be "like God," rather than "dependent on him" (Bonhoeffer, 1955, 1959), humankind has suffered from several ongoing consequences, including being separated from God, removed from the perfect safety found in the Garden of Eden, and the tendency to veer off course, heading in our own direction (away from God) on the roads of life (McGrath & McGrath, 2002).

Based on this reality, humankind struggles on a physical (e.g., death, illness, disordered functioning), personal (e.g., we are no longer perfectly dependent on God as our source of safety and security), and moral (e.g., we constantly make mistakes, we fail to live up to God's standards for living) level (McGrath & McGrath, 2002). In fact, within the pages of the Bible, our suffering extends to a wide variety of scenarios and circumstances, including personal decisions, relational betrayals, grief and loss, the uncertainties of life, and so on (Keller, 2013). Although, from a Christian perspective, the impact of sin is far-reaching, Jesus has restored our relationship with God via his work on the cross (e.g., 2 Corinthians 5:18–20). Due to Jesus' saving act, Christians have been rescued from the consequences of sin, and can turn from sinful behavior with the help of Christ (Bloesch, 2017). Because of Jesus' atoning, sacrificial act, we can experience the love, grace, mercy, and forgiveness of God from moment to moment. In other words, God offers us his compassion as an antidote to our shame. We will be covering compassion as a remedy for shame in the third chapter; until then, I would like to review the characteristics of shame-proneness, including the ways in which recurrent shame can get in the way of daily living.

Shame-Proneness

From a psychological perspective, shame involves negative self-evaluations, which tend to be internal ("It's my fault"), stable ("I'll always be this way"), and global ("I'm totally worthless") (Cohen, Wolf, Panter, & Insko, 2011). Shame results from evaluating the "self," rather than merely our "behavior," as somehow "missing the mark," and tends to arise when our perceived behavior is publicly exposed, rather than privately experienced (Cohen et al., 2011). When shame is experienced, a natural reaction is to hide, conceal, and cover up (Tangney, Wagner, & Gramzow, 1992), reminiscent of the Genesis account in the third chapter of the Bible. In struggling with shame, we are also more likely to experience anger, anxiety, and depression, among other psychological symptoms (Tangney et al., 1992).

"Shame-proneness" is a propensity to struggle with shame in the context of life events; in other words, proneness to shame is more of a trait, rather than an isolated state (Tangney & Dearing, 2002). When we experience shame on a regular basis, we can end up constantly attacking ourselves as "bad," feeling publicly "exposed" before God, and repeatedly "hiding" from him. Yet, God is the very source of the soothing comfort we vitally need in the midst of our pain.

Shifting to a distinctly Christian interpretation, the chronic experience of shame-proneness is an inevitable reality of the fall of humankind, with Christians struggling with shame due to our original decision to "be like God," rather than "dependent on God" (Bonhoeffer, 1955, 1959). Shame, from a Christian perspective, emanates from seeing ourselves as "incomplete" and "broken," being publicly exposed before God, and constantly trying to hide from him. Unfortunately, we end up turning away from the missing piece of the proverbial puzzle, conflating the solution with the problem. Rather than pivoting away from God to hide in shame, the solution involves returning to God, who resides in the middle of the Garden. Instead of trying to be "like God," the antidote involves being "dependent on God" (Bonhoeffer, 1955, 1959).

In sum, shame-proneness within the Christian tradition accurately captures our enduring estrangement from God; still, from moment to moment, we can reach for him in the midst of our shame, in that God offers us soothing comfort, redemption, and the hope of his eventual restoration of all things. Because of this restored relationship with God—based on Jesus' redeeming work on the cross—we can persevere when faced with the inconsistencies of a world that is currently incomplete, fragmented, and broken.

Your First Experience of Shame: An Exercise

Shame-proneness can gradually develop over time, with early experiences of shame influencing later ones. In this exercise, I would like you to spend a few minutes reflecting on your first experience of shame. In particular, in the space that follows, see if you can answer the following questions in the context of your first experience of shame:

What thoughts did you think about yourself?

___

___

___

What emotions did you feel?

___

___

___

What actions did you take?

___

___

___

How did this experience impact your relationships?

___

___

___

What impact did this experience have on your relationship with God?[1]

Shame-Proneness in the Bible

Beyond the first recorded instance of shame in Genesis, other biblical figures have struggled with this ubiquitous human experience. Certainly, many people in the Bible, who were called by God to fulfill his purposes, felt an enduring sense of "deficiency" (Albers, 1995). For example, in Exodus 3–4, God appeared to Moses in the form of a burning bush, telling Moses to go to the Pharaoh to set the Israelites free. However, Moses expressed significant self-doubt when faced with God's firm request: "Who am I that I should go to Pharaoh and bring the Israelites out of Egypt?" In response to this protest, God told Moses, "I will be with you."

A few verses later, Moses once again verbalized his deep sense of inadequacy: "What if they do not believe me or listen to me?" In turn, God gave Moses "signs" to convince the Pharaoh; still, Moses revealed his perceived self-deficiency once more: "Pardon your servant, Lord, I have never been eloquent, neither in the past nor since you have spoken to your servant. I am slow of speech and tongue." This exchange continued for several more passages, with Moses expressing his self-doubt each step of the way.

Although we do not know for sure if Moses struggled with shame-proneness on a daily basis, Exodus 3–4 reveals that he definitely had a hard time responding to God's call with an unwavering, "yes, Lord." Yet, in spite of Moses' hesitation, God told Moses, "I will be with you," which reveals the Christian antidote to shame. Although we continue to struggle with self-doubts, self-criticisms, and negative self-evaluations in the 21st century—long after the initial effects of the fall—God is with us, strengthening our ability to persevere in the midst of both inner and outer trials. In fact, God's "power is made perfect in [our] weakness" (2 Corinthians 12:9).

Repetitive Negative Thinking and Shame

Because of the fall of humankind, Christians are vulnerable to repetitive negative thinking. Unfortunately, in trying to be "like God" in "knowing good and evil" (Genesis 3:5), we can strive, on our own and independent of God's infinite wisdom (Proverbs 3:5), to make sense of our inner and outer world. This type of thinking can involve ruminating about the past or worrying about the future. When we ruminate about the past, we constantly "chew on" prior events, going over and over the information in our head. Ruminating can take the form of thinking about a past mistake or conversation, with the central theme involving getting stuck in this perseverative process. Or, we may worry about a yet-to-be-determined future, attempting to "fill in the blanks" with "what-ifs" by striving to predict what lies ahead. Yet, only God knows the future (Psalm 139:16; James 4:14–15); therefore, trusting in him, and yielding to his will, is key (Matthew 6:25–34).

In either case, we can get stuck in these types of thinking patterns, which means we may spend a good deal of our day fixated on negative cognitions, resulting in depression, anxiety, and shame. In fact, recent research has revealed that repetitive negative thinking is linked to both depression and anxiety (Arditte, Shaw, & Timpano, 2016), as well as shame (Mahoney, McEvoy, & Moulds, 2012). Ultimately, this style of perseverative thinking can be especially problematic in contributing to a range of psychiatric disorders.

In the context of shame, ruminating about the past may involve being highly critical of yourself in past situations or conversations. You might find that you are going over and over a mistake you have made, blaming yourself and assigning global self-ratings of worthlessness, unlovability, and so forth. Or, you may worry about an unknown future, predicting that you will inevitably "fail again." Whether you are looking forwards or backwards, constantly "chewing on" self-criticism can take up all of your time and energy so that you are unable to see what is right in front of you—God's unending, perfect love. Certainly, if you are "chewing the cud" of self-criticism all day long, partially digesting the information, only to regurgitate it again to chew on it some more, the accompanying shame can feel like a permanent, unwavering, and unrelenting inner experience.

The Apostle Paul and Christian Thinking: Focusing on "Things Above"

In the New Testament, the Apostle Paul had several things to say about Christian thinking. When writing to the Colossians (3:1–3), he stated the following:

> Since, then, you have been raised with Christ, set your hearts on things above, where Christ is, seated at the right hand of God. Set your minds on things above, not on earthly things. For you died, and your life is now hidden with Christ in God.

In this passage, Paul was encouraging believers in Christ to focus on the right things, viewing the world from Jesus' perspective (Bruce, 1984). In other words, rather than being narrowly preoccupied with our own perceived flaws, as is the case with shame-proneness, regularly pivoting towards our identity in Christ is central to healthy Christian living (Bruce, 1984).

As another example, when concluding his letter to the Philippians (4:8), Paul advocated the following:

> Finally, brothers and sisters, whatever is true, whatever is noble, whatever is right, whatever is pure, whatever is lovely, whatever is admirable—if anything is excellent or praiseworthy—think about such things.

Here, Paul offered a list of virtues for Christians to "think about," possibly in the context of persecution (Thielman, 1995). Stated differently, even though society may have seemed to be against them, the Philippians were to actively strive to see the good in the world, given that God's plan was still being carried out (Thielman, 1995).

In these two 1st-century letters, Paul emphasized focusing on "things above," as well as a list of virtues so as to shift away from "earthly things." Although Christians are certainly vulnerable to repetitive negative thinking and shame, the Apostle Paul encouraged believers in Christ to think about both God and his creation in the best possible manner. One such group of Christians who wrote extensively on this salient cognitive shift was the Puritans.

The Puritans and Christian Thinking: Cultivating "Heavenly-Mindedness"

The Puritans were a group of Protestants from England in the 1500s and 1600s. They advocated for drawing directly from the Bible to guide all aspects of life. One Puritan author, Joseph Hall, argued that we are always meditating on something; thus, what we choose to meditate on is key (Hall, 2016). In other words, we can choose to focus on self-doubts, self-criticisms, and negative self-evaluations, or meditate on both God and his promises in the Bible (Ball, 2016). The Puritans referred to this deep shift in thinking as meditation, which is "a serious and solemn thinking about God" (Watson, 2012). As Christians pivot from "earthly-mindedness" to "heavenly-mindedness" via "gathering together the thoughts" (Watson, 2012), we are able to "keep them under check" (Ball, 2016).

John Ball, a Puritan writer in the 1600s, further elaborated on "heavenly-mindedness":

> Frequent and daily repetition and regard for heavenly things brings us to better and more inward acquaintance with God and a most comfortable fellowship and communion with Him. The more we speak and converse with a man, the better we know him, the further we see into his worth, faithfulness and excellency.
>
> (Ball, 2016, p. 43)

In this workbook, you will be practicing this shift from "earthly-mindedness" to "heavenly-mindedness" so as to ameliorate shame and negative self-judgments. Yet, it is easy for the mind to wander towards negative thinking. In fact, recent research has revealed that half of a sample of adults indicated their mind was wandering while they were attempting to focus on another activity (Killingsworth & Gilbert, 2010). When mind wandering turns into repetitive negative thinking, we can quickly experience painful emotions like shame. It is almost as if we wander into the wrong part of town and cannot seem to find our way home. Our mind may begin to drift, quickly turning towards self-doubt, self-criticism, and self-judgment. When this happens, we may end up feeling a tremendous amount of shame, leading to withdrawal and concealment from others. Just like being in the wrong part of town after dark, a straying mind can experience serious emotional and behavioral consequences.

In the fourth chapter, you will work on thinking with compassion to pivot from self-criticism to an awareness of God's loving presence. In the meantime, I would like you to begin to consider the types of thoughts you "chew on" from moment to moment, reminiscent of a cow chewing cud in a field all day long. Interestingly, cud is food that has only been partially digested in that it goes from the mouth to the stomach, then back to the mouth to be chewed all over again. Consistent with this process, "chewing on" self-judgments and self-criticisms all day long can take up all of your time and energy, especially when you struggle to fully digest this type of proverbial food so as to move on to the next challenge in life.

What Do You Think About Throughout Your Day?: An Exercise

For this exercise, see if you can monitor your thoughts throughout your day, especially your self-doubts, self-criticisms, and self-judgments. At times, we can struggle to notice our negative self-evaluations, in that they are so common. Reminiscent of a cow slowly chewing cud in a grassy field all day long, we may not even notice that we are "chewing on" the proverbial grass of negative self-evaluations throughout our day.

After recording your thoughts throughout the week, try to reflect on the thought patterns you have engaged in. What types of negative self-evaluations do you struggle with the most? Do they involve a certain perceived flaw? Does your thinking consist of how you believe you come across to others or how you believe God views you? How do these negative self-views impact your daily life and relationships with others?

Day of the Week	*Self-Doubts, Self-Criticisms, and Self-Judgments (Morning)*	*Self-Doubts, Self-Criticisms, and Self-Judgments (Afternoon)*	*Self-Doubts, Self-Criticisms, and Self-Judgments (Night)*
Monday			
Tuesday			
Wednesday			
Thursday			
Friday			
Saturday			
Sunday			

In addition to "chewing on" self-criticism all day long, you may struggle with shame because of an overreliance on the "danger" system of emotion regulation. In this workbook, you will be working on transitioning from the "danger" to the "contentment" system (via several types of Christian practices). In the remainder of this chapter, you will learn about three God-given emotion regulation systems, as well as a strategy for shifting from the "danger" to the "contentment" system so as to relate differently to shame (Burroughs, 2010; Gilbert, 2010).

Emotion Regulation: The "Danger," "Drive," and "Contentment" Systems

When it comes to managing our emotions, we have three overarching systems: "danger," "drive," and "contentment" (or "safeness") (Gilbert, 2009).[2] Each system serves a useful function and is linked to a range of emotional experiences and behavioral outcomes. To begin, the "danger" system helps us to take action ("fight, flight, or freeze" responses via the sympathetic nervous system) when we encounter a dangerous situation, with fear, anxiety, and anger allowing us to quickly make sense of a threat so as to respond in the most appropriate manner (Gilbert, 2009; Kolts, 2016). Biologically, the stress hormone cortisol is linked to the "danger" system.

Next, the "drive" system is implicated in motivating us to attain the necessary life resources to survive (e.g., food, shelter, clothing, relationships, reproduction), with positive feelings (e.g., excitement, pleasure) helping us to press forward in order to continuously acquire these requisite building blocks for optimal living (Gilbert, 2009; Kolts, 2016). Within the brain, the neurotransmitter dopamine is linked to these types of behavior.

Finally, the "contentment" (or "safeness") system is linked to "not-seeking" behavior (via the parasympathetic nervous system), given that we are accessing this system when we are content, calm, at peace, and feeling a sense of safety, rather than moving towards something we want or away from something we do not want; in other words, when we are *not* in danger or preoccupied with pursuing resources, we are in a relaxed state of being (Gilbert, 2009; Kolts, 2016). From a biological perspective, the hormone oxytocin is linked to a sense of safety in the context of close relationships. Interestingly, in a recent study on the link between oxytocin and spirituality among Christians, findings revealed a positive relationship between levels of oxytocin detected in Christians' saliva and their self-described level of spirituality (Holbrook, Hahn-Holbrook, & Holt-Lunstad, 2015).

These three systems, biologically and psychologically speaking, are absolutely essential. We need to be able to detect threatening situations as soon as possible (via the sympathetic nervous system), whether in the present moment (with the emotion of fear) or just around the corner (when we experience anxiety). In turn, we are able to fight for survival, flee the situation, or yield to the situation or person. We also need to regularly pursue vital resources for our own survival—this behavior is reinforced by way of pleasurable emotional experiences. Finally, we need to experience a sense of safety and contentment in the context of trusting relationships (via the parasympathetic nervous system); this feeling of peace and calm occurs when we are not distracted by anticipating threats or acquiring material possessions.

Tragically, we may end up struggling to utilize the "contentment" system on a regular basis due to a lack of trusting, supportive relationships in childhood; instead, we might overly utilize the "danger" system, leading to chronic experiences of shame and negative self-evaluations (Gilbert, 2009). To be sure, we can end up constantly anticipating danger in the context of social interactions, predicting that others are judging us; when this happens, we may turn on ourselves with self-doubt and self-criticism. Stated differently, early life experiences that involved other people criticizing us can lead to criticizing ourselves on a regular basis, triggering the "danger" system (Gilbert, 2013). Over time, an overactive "danger" system can result in repetitive negative thinking and painful emotional states like shame. Or, we may engage in addictive or compulsive behaviors so as to pursue pleasure and avoid pain, overly relying on the "drive" system in our misguided efforts to numb our suffering (Gilbert, 2010).

Ultimately, we need the feelings of safety and support that come from close, intimate relationships with others. When we do not have access to healthy interpersonal interactions, we may struggle to access the "contentment" system (via parasympathetic activity) on a regular basis, overly relying on the "danger" system (by way of sympathetic activity) because of early life experiences (Gilbert, 2010). As a result, we may seldom (or never) feel the contentment, peace, and security that come from safe connections.

The Three Traveling Companions: Nicknamed "Danger," "Drive," and "Contentment"[3]

A metaphor may help you to better understand the importance of these three systems, including the ways in which they must work together in order to survive on the roads of life. Imagine there is a man, nicknamed "Danger," walking down the road. "Danger" is known for being able to spot threatening situations from a mile away. As he walks along the street, he can see rattlesnakes in the distance, quickly get out of the way of moving cars, and avoid other mishaps along the roads of life. Yet, because he focuses all his attention on anticipating danger, he fails to build a life for himself. In other words, he does not devote his time and energy to securing the necessary resources (e.g., food, shelter, clothing) to succeed in life. Undoubtedly, he has a hard time slowing down to find contentment, enjoyment, and peace in this world. Although he is always "on guard" to anticipate catastrophe, he does not find rest.

As he is walking, he meets another man, nicknamed "Drive," quickly befriending him. "Drive" is known for focusing on getting the requisite material possessions needed to survive. Thus, he has a house just down the road, with a new car parked in the driveway. He also has a refrigerator full of food, and comfortable clothes in his closet. Unfortunately, though, "Drive" struggles to notice the dangers that lie ahead; as a result, he is late on his bills, and is probably going to lose his job in the next year or so. As the two talk, "Danger" quickly realizes that "Drive" struggles with the ability to anticipate threatening situations, and "Drive" discovers that "Danger" devotes all of his energy to predicting the future, which means he has no time to acquire life's much-needed possessions. The two, in turn, decide to combine efforts, recognizing that they can work more effectively if they travel along the roads of life together.

Over time, though, the two begin to get extremely exhausted, recognizing that they are seldom, if ever, able to find rest. Although they work well together—they are able to collaboratively look ahead to predict threats and acquire vital possessions to survive in life—both quickly realize they are unable to slow down enough to actually enjoy life. Stated differently, they do not feel content, in that their ability to "approach" and "avoid" is not balanced with the capacity to enjoy what life has to offer.

One day, "Danger" and "Drive" meet a third man, nicknamed "Contentment," who is known for being able to slow down enough to find peace, contentment, and a sense of safety. "Contentment," though, struggles to anticipate disasters and accumulate the possessions necessary to survive. Thus, the three of them discover that they can work well together; yet, the most important component of success, which they have been missing, is balancing their three distinct strengths. "Danger" can anticipate future doom, but needs to also focus on working hard to survive and finding time to rest. "Drive" needs to acquire possessions, but must do so while also enjoying the present moment and looking ahead. Finally, "Contentment" needs to rest in the present moment, but must balance this "non-striving" tendency with the ability to predict threats and secure life's essential resources.

As this metaphor reveals, balancing the three systems is the most important part of the journey. Unfortunately, you may overly rely on the "danger" system, at the expense of finding rest and contentment in the moment. Within the Christian tradition, however, God offers you rest, and can help you to balance the three systems so as to change the way you relate to your self-critical thoughts.

A Christian View of the God-Given "Danger," "Drive," and "Contentment" Systems

From a Christian point of view, God created humankind to be in relationship with him; this means that a true reflection of our humanness—the *imago Dei*—lies in our "self-in-community" identity with God and others (Olson, 2004). However, due to the fall, we continue to struggle with our own imperfections, and have a hard time navigating a dimly lit, broken world. One such area of brokenness involves the reality that people do not always measure up to our standards, letting us down in a wide variety of ways; we, too, come up short in our own attempts to pursue goals, deepen relationships, and so on. Along the way, we need to rely on the three systems—"danger," "drive," and "contentment" (Gilbert, 2010)—in that we live in an inherently dysfunctional, fragmented world. In particular, we need to utilize our God-given "danger" system to better understand current and future threats. Moreover, we need to use our God-given "drive" system so as to provide for ourselves and those who count on us. Finally, we need to connect to our "contentment" system to find God's peace in a fast-paced, dangerous world.

Still, when we overly rely on our "danger" system because of early life experiences of abuse, neglect, or repeated criticism from others, we may have a hard time tapping into the "contentment" system (Gilbert, 2010). In other words, the "contentment" system may seem like a foreign land you have never visited, only to be shown pictures of a vast, unfamiliar landscape. Yet, God wants you to rest in his loving arms, constantly welcoming you home when you wander away; more importantly, he is actively pursuing you even when you veer off course (Luke 15). As the introduction chapter revealed, God is offering you nothing short of himself (including his love, compassion, mercy, grace, and forgiveness) so as to function like the proverbial glue that holds you together.

Within the Old Testament, Psalm 46 seems to accurately capture the perfect security and contentment that is found only in God:

> God is our refuge and strength, an ever-present help in trouble. Therefore we will not fear, though the earth give way and the mountains fall into the heart of the sea, though its waters roar and foam and the mountains quake with their surging. There is a river whose streams make glad the city of God, the holy place where the Most High dwells. God is within her, she will not fall; God will help her at break of day. Nations are in uproar, kingdoms fall; he lifts his voice, the earth melts. The Lord Almighty is with us; the God of Jacob is our fortress. Come and see what the Lord has done, the desolations he has brought on the earth. He makes wars cease to the ends of the earth. He breaks the bow and shatters the spear; he burns the shields with fire. He says, '*Be still, and know that I am God*; I will be exalted among the nations, I will be exalted in the earth.' The Lord Almighty is with us; the God of Jacob is our fortress. (italics added)

In this famous chapter, the main point is to "unconditionally trust in God no matter what should happen," and "safety and security are to be found in God" (Dunn & Rogerson, 2003, p. 391). In the first few verses, the author indicated that God is with his people, in spite of a range of natural disasters. Indeed, the author went on to state that God even offers his help in the midst of human-made disasters. To conclude, the psalmist noted that God says to his people, "Be still, and know that I am God." Interestingly, the Hebrew word, *raphah*, is translated as "be still," meaning to "cease striving" (Strong, 2001b). Right after the writer indicated that God "breaks the bow," "shatters the spear," and "burns the shields with fire," the command to "be still" is used. Consequently, *raphah* can potentially be interpreted as a command to "set down your weapons" (Earwood, 1989). In this context, the text seems to capture dropping your weapons on the battlefield because God is in control.

To "set down your weapons" because God is in control, offering "safety and security," is what you will be practicing in this workbook, shifting from the "danger" to "contentment" system (Burroughs, 2010; Gilbert, 2010) in your relationship with him. As will be revealed in the third chapter, compassion plays an important role in this intentional pivot. Compassion, from a Christian perspective, comes from the outside in, meaning we can have compassion for ourselves because God has already clothed us with his love, mercy, grace, and forgiveness, leading to true Christian contentment. Certainly, when we put our trust in God's providential care, like the Apostle Paul, we can learn to be "content whatever the circumstances" (Philippians 4:11–13). In fact, I will spend more time on this in the third chapter, given that Christians throughout the centuries have written extensively on the role that contentment plays in psychological and spiritual functioning. For now, I will offer a concise definition of Christian contentment from the Puritan author Jeremiah Burroughs (2010):

> Christian contentment is that sweet, inward, quiet, gracious frame of spirit, which freely submits to and delights in God's wise and fatherly disposal in every condition.
>
> (p. 3)

What follows is an exercise for getting to know your three systems, which can help to prepare you for drawing upon God when you are overly relying upon the "danger" system to navigate the roads of life. Certainly, Psalm 46 captures the unpredictability and instability of a dangerous world, with the psalmist encouraging the reader to trust in God in spite of a wide variety of calamities.

Getting to Know Your Three Systems: An Exercise

In the space below, please identify the thoughts, feelings, and behaviors associated with your three systems, along with the most frequent types of situation that lead to the use of your three systems:

What thoughts, feelings, and behaviors do you typically experience when you are utilizing your "danger" system (Gilbert, 2010)? What types of situations trigger your "danger" system? What are some common outcomes when you utilize your "danger" system? How do these "danger" system-related experiences impact your relationship with God?

____
____
____
____
____
____

What thoughts, feelings, and behaviors do you typically experience when you are utilizing your "drive" system (Gilbert, 2010)? What types of situations trigger your "drive" system? What are some common outcomes when you utilize your "drive" system? How do these "drive" system-related experiences impact your relationship with God?

____
____
____
____
____
____

What thoughts, feelings, and behaviors do you typically experience when you are utilizing your "contentment" system (Gilbert, 2010)? What types of situations trigger your "contentment" system? What are some common outcomes when you utilize your "contentment" system? How do these "contentment" system-related experiences impact your relationship with God?

____
____
____
____
____
____

In this workbook, my hope is that you will begin to balance your use of the three God-given systems, employing the "danger" system to help you take action in the face of threatening situations, utilizing the "drive" system to provide for yourself and your loved ones, and turning to God in order to access the "contentment" system (Burroughs, 2010; Gilbert, 2010). More specifically, you will be learning to recognize that he designed you to find comfort, protection, peace, and a deep sense of calm in your unique relationship with him. One of the ways to do so, as revealed throughout this workbook, is by way of Christian *apophatic* meditation. With this form of meditation, you will be practicing a Christian alternative to mindfulness meditation, which has empirical support in the psychology literature for cultivating self-compassion in response to shame and negative self-judgments. From a Christian perspective, contemplation is about "resting in God" (a term originally used by Gregory the Great) from moment to moment, accessing the "contentment" system so as to ameliorate the shame and self-criticisms that emanate from overly relying on the "danger" system. When this happens, my hope is that you will be able to work on extending God's compassion to yourself and others.

Mindfulness Versus Contemplation: Focusing on the "Self" or God to Access Compassion?

Within the last several decades, mindfulness meditation has had a significant influence upon several Western institutions. As revealed in the vast array of publications on the topic, mindfulness as a meditative practice is currently employed within elementary schools, higher education, corporations, psychotherapy rooms, and so on. Commonly defined as "paying attention in a particular way; on purpose, in the present moment, and nonjudgmentally" (Kabat-Zinn, 2012, p. 1), practitioners of mindfulness meditation typically focus on the breath or one of the five senses for a formal period of time (e.g., ten minutes) in a quiet environment so as to cultivate non-judgmental, focused attention. Although mindfulness in American society has been secularized (i.e., separated from its religious roots and researched within Western psychology), it has been historically grounded in Buddhism.

Within the Buddhist tradition, there are four "noble truths," including (a) life is suffering, (b) the cause of suffering is desire, (c) suffering can be ended, and (d) the way to end suffering is through the "Eightfold Noble Path" (Morgan, 2010). One of the steps to end suffering along the "Noble Path" involves "right mindfulness."

With Buddhism's "right mindfulness," practitioners attempt to get to know the mind, including fluctuating inner states; whether focusing on being mindful of the body, feelings, or other mental events, the ultimate aim is "enlightenment" (Morgan, 2010). In formal mindfulness meditation, practitioners are attempting to better understand the "Three Marks of Existence," including "impermanence," "no-self," and "suffering" (Morgan, 2010; Tirch, Silberstein, & Kolts, 2016). Getting to know impermanence involves recognizing that the inner world is constantly changing, and cultivating no-self is about getting to know the "self" as a process, rather than a fixed, permanent state; finally, mindfulness can help practitioners get to know the nature of suffering, including the notion that we can understand suffering (i.e., "pervasive unsatisfactoriness") on a deeper level, and respond to suffering via acceptance and compassion (Tirch, Silberstein, & Kolts, 2016). Overall, the Buddhist ingredients of "impermanence" and "no-self"—cultivated by way of mindfulness meditation—are different from those within Christian contemplation, which are about deepening your relationship with God.

Turning to the history of Christian *apophatic* meditation (often referred to in the 21st century as "contemplative prayer"), Christians started to move to the deserts of Egypt, Palestine, and Syria in the 4th century in order to reject the materialism that was rampant in secular society. As they moved to the desert, they simultaneously strived to face their inner temptations and deepen their relationship with God (Burton-Christie, 1993). Just like Jesus' 40 days in the wilderness (Matthew 4:1–11), these desert monks moved to the desert to wholeheartedly rely on God, cultivating a mindful attention on his presence (Burton-Christie, 1993).

Originally, they would recite Scripture in an effort to focus their mind on God, turning away from tempting, compulsive thoughts (which they believed came from demons in the desert) (Laird, 2011). Over time, they shortened these passages in Scripture, and eventually recited the Jesus Prayer: "Lord Jesus Christ, Son of God, have mercy on me" (Laird, 2011). With the Jesus Prayer, Christian practitioners are attempting to accomplish several goals (adapted from Johnson, 2010):

- Focusing on God (the Greek word, *proseuch*).
- Remembering God (the Greek phrase, *mneme theou*).
- Watching the inner world (the Greek word, *nepsis*), including tempting thoughts (the Greek word, *logismoi*).
- Developing a peaceful inner state (the Greek word, *hesychia*).
- Relating differently to negative thoughts in an indirect manner by shifting the focus to God (Ware, 2000).

Other forms of Christian *apophatic* meditation include the instructions from *The Cloud of Unknowing* (Bangley, 2006), a 14th-century anonymous writing, which inspired a 21st-century version, centering prayer (Keating, 2009). In centering prayer, you simply (a) select a "sacred word," which captures your attitude of surrender to God's loving action within your innermost being, and (b) utilize the word whenever you get distracted with your own thoughts in order to—again and again—yield to God's active, loving presence (Keating, 2009).

Of course, there are several differences between Buddhist-informed mindfulness and Christian *apophatic* meditation, including the following:

- The point of focus, concentration, or attention
  - The breath or the five senses (Buddhism) versus God (Christianity).
- Views about suffering
  - Suffering is due to human desire (Buddhism) versus suffering is due to humans originally turning away from God (Christianity).
- Views about the inner world
  - Impermanence (Buddhism) versus brokenness due to the fall of humankind (Christianity).
- Views about the self
  - The independent self is an illusion (Buddhism) versus humans were created in God's image to be in union with him (but are fallen due to originally turning away from him) (Christianity).

Because of these differences, as a Christian, you may wish to turn towards your own faith tradition, rather than mindfulness meditation. Although mindfulness meditation in the 21st century has been secularized in the clinical psychology literature, it still has roots in Buddhism. Therefore, to familiarize yourself with the meditative foundations within your own religious heritage, you will be practicing a modified version of Christian *apophatic* meditation via the powerful word, "Lord."

Contemplation and the "Contentment" System: An Exercise

In this ten-minute exercise, I would like you to begin to practice Christian *apophatic* meditation by focusing on the word, "Lord." Within the pages of the New Testament, the Greek word for "Lord," *kurios*, is used when referring to Jesus. Translated as "supreme in authority," the word can also mean "master" or "owner" (Strong, 2001a). In this practice, you will be using modified instructions from centering prayer (Keating, 2009). In addition, please consider using the corresponding audio recording, "Track 1," available at https://www.routledge.com/The-Compassion-Based-Workbook-for-Christian-Clients-Finding-Freedom-from/Knabb/p/book/9780815394365.

Find a quiet, comfortable location, sitting in a chair with your hands rested in your lap. In the next ten minutes, you will be repeating, "Lord," as a way to find rest in Jesus as *the* source of security. Because Jesus is in control of your inner word, serving as your "master," there is nothing else you need to be doing, other than yielding to his loving control. Once you are ready, close your eyes, and begin to recite the word, "Lord," surrendering to God's authority over your inner world. Whenever a distracting thought emerges, gently pivot towards "Lord" to capture your willingness to yield to God as the "owner" of your thoughts and feelings. In other words, God is your source of security; thus, you do not need to anticipate danger or accumulate possessions during this time spent with him. When the ten minutes comes to a close, thank God for the ability to spend this time with him. Ask him to remind you of his loving presence throughout your day.

The above instructions can be condensed into two steps (adapted from Keating, 2009) for ease of use:

- Begin to silently, slowly, and gently repeat the word, "Lord," which captures your attitude of surrender to God's loving action within your innermost being.
- Pivot back to the word, "Lord," whenever you get distracted with your own thoughts in order to—again and again—yield to God's active, loving presence.

After you have concluded the ten-minute practice, try to reflect on your experience, answering the following questions:

What was it like to use the word, "Lord," for the ten-minute block of time as a way to yield to God's loving care?

What thoughts and feelings came up as you attempted to surrender to God via the word, "Lord," for the ten-minute block of time?

How can this practice help you shift your attention from shame and negative self-judgments to Jesus' loving control over your inner world?

Before concluding the chapter, I would like you to read about Rebecca, who struggles with overly relying on the "danger" system (Gilbert, 2010). By getting to know her, my hope is you can identify with her challenge before moving on to one of the next steps in this workbook—using compassion as an antidote for shame.

The "Danger," "Drive," and "Contentment" Systems in the Real World: A Case Example

Rebecca grew up with a mother who was chronically depressed. As a result, she struggled to feel supported. In that her father was not around, she was often left by herself for long periods of time, with her mother barely managing to get out of bed long enough to take care of basic household responsibilities. Over time, Rebecca started to believe she was defective, unworthy of her mother's love. On occasion, her mother would take her to church, with Rebecca feeling a deep sense of shame before God. In particular, she felt invisible and flawed, struggling to understand how a God so big could love someone so small. Even though she knew the Bible said that God loved "the world" (John 3:16), she was convinced she was not part of "the world" God created and cared for.

In her young adult years, she continued to struggle with feeling God's love for her; instead, she would constantly anticipate others' rejection, reminiscent of her mother's emotional unavailability. Her "danger" system (Gilbert, 2010) seemed to be working overtime, given she was highly sensitive to perceived criticism from others. Gradually, she started to criticize herself, firmly believing that her mother would have healed from the chronic depression if Rebecca was lovable. As the judgmental voice inside her head got louder by the day, she turned to alcohol as a way to numb the pain. Yet, this short-term attempt to mask her shame only made matters worse.

Above all else, she longed for the sense of safety, closeness, and connection her classmates in Sunday School expressed in describing their relationship with God, and wondered how she could feel an unshakable faith in God's active, loving presence in her life. She knew she was exhausted, fatigued by her pattern of "striving," only to "come up short" on a daily basis.

As you move into the next chapter, try to consider your own struggles with shame. How might self-compassion, which first comes from God, help you in your efforts to feel God's love, grace, mercy, and forgiveness? In what specific ways can compassion help you to live the life you want, radically following Jesus in the process?

Conclusion

In this chapter, you explored the definitions and characteristics of shame from both psychological and Christian perspectives. You also learned about shame-proneness, repetitive negative thinking, and the "danger," "drive," and "contentment" systems (Gilbert, 2010). Finally, you were able to compare and contrast mindfulness and Christian *apophatic* meditation, learning about how the latter can be used to simultaneously (a) relate differently to your difficult inner experiences of shame and negative self-judgments, and (b) turn to God to connect to your "contentment" system.

Although shame and self-criticism are unfortunate realities because of the fall of humankind, the practices in this workbook can help you to shift from "earthly-mindedness" to "heavenly-mindedness" so as to find rest in God—the author of the "contentment" system (Burroughs, 2010; Gilbert, 2010). Before transitioning to the role that compassion plays in this process—in the third chapter—I would like to explore your relationship with God in more detail, given that he is the ultimate source of security, contentment, and compassion, offering you an antidote to chronic shame and self-judgments.

Notes

1 If you did not have a relationship with God at the time, please consider how this early experience of shame currently influences your relationship with God.
2 Worth mentioning, some authors have pointed out the difference between "safety" and "safeness," with the former describing attempts to protect against threatening situations via the sympathetic nervous system and the latter capturing a sense of contentment and calm by way of the parasympathetic nervous system in the context of close relationships (Gilbert, 2005).
3 In this metaphor, "danger," "drive," and "contentment" are based on Gilbert (2010).

References

Albers, R. (1995). *Shame: A faith perspective*. New York: The Haworth Pastoral Press.
Arditte, K., Shaw, A., & Timpano, K. (2016). Repetitive negative thinking: A transdiagnostic correlate of affective disorders. *Journal of Social and Clinical Psychology, 35*(3), 181–201.
Ball, J. (2016). *A treatise of divine meditation*. Crossville, TN: Puritan Publications.
Bangley, B. (Ed.). (2006). *The cloud of unknowing: Contemporary English edition*. Brewster, MA: Paraclete Press.
Bloesch, D. (2017). Sin. Biblical understanding. In D. Treier & W. Elwell (Eds.), *Evangelical dictionary of theology* (p. 808). Grand Rapids, MI: Baker Academic.
Bonhoeffer, D. (1955). *Ethics*. New York: Touchstone.
Bonhoeffer, D. (1959). *Creation and fall*. New York: Touchstone.
Bruce, F. (1984). *The epistles to the Colossians, to Philemon, and to the Ephesians*. Grand Rapids, MI: William B. Eerdmans Publishing Company.
Burroughs, J. (2010). *The rare jewel of Christian contentment*. Pensacola, FL: Chapel Library.
Burton-Christie, D. (1993). *The word in the desert: Scripture and the quest for holiness in early Christian monasticism*. New York: Oxford University Press.
Cohen, T., Wolf, S., Panter, A., & Insko, C. (2011). Introducing the GASP scale: A new measure of guilt and shame proneness. *Journal of Personality and Social Psychology, 100*(5), 947–966.
Dunn, J., & Rogerson, J. (Eds.). (2003). *Eerdmans commentary on the Bible*. Grand Rapids, MI: William B. Eerdmans Publishing Company.
Earwood, G. (1989). Psalm 46. *Review and Expositor, 86*, 79–86.
Erickson, M. (2013). *Christian theology* (3rd ed.). Grand Rapids, MI: Baker Academic.
Gilbert, P. (1998). What is shame? Some core issues and controversies. In P. Gilbert & B. Andrews (Eds.), *Shame: Interpersonal behavior, psychopathology, and culture* (pp. 3–38). New York: Oxford University Press.
Gilbert, P. (2005). Compassion and cruelty: A biopsychosocial approach. In P. Gilbert (Ed.), *Conceptualisations, research and use in psychotherapy* (pp. 9–75). New York: Routledge.
Gilbert, P. (2009). Introducing compassion-focused therapy. *Advances in Psychiatric Treatment, 15*(3), 199–208.
Gilbert, P. (2010). *Compassion focused therapy: Distinctive features*. New York: Routledge.
Gilbert, P. (2013). *The complete guide to overcoming depression*. London: Robinson.
Gilbert, P., & Irons, C. (2009). Shame, self-criticism, and self-compassion in adolescence. In N. Allen & L. Sheeber (Eds.), *Adolescent emotional development and the emergence of depressive disorders* (pp. 195–214). Cambridge: Cambridge University Press.
Hall, J. (2016). *The art of divine meditation* [Kindle version]. Retrieved from Amazon.com
Holbrook, C., Hahn-Holbrook, J., & Holt-Lunstad, J. (2015). Self-reported spirituality correlates with endogenous oxytocin. *Psychology of Religion and Spirituality, 7*(1), 46–50.
Johnson, C. (2010). *The globalization of hesychasm and the Jesus prayer: Contesting contemplation*. New York: Continuum.
Kabat-Zinn, J. (2012). *Mindfulness for beginners: Reclaiming the present moment—and your life*. Boulder, CO: Sounds True, Inc.
Keating, T. (2009). *Intimacy with God: An introduction to centering prayer*. New York: The Crossroad Publishing Company.
Keller, T. (2013). *Walking with God through pain and suffering*. New York: Riverhead Books.
Killingsworth, M., & Gilbert, D. (2010). A wandering mind is an unhappy mind. *Science, 330*(6006), 932.

Kolts, R. (2016). *CFT made simple: A clinician's guide to practicing compassion-focused therapy*. Oakland, CA: New Harbinger Publications, Inc.
Laird, M. (2011). *A sunlit absence: Silence, awareness, and contemplation*. New York: Oxford University Press.
Mahoney, A., McEvoy, P., & Moulds, M. (2012). Psychometric properties of the repetitive thinking questionnaire in a clinical sample. *Journal of Anxiety Disorders, 26*(2), 359–367.
McGrath, A. (2011). *Christian theology: An introduction*. Malden, MA: Wiley-Blackwell.
McGrath, J., & McGrath, A. (2002). *Self-esteem: The cross and Christian confidence*. Wheaton, IL: Crossway Books.
Morgan, D. (2010). *Essential Buddhism: A comprehensive guide to belief and practice*. Santa Barbara, CA: Praeger.
Olson, R. (2004). *The Westminster handbook to Evangelical theology*. Louisville, KY: Westminster John Knox Press.
Strong, J. (2001a). *The Greek dictionary of the New Testament*. Nashville, TN: Thomas Nelson.
Strong, J. (2001b). *The new Strong's expanded dictionary of the words in the Hebrew Bible*. Nashville, TN: Thomas Nelson.
Tangney, J., & Dearing, R. (2002). *Shame and guilt*. New York: The Guilford Press.
Tangney, J., Wagner, P., & Gramzow, R. (1992). Proneness to shame, proneness to guilt, and psychopathology. *Journal of Abnormal Psychology, 101*(3), 469–478.
Thielman, F. (1995). *The NIV application commentary: Philippians*. Grand Rapids, MI: Zondervan.
Tirch, D., Silberstein, L., & Kolts, R. (2016). *Buddhist psychology and cognitive-behavioral therapy: A clinician's guide*. New York: The Guilford Press.
Ware, K. (2000). *The inner kingdom*. Crestwood, NY: St. Vladimir's Seminary Press.
Watson, T. (2012). *A treatise concerning meditation*. Charleston, SC: Waxkeep Publishing.

CHAPTER 2

Attachment to God and the "Contentment" System

Introduction

In this chapter, you will explore the basics of attachment theory, including the development of secure and insecure attachments. You will also review the neurobiology of attachment, especially the role that oxytocin (a hormone and neurotransmitter) plays in your "contentment" system and a felt sense of interpersonal security (Buchheim et al., 2009; Gilbert, 2010). Moreover, you will learn about the relationship between attachment and compassion,[1] including recent research suggesting compassion helps to explain the link between insecure attachments and depression and anxiety (Joeng et al., 2017). Overall, attachment theory can help you to better understand the central role that relationships play in connecting you to your "contentment" system as an antidote to shame and self-judgments.

Beyond human attachments, you will explore your attachment to God, including basic definitions of God concept, God image, and God attachment (and how they relate to one another in your own life). You will learn about emerging research on God attachment and the brain, such as the role that oxytocin plays in your spiritual functioning (Holbrook, Hahn-Holbrook, & Holt-Lunstad, 2015), as well as research on the function of self-compassion in explaining the link between God attachment and mental health: "Essentially, those who perceive God as compassionate are able to extend compassion to themselves" (Homan, 2014, p. 985). Although compassion will be explored in more detail in the next chapter, for now, you will have the opportunity to review the important connection between God attachment and self-compassion, unpacking this dynamic by applying it to your own life.

The information on attachment in this chapter will assist you, as a Christian, to utilize the "contentment" system (rather than overly relying on the "danger" system) (Gilbert, 2010; Kolts, 2016) to cultivate a secure attachment with God, which can help you with shame and negative self-judgments. Interestingly, recent research has revealed that our God image and God attachment can change (Knabb, Frederick, & Cumming, 2017; Thomas, Moriarty, Davis, & Anderson, 2011). Our God image functions like an "attachment filter," helping to explain the connection between God (commonly referred to as your "divine attachment figure") and our deeper, emotional experience of our "divine action figure" (Thomas et al., 2011). This emerging research has illuminated that our God image and God attachment can be modified via cognitive interventions (Thomas et al., 2011), and our God image can change by way of Christian meditation (Knabb et al., 2017). Although the next chapter will more fully expand upon compassion, for now, you will focus on how your understanding of God relates to compassion and begin to consider a strategy for change.

In the second half of this chapter, the story of Mary and Martha in the gospel of Luke (10:38–42) will be used to highlight the difference between the "contentment" and "danger" systems (Gilbert, 2010), with Mary sitting at Jesus' feet. Mary's yielding posture represents the contemplative life, wherein you can learn to surrender to God's presence in the here-and-now (Knabb, 2016a). By learning to rest at the feet of Jesus during instances of shame and self-criticism, you will be working towards experiencing the peace and contentment that God generously offers from moment to moment. As one more biblical example, Jesus' teaching on worry (Matthew 6:25–34) will be presented to contrast relying on the "danger," "drive," and "contentment" systems (Gilbert, 2010) when faced with the uncertainties of life. Then, this story will be expanded upon to include the ways in which you can learn to rely on God (including his providential care) as a source of safety when you are stuck in repetitive thinking during moments of shame.

Most importantly, the research reviewed in this chapter will be built upon throughout the remainder of the workbook, helping you to cultivate a biblically based God concept (through Scripture), positive God image (especially God's providence, developed through cognitive, affective, and experiential exercises), and secure attachment with God (via Christian meditation) so as to access your God-designed "contentment" system (Burroughs, 2010; Gilbert, 2010) and attain a deeper compassion for yourself and others. Along the way, exercises, writing assignments (e.g., journaling), and a case example will be employed to help you better understand the role that your "contentment" system, including an accurate God concept, healthy God image, and secure attachment to God, plays in buffering against your shame and negative self-judgments.

Attachment Theory: Basic Concepts

Attachment theory first began to develop around the 1940s with John Bowlby's observations of the impact that separation from caregivers has on children (Bretherton, 1985, 1992). Specifically, Bowlby found that children often experience predictable attachment behaviors—protest, despair, and detachment—when their parents are absent for an extended period of time (Karen, 1994). With protest, there is an initial attempt by the child to restore the distance in the relationship, followed by a period of despair when the child realizes the parent is not returning. After despair, children typically begin to live life again, although they may come across as distant and uninterested in restoring the connection when the parent returns.

Gradually, Bowlby and colleagues developed a comprehensive relational theory that helps to explain the importance of interpersonal connections during each phase of life (Bretherton, 1985, 1992). Within attachment theory, several concepts are important for you to consider at this point in the workbook, including attachment-related behaviors, bonds, and styles (Rholes & Simpson, 2004), as well as the overarching attachment system. Attachment behaviors include the ways in which you attempt to, psychologically and behaviorally, secure or maintain a close connection with a trusted other (Rholes & Simpson, 2004). Attachment bonds involve your emotional connection to a caregiver, intimate partner, and so on (Rholes & Simpson, 2004). Attachment styles reflect your "stable" and "global" patterns in pursuing and attaining closeness, connection, and safety from attachment figures, along with your beliefs about the willingness of the attachment figure to respond to your pursuits for closeness (Rholes & Simpson, 2004).

Over the years, researchers have focused their efforts on identifying several distinct attachment styles—an amalgam of emotions, behaviors, and relational needs and expectations—including secure, anxious, dismissive avoidant, and fearful avoidant (Mikulincer & Shaver, 2007). In the space below, see which statements you most identify with (adapted from Bartholomew & Horowitz, 1991; Brennan, Clark, & Shaver, 1998; Mikulincer & Shaver, 2007, 2017):

- Secure
  - I have a positive view of myself and others in close relationships.
  - I believe I am lovable in close relationships.
  - I believe other people will respond to my needs in close relationships.
  - I am able to lean on others, and am willing to allow others to lean on me.
  - I spend no time worrying about being abandoned, rejected, or experiencing intimacy.
  - People want to be as close to me as I do to them.

  - When my close relationships are not going well, I communicate my true feelings without getting overly upset.
- Anxious
  - I have a negative view of myself and a positive view of others in close relationships.
  - I believe I am unlovable in close relationships.
  - I believe other people are responsive in general, but I worry that others will reject or abandon me in particular.
  - I want to be able to lean on others, but they seem to have a hard time leaning on me.
  - I am preoccupied with intimate relationships.
  - I worry about being abandoned or rejected, and fear that others do not want to be intimate with me.
  - I want to be closer to others than they want to be to me.
  - When my close relationships are not going well, I get frustrated, anxious, upset, or feel bad about myself as a person.
- Dismissive avoidant
  - I have a positive view of myself and a negative view of others in close relationships.
  - I believe I am lovable in close relationships.
  - I do not believe other people will respond to my needs in close relationships.
  - I do not want to lean on others or allow others to lean on me.
  - I am dismissive of intimate relationships.
  - I do not worry about being abandoned or rejected by others.
  - I get nervous when people get too close to me.
  - People want to be closer to me than I want to be to them.
  - I do not express vulnerable feelings in close relationships.
- Fearful avoidant
  - I have a negative view of both myself and others in close relationships.
  - I believe I am unlovable in close relationships.
  - I do not believe other people will respond to my needs in close relationships.
  - I do not want to lean on others or allow others to lean on me.
  - I am avoidant of intimate relationships.
  - I worry about being abandoned or rejected by others.
  - I get nervous when people get too close to me.
  - People want to be closer to me than I want to be to them.
  - I do not express vulnerable feelings in close relationships.

Finally, your attachment system, which is a "biologically evolved regulatory system," includes all of the aforementioned behaviors that you utilize in response to threatening situations (Mikulincer & Shaver, 2004). Throughout the lifespan, you employ trusted others as a secure base and safe haven, with a secure base functioning as someone to launch out into the world from so as to confidently explore the environment; this same person is utilized as a safe haven for soothing comfort when the environment is unsafe, threatening, or distressing (Mikulincer & Shaver, 2004). Think of this dynamic almost like a "circle of security," first using the caregiver as a launching pad so as to explore your environment, pursue life goals, and so on; when the world gets difficult, scary, or distressing, the caregiver becomes your source of support, security, and safety (Feeney & Collins, 2004).

Overall, attachment behaviors help you to form and maintain attachment bonds, leading to the development of an attachment style, which consists of your strategies to secure closeness and expectations about the reliability of others in getting these vital interpersonal needs met.

The Three Phases of the Attachment System: Safety as the Central Goal

One of the most important benefits of secure attachments involves the protection that is offered to us by a caregiver, or "attachment figure," who is typically seen as "stronger and wiser" (Mikulincer & Shaver, 2007). When in danger, we can reach for the safety of another person, who offers support in this crucial time of need. If faced with a threatening situation, we commonly go through three phases (adapted from Mikulincer & Shaver, 2007):

- The detection phase: in this phase, we monitor the situation to determine if a threat is present; if a dangerous situation arises, our attachment system is activated, and we search for closeness with an attachment figure, whereas a nonthreatening scenario leads to us going about our day.
- The availability phase: in this phase, we search for an attachment figure in the face of a dangerous situation; if the trusted person is available for closeness and connection, we feel a sense of safety and security, and experience positive feelings, whereas the unavailability of an attachment figure leads to heightened distress and insecure attachment.
- The seeking phase: in this phase, we determine if it is possible to make further attempts at closeness and connection; if these attempts are an option, "hyperactivating" tendencies are utilized, whereas "deactivating" tendencies are employed if closeness is not possible.

Both "hyperactivating" and "deactivating" approaches to threat emanate from the unavailability of an attachment figure, with children of parents who use hyperactivating styles internalizing these tendencies so as to become hyperactivating themselves, and a similar pattern emerging among children with parents with deactivating styles (Mikulincer & Shaver, 2007; Wallin, 2007). See if you can identify with using (at least some of the time) either of the following strategies, whether hyperactivating or deactivating (adapted from Mikulincer & Shaver, 2007; Wallin, 2007):

- Hyperactivating strategies
  - I overly rely on others for support.
  - I have unrealistic expectations about the need for support from others.
  - I have clinging tendencies.
  - I exhibit controlling behavior.
  - I exaggerate the level of threat, danger, or vulnerability.
  - I struggle with self-blame.
  - I have escalating emotions.
  - I struggle with a devalued sense of self.
  - I am preoccupied with others' needs.
- Deactivating strategies
  - I overly rely on myself and maintaining autonomy.
  - I deny realistic threats, dangers, vulnerabilities, or needs.
  - I suppress emotions.
  - I have an inflated sense of self.
  - I dismiss others' needs.

Typically, a "hyperactivating" strategy is used with anxious attachment, whereas a "deactivating" strategy is utilized with avoidant attachment. In both instances, our "contentment" system (Gilbert, 2010) is not fully employed. In other words, with insecure attachment, we struggle to feel safe and content in the context of intimate relationships.

In relating attachment styles to the experience of shame, with secure attachment, we often have healthy self-esteem, experience guilt (as opposed to shame) when our behavior is not reflective of a preferred interpersonal standard, and strive to ameliorate perceived relational ruptures as best we can (Mikulincer & Shaver, 2007). With anxious attachment, though, we may blame ourselves (rather than focus on our behavior) when we experience relational discord, resulting in the experience of shame (Karen, 1994; Mikulincer & Shaver, 2007). This tendency to exercise self-blame when dealing with interpersonal challenges may develop over time, with parents or caregivers rejecting repeated efforts for comfort and connection (Schore, 1998). In other words, shame can first be external via criticism from family or discrimination from a social group, resulting in internalized shame, self-criticism, and self-blame (Gilbert & Irons, 2009).

With avoidant attachment, we typically have a negative view of others and a positive or negative view of ourselves (Bartholomew & Horowitz, 1991). When experiencing external shame in a family or social group, we may end up attributing blame to others (rather than internalizing shame and blaming ourselves), leading to anger and retaliation (Gilbert & Irons, 2009). However, this possibly elevated view of ourselves and devalued view of others may actually serve as a defense against a deeper experience of shame, which emanates from a negative view of ourselves that resides underneath an inflated, protective layer of pseudo-self-worth (Gross & Hansen, 2000; Martins, Canavarro, & Moreira, 2016). Although we may not express our vulnerabilities with avoidant attachment, shame can be an underlying experience (Gilbert, 2000), and we may end up expressing anger instead (Gilbert, 1998).

Ultimately, recent research has revealed that shame is correlated with both attachment anxiety and avoidance (Martins et al., 2016), and chronic experiences of external shame can lead to the underutilization of our "contentment" system for soothing comfort when experiencing criticism, bullying, and so forth within our environment (Gilbert & Irons, 2009). Yet, throughout the lifespan, we need to be safely connected, and innately need soothing comfort from trusted others when experiencing environmental stressors (Gilbert & Irons, 2009).

Understanding Attachment Styles: An Exercise

Attachment theory suggests that we form a lens—an internal working model—through which to view close relationships. With this lens, we have a view of ourselves (positive or negative) and others (positive or negative) (Bartholomew & Horowitz, 1991). In addition, we exhibit a certain level of anxiety and avoidance in our close relationships, which leads to an attachment style (Mikulincer & Shaver, 2017). Based on past and current relational experiences, you may tend to have secure or insecure attachments. Common insecure styles include anxious (negative view of self and positive view of others; high anxiety and low avoidance), fearful avoidant (negative view of self and others; high anxiety and high avoidance), and dismissive avoidant (positive view of self and negative view of others; low anxiety and high avoidance) (Bartholomew & Horowitz, 1991). In this exercise, you will begin to explore the life experiences that have shaped how you view yourself and others in the context of close relationships. Please spend some time reflecting on the following questions (adapted from Bartholomew & Horowitz, 1991; Clinton & Sibcy, 2002). In turn, please journal your responses in the space that follows so as to get a better sense of your views about yourself and others. Once you have completed these four question areas, please move on to the next section, which asks you to consider the pattern of your answers. Worth mentioning, you may want to review your answers with your therapist or counselor in order to explore these dynamics further.

Do you believe you have worth and are deserving of others' love, especially those who are closest to you?

When did you first begin to conclude this? What early experiences do you have of this belief that you are or are not worthy and deserving of love?

Are the people closest to you reliable? Are they accepting of you? Can you trust them? Are they available when you need them the most? Will they respond to your needs if you ask for their support?

When did you first begin to form these beliefs about others? What early experiences do you have of others' reliability, acceptance, trustworthiness, availability, and responsiveness?

Now that you have answered the above questions, please consider whether or not your answers about yourself and others tend to be positive or negative.

What were some of the themes that emerged in your answers? Do you tend to have a positive view of yourself and others (a secure attachment style)? A negative view of yourself and a positive view of others (an anxious attachment style)? A positive view of yourself and a negative view of others (a dismissive avoidant attachment style)? A negative view of yourself and negative view of others (a fearful avoidant attachment style)?

Based on your answers, what are the implications for your ability to be soothed and comforted in the context of a safe, supportive relationship with a trusted other? In other words, does a negative view of yourself prevent you from reaching for a loved one in your time of need? Or, does a negative view of others undermine your willingness or ability to reach for someone to help you get through a difficult time?

Before moving on to an exploration of the relationship between attachment, compassion, and your relationship with God, I would like to briefly review some of the more recent findings on the neurobiology of attachment. From a Christian perspective, God designed both the world and the human beings who inhabit this God-given planet; as a result, understanding his blueprint for your close, intimate bonds is especially important at this stage of the workbook.

The Neurobiology of Attachment

For Christians, God created this world, which includes human beings (Genesis 1). From a biological perspective, love is the motivating force that allows us to form attachments, leading to the increased likelihood of survival in close-knit groups (Insel & Young, 2000). In terms of brain functioning, early caregiver–infant exchanges (e.g., "mutual gaze episodes" or "face-to-face transactions," wherein the mother picks up on the infant's nonverbal facial expressions and is attuned to his or her emotional state) in the first year of life allow the caregiver to help regulate the infant's autonomic nervous system (ANS) (Schore, 2000; Schore & Schore, 2008). These repeated interactions lead to the development of key neural connections in the right brain, which play a central role in autonomic brain functioning (Schore & Schore, 2008). Over time, relational interactions between the child and parent allow the child to manage distressing emotions and form a felt sense of the attachment bond via procedural memory in the right brain (Schore, 2000). Stated differently, the caregiver is available to collaborate with the child so as to regulate his or her distressing emotions (Schore, 2000). To situate this discussion within our larger conversation on attachment, shame, and compassion, we can activate the parasympathetic nervous system when we experience compassion in the context of safe, supportive relationships, and the sympathetic nervous system when we are self-critical (Neff, 2016). If you did not experience safe, supportive relationships early on in life, you may currently struggle with relying on trusted others to access parasympathetic activity and the "contentment" system (Gilbert, 2010).

In addition to right brain development and regulation of the ANS, oxytocin (a hormone) is involved in human bonding. Primarily produced in the hippocampus, this hormone contributes to the management of stress and anxiety, and may play a role in caregiving, trust, and empathy, among other social behaviors (Krause et al., 2017). Although additional research is necessary to better understand this unique hormone, it is often referred to as the "cuddle hormone" due to its potential role in human connections.

From a Christian perspective, given that God designed human beings, he is the author of the neurobiological mechanisms of attachment. As a result, we can better comprehend his intentions for human relations by deepening our understanding of the biological underpinnings of interpersonal interactions. Before moving on to an exploration of God attachment—given this is a central focus within the workbook—I would like to briefly touch on the role that compassion plays in attachment-related behavior and accessing the "contentment" system (Gilbert, 2010).

Attachment, Compassion, and the "Contentment" System

When we are securely attached, we can more easily access the "contentment" system in the context of supportive relationships, receiving soothing comfort from trusted others (Colonnello, Petrocchi, & Heinrichs, 2017; Gilbert, 2010). One way we are comforted is through the compassionate responses (e.g., affection, care, kindness, warmth) we receive from those close to us, including caregivers in childhood and romantic partners and friendships in adulthood (Gilbert, 2010). If compassion is defined as the ability to be moved by, and responsive to, suffering (Ekman & Ekman, 2017), it is easy to see the importance of a well-timed compassionate response when we are in pain. Certainly, when we experience compassion from others as they attempt to alleviate our suffering, we are able to access the "contentment" system in that we are being cared for by a "stronger and wiser" other (Mikulincer & Shaver, 2007); this experience, in turn, leads to a corresponding feeling of contentment. Early in life, repeated experiences of receiving compassion from caregivers can result in our ability to be compassionate towards both ourselves and others as we grow older (Mikulincer & Shaver, 2017; Raque-Bogdan, Ericson, Jackson, Martin, & Bryan, 2011). To be sure, when we are treated with worth in securely attached relationships, we go on to treat other people with worth, too (Raque-Bogdan et al., 2011).

Recent research has revealed that self-compassion can explain the link between insecure attachments and depression, anxiety, and mental health (Joeng et al., 2017; Raque-Bogdan et al., 2011). These results suggest that teaching self-compassion and self-kindness strategies to people with anxious and avoidant attachment styles may help to address the depression and anxiety that can emanate from a lack of attachment security (Joeng et al., 2017). In other words, self-compassion can enhance our ability to unilaterally access the safety, contentment, and peace that otherwise flow from healthy interpersonal connections. On the other hand, if we already have a secure attachment style, we are better positioned to be compassionate towards ourselves and others, given we are not focusing all of our attention, thoughts, emotions, and so on towards insecure attachments (Mikulincer, Shaver, Gillath, & Nitzberg, 2005). To summarize, when we are insecurely attached, all hope is not lost, given we can still learn to cultivate self-compassion so as to ameliorate psychological pain and access the "contentment" system (Gilbert, 2010). What is more, when we are securely attached, we are in an optimal position to naturally access the "contentment" system in the context of healthy relational connections, as well as function as a source of compassionate support for others.

In either case, for Christians, God is the ultimate source of compassion. Therefore, I would like to turn to the God attachment literature in order to help you better understand the role that God—as a "divine attachment figure" (DAF)—can play in helping you to access the "contentment" system (Gilbert, 2010) to ameliorate your shame and self-judgments.

God Attachment: Reaching for the "Stronger and Wiser" Other[2]

In recent years, researchers have investigated the psychological formation of both a God concept and God image. The former involves your beliefs about God (God is often referred to as your "divine attachment figure" [DAF]), including views about God's traits, how God interacts with humankind (e.g., God's thoughts, feelings, and behaviors), and how you interact with God (e.g., your thoughts, feelings, and behaviors) (Davis, Moriarty, & Mauch, 2013). The development of your God concept is intentional and occurs based on what you learn in Sunday School, the Bible, popular Christian writings, and so on (Davis et al., 2013). This process is left-brain-dependent and driven by your conscious, theological understanding and "head knowledge" of God (Davis et al., 2013).

Your God image develops unintentionally, based on life experiences (Davis et al., 2013). This image is a deeper, unconscious relational and emotional experience of God (Davis et al., 2013). Sometimes referred to as "heart knowledge," the development of your God image takes place through experiential learning and is right-brain-dependent (Davis et al., 2013). See the following lists to better understand the difference between your God concept and image (adapted from Davis et al., 2013):

- God concept
  - Left-brain activity
  - "Head knowledge"
  - Cognitive understanding of God
  - Develops based on intentional learning
  - Conscious/explicit level
  - Verbal level
- God image
  - Right-brain activity
  - "Heart knowledge"
  - Emotional understanding of God
  - Develops based on incidental learning
  - Unconscious/implicit level
  - Nonverbal level

Returning to the discussion from a previous section of this chapter, we form a view of ourselves and others over time—an internal working model of relationships—which leads to an attachment style. This attachment style involves a certain level of anxiety and avoidance, with the former relating to our experience of anxiety in relationships and the latter pertaining to our level of distance in relationships. Commonly, our working model of relationships and attachment style develop based on early life experiences with caregivers.

For the last few decades, researchers have been debating just how our God image develops, and how our God image relates to God attachment. One of the more popular explanations is that our internal working model/attachment style in human relationships tends to overlap—or correspond—with our internal working model/attachment style with God (Davis et al., 2013; Hall, Fujikawa, Halcrow, Hill, & Delaney, 2009), and our internal working model of God corresponds with our God image (Moriarty, Hoffman, & Grimes, 2006). In other words, as overlapping concepts, your early relational experiences with caregivers can influence your internal working model of God, attachment to God, and image of God in that these terms share common ground. If this is the case, the ways in which you experience God on a deeper level may be consistent with how you have historically experienced others (e.g., parents, a romantic partner). Consequently, your God image ("heart knowledge") may be either consistent or inconsistent with your God concept ("head knowledge"), given that your God image is dependent on your relational experiences and your God concept is reliant upon Christian sources of knowledge (e.g., the church, the Bible, Christian leaders) (Thomas et al., 2011). Ultimately, you may have one of several combinations, including a positive God concept and image, a negative God concept and image, or a positive God concept and negative God image.

Nevertheless, ideally, you will have a healthy, accurate, and positive concept of how you think about God that is consist with a healthy, accurate, and positive image of how you feel about God (Thomas et al., 2011). For example, recent research has revealed that a cognitive concept of God's providential care is correlated with a deeper emotional image of his providence (Knabb, Vazquez, Wang, & Bates, 2018). In this workbook, you will have opportunities to relate to God both cognitively and experientially, trusting in his providential care along the way, so as to access the "contentment" system (Gilbert, 2010) during moments of shame and self-judgment.

Returning to the different types of attachment, common insecure styles with God can include the following (adapted from Bartholomew & Horowitz, 1991):

- Anxious
    - Negative view of yourself
    - Positive view of God
    - High anxiety
    - Low avoidance
- Fearful avoidant
    - Negative view of yourself
    - Negative view of God
    - High anxiety
    - High avoidance
- Dismissive avoidant
    - Positive view of yourself
    - Negative view of God
    - Low anxiety
    - High avoidance

Unfortunately, when we have an insecure attachment style with God, we may not be able to access the "contentment" system (Gilbert, 2010) to help us when we are distressed, especially since we might experience high anxiety, high avoidance, or both in our relationship with him. In the context of shame and self-criticism, you may especially struggle to reach for God for soothing comfort. Before moving on to the role that compassion plays in this process, I would like to briefly review the role that the brain plays in our attachment to God, given that God is the designer of the human brain.

God and the Brain

One of the most important components of your attachment to God involves your ability to access your "contentment" system (Burroughs, 2010; Gilbert, 2010) in your time spent with him. By learning to find rest in your awareness of God's active, loving presence, you will be able to work towards addressing the shame and self-criticism that is holding you back in life. Along the way, you will be striving to change your image of God through Christian meditation and other strategies (Garzon, 2008; Knabb et al., 2017), given that the sense of safety you cultivate in your fellowship with him can buffer against the inevitable pain of daily living.

Interestingly, your image of God is right-brain dependent, whereas your concept of God is linked to the left brain; as a result, using strategies to integrate your concept and image of God so that they are working together is especially important (Garzon, 2008). Thus, you will be learning more about God's providential care, as well as entering into experiences that help you more deeply embrace his care for you.

In addition, recent research has found that, for Christians, the link between spirituality ("a feeling of personal connection to a sacred reality such as God") and peace and comfort may be explained by the hormone oxytocin (Holbrook et al., 2015). In a sample of Christians, researchers found a relationship between oxytocin (measured in the saliva) and spirituality, after excluding the influence of factors like being in a relationship, attending church, and feeling certain emotions (Holbrook et al., 2015). Given that oxytocin plays a role in bonding and the regulation of stress, deepening your ability to connect to God on a spiritual level is especially important. One way to do so is to engage in spiritual practices that will help you experience God's compassion.

God Attachment and Compassion

Beginning in the next chapter, you will explore the role that compassion can play in helping you with shame and negative self-evaluations. As a Christian, the ultimate source of compassion is God, revealing that compassion comes from the outside in. Stated differently, your ability to have self-compassion emanates from God's compassion for you. This understanding is consistent with recent research, which has revealed that self-compassion helps to explain the relationship between God attachment and depression and anxiety (Homan, 2014).

When we experience God's kindness towards us, we are able to extend this kindness to ourselves, which has implications for recurrent struggles with shame. If we revisit the notion of an internal working model of God, deeply held beliefs that we are worthy of God's love and he will be responsive to our needs can help us to be more loving to ourselves. Stated differently, when we perceive that an attachment figure (such as a "divine attachment figure") is kind and responsive, we can begin to integrate this understanding into our self-representation (Homan, 2014). Indeed, this understanding is consistent with a biblical view—Jesus' compassionate response to humanity's separation from God involved the ultimate self-sacrificial act on the cross. In his ministry, moreover, Jesus consistently had compassion for those he came into contact with (Matthew 9:35–36, 15:29–39, 20:29–34). In addition, a variety of passages in the Old Testament elucidate the role that God plays in extending his compassion to his people (Isaiah 49:13, 63:7; Psalm 51:1, 103:1–5, 103:13, 119:77, 145:9). When God offers us his perfect compassion, and we allow ourselves to receive it, we can experience a changed life (see Psalm 103).

A Christian View of Secure God Attachment and the "Contentment" System

Taking the previous sections of this chapter into consideration, secure God attachment involves having a healthy view of your relationship with him. In particular, you are worthy of God's love, and God is responsive to your needs. Rather than being preoccupied with his abandonment or avoidant of him for fear of his rejection, you can rest safely in his loving arms. In addition, instead of employing a hyperactivating or deactivating style, you can access the "contentment" system to find peace and contentment in your time with him (Burroughs, 2010; Gilbert, 2010). Although your God image and concept might not currently align because of relational hurts from the past, you will be working towards deeply resonating with God's promises in the Bible, reconciling your God concept and image as you receive his compassion from moment to moment. As a next step, you will be completing exercises to better understand the difference between your God concept and image, as well as your attachment style with God.

God Concept Versus Image: An Exercise

In the space that follows, please begin to reflect on your God concept, before moving on to your God image. Think of your God concept in terms of the information you know about God on an abstract level, whereas your God image is a deeper, felt sense of God.

If someone asked you about who God is, how would you answer him or her? What information would you give this person in terms of God's attributes and actions? In the traditional Christian sense, do you believe God is infinitely loving, powerful, and wise (Gorsuch, 1968)? Do his providential actions extend to all of his creation, including human beings? If these do not apply, what other attributes do you "know" about God "in your head?" Is God comforting, forgiving, gentle, gracious, kind, merciful, protective, supporting, and warm (Gorsuch, 1968)?

____
____
____
____
____
____

Turning to your image of God, please answer the next set of questions (adapted from Lawrence, 1997) by considering your answers on a deeper, experiential level in your relationship with him. Is God available when you need him? Does God want you to improve and grow? Does God unconditionally love you and accept you? Does God have an influence over you? Do you have an influence over God?

____
____
____
____
____
____

After writing about your God concept and image, spend a few minutes reflecting on the similarities and differences between the two. In other words, are there any noticeable gaps between what you know about God "in your head" versus "in your heart" (Davis et al., 2013)? If you were to close this gap, how might your life be different? In what ways might you be more compassionate towards yourself and others?

____
____
____
____
____
____

Understanding Your Attachment Style with God: An Exercise

Slightly adapted from the previous "Understanding Attachment Styles" exercise, I would like you to now spend some time reflecting on your relationship with God. Remember, we form a lens—an internal working model—through which to view our relationship with God. With this lens, we have a view of ourselves (positive or negative) and God (positive or negative) (Davis et al., 2013; Clinton & Straub, 2010). In addition, we exhibit a certain level of anxiety and avoidance in our relationship with God, which leads to an attachment style with him (Davis et al., 2013; Clinton & Straub, 2010). Common insecure styles with God include anxious (negative view of self and positive view of God; high anxiety and low avoidance), fearful avoidant (negative view of self and God; high anxiety and high avoidance), and dismissive avoidant (positive view of self and negative view of God; low anxiety and high avoidance) (adapted from Bartholomew & Horowitz, 1991; Clinton & Straub, 2010).

In this exercise, you will begin to explore the life experiences that have shaped how you view yourself and God. Please spend some time reflecting on the following questions (adapted from Bartholomew & Horowitz, 1991; Clinton & Sibcy, 2002). In turn, please journal your responses in the space that follows so as to get a better sense of your views about yourself and God. Once you have completed these four question areas, please move on to the next section, which asks you to consider the pattern of your answers.

Do you believe you have worth in God's eyes and are deserving of God's love?

____
____
____
____
____
____

When did you first begin to conclude this? What early experiences do you have of this belief that you are or are not worthy and deserving of God's love?

____
____
____
____
____
____

Is God reliable? Is he accepting of you? Can you trust him? Is he available when you need him the most? Will he respond to your needs if you ask for his support?

____
____
____
____
____
____

When did you first begin to form these beliefs about God? What early experiences do you have of God's reliability, acceptance, trustworthiness, availability, and responsiveness?

Now that you have answered the above questions, please consider whether or not your answers about yourself and God tend to be positive or negative.

What were some of the themes that emerged in your answers? Do you typically have a positive view of yourself and God (a secure attachment style)? A negative view of yourself and a positive view of God (an anxious attachment style)? A positive view of yourself and a negative view of God (a dismissive avoidant attachment style)? A negative view of yourself and a negative view of God (a fearful avoidant attachment style)?

Based on your answers, what are the implications for your ability to be soothed and comforted in the context of a safe, supportive relationship with God? In other words, does a negative view of yourself prevent you from reaching for God in your time of need? Or, does a negative view of God undermine your willingness or ability to reach for him to help you get through a difficult time?

Before completing several additional exercises and reading about a case example to conclude the chapter, I would like you to consider the "contentment" system (Gilbert, 2010) in the context of two passages in Scripture—the story of Mary and Martha and Jesus' teaching on worry.

Mary and the "Contentment" System: A Biblical Example

In the gospel of Luke (10:38–42), the story of Mary and Martha is presented:

> As Jesus and his disciples were on their way, he came to a village where a woman named Martha opened her home to him. She had a sister called Mary, who sat at the Lord's feet listening to what

> he said. But Martha was distracted by all the preparations that had to be made. She came to him and asked, "Lord, don't you care that my sister has left me to do the work by myself? Tell her to help me!" "Martha, Martha," the Lord answered, "you are worried and upset about many things, but few things are needed—or indeed only one. Mary has chosen what is better, and it will not be taken away from her."

To interpret this story, I would like to turn your attention to *The Conferences*, a collection of interviews by John Cassian in the deserts of Egypt. Based on his conversations with the early desert Christians, *The Conferences* sheds light on the teachings of Christian monks in the 5th century. For these early desert dwellers, they had to face harsh environmental and psychological conditions, such as the heat, a lack of food, hunger, boredom, sadness, loss, and anxiety. As they faced these realities, they were able to get to know the inner world, and developed strategies for dealing with difficult thoughts and feelings. Despite these challenges, they repeatedly turned towards God, cultivating a deeper relationship with him as a way to cope with physical and psychological suffering.

Of particular importance to the story of Mary and Martha in Luke's gospel, Cassian interviewed Moses, an early desert Christian, on the ultimate goal for desert monks. This conversation seems to have relevance for our discussion on God attachment and the "contentment" system (Burroughs, 2010; Gilbert, 2010). Specifically, Moses noted that the ultimate goal of desert monks was "purity of heart" (Matthew 5:8), which is a way of saying that Christians should get to know our thoughts and feelings so as to better discern if they come from ourselves or God (Harmless, 2004). Moreover, "tranquility of mind" is another component of "purity of heart," which means that we can attain an inner peace, stillness, and sense of calm by focusing our attention on God (Harmless, 2004).

In elaborating further on this aim, Moses stated the following:

> It is inevitable that the mind which does not have a place to turn to or any stable base will undergo change from hour to hour and from minute to minute due to a variety of its distractions, and by the things that come to it from outside it will be continually transformed to whatever occurs to it at any given moment.
>
> (Cassian, 1997, p. 44)

In the context of the story of Mary and Martha, Mary was focused on Jesus and engaging in divine contemplation (the Greek word, *theoria*) (Cassian, 1997). On the other hand, Martha's frantic activity was secondary to the most important part, which is sitting at Jesus' feet and focusing all our attention on him. Moses elaborated further on this salient dynamic:

> This should be our principal effort, then; this should be constantly pursued as the fixed goal of our heart, so that our mind may always be attached to divine things and to God. Whatever is different from this, however great it may be, is nevertheless to be judged as secondary or even as base, and indeed as harmful.
>
> (Cassian, 1997, p. 46)

When you are struggling with shame and negative self-evaluations, shifting your focus from the dangers that reside ahead or accumulating possessions or other "things" to an awareness of God's active, loving presence is key. Consistent with Mary's simple effort to sit at Jesus' feet, accessing the "contentment" system by cultivating contentment and "non-doing" as you spend time with him is "what is better," as Jesus revealed (Burroughs, 2010; Gilbert, 2010; Segal, Williams, & Teasdale, 2012).

Jesus and the "Danger," "Drive," and "Contentment" Systems: A Biblical Perspective

In addition to the story of Mary and Martha, Jesus' teaching on worry in Matthew's gospel (6:25–34) may help you to better understand the value of learning to trust in God's providential care by accessing the "contentment" system (Burroughs, 2010; Gilbert, 2010):

> "Therefore I tell you, do not worry about your life, what you will eat or drink; or about your body, what you will wear. Is not life more than food, and the body more than clothes? Look at the birds of the air; they do not sow or reap or store away in barns, and yet your heavenly Father feeds them. Are you not much more valuable than they? Can any one of you by worrying add a single hour to your life? And why do you worry about clothes? See how the flowers of the field grow. They do not labor or spin. Yet I tell you that not even Solomon in all his splendor was dressed like one of these. If that is how God clothes the grass of the field, which is here today and tomorrow is thrown into the fire, will he not much more clothe you—you of little faith? So do not worry, saying, 'What shall we eat?' or 'What shall we drink?' or 'What shall we wear?' For the pagans run after all these things, and your heavenly Father knows that you need them. But seek first his kingdom and his righteousness, and all these things will be given to you as well. Therefore do not worry about tomorrow, for tomorrow will worry about itself. Each day has enough trouble of its own."

In this passage, Jesus highlighted the tendency that we have to worry about tomorrow, which includes efforts to accumulate "things," reminiscent of both the "danger" and "drive" systems (Gilbert, 2010). Yet, his solution is to depend on God (Keener, 1999), pointing to God's care of his creation as an example of the reality that God will provide. Here, we see the importance of shifting our attention from catastrophizing about tomorrow and overly planning by pursuing the wrong things to God's loving, compassionate care. Jesus, in emphasizing God's care for his creation, is suggesting that anxious striving is futile; thus, learning to trust in God's sovereign, loving responsiveness is key (Keener, 1999). In order to begin to work on pivoting from "danger" and "drive" to "contentment" (Gilbert, 2010), I would like you to complete a short exercise.

Sitting at Jesus' Feet: An Exercise

In this exercise, you will be spending ten minutes with Jesus, in silence. You will be imagining that you are sitting at his feet, similar to Mary's yielding posture in the gospel of Luke (10:38-42). For St. Gregory, a theologian who lived around the 6th century, Mary captures the contemplative life, which consists of rest, non-action, an awareness of God's love, and an attitude of surrender towards God's will (Cutler, 2003; Knabb, 2016b). Conversely, Martha symbolizes the active life, which involves acts of servanthood and self-sacrifice (Cutler, 2003; Knabb, 2016b). In his lifetime, Jesus Christ reflected contemplation and action, engaging in healing and spending time with God in solitude (Cutler, 2003; Knabb, 2016b).

At times, you will focus on following Jesus in a state of action; however, you also need to learn to rest at Jesus' feet in order to slow down enough to access the "contentment" system (Burroughs, 2010; Gilbert, 2010). Characteristics of this contemplative state of "non-doing" include the following (adapted from Frenette, 2012; Gilbert, 2010; Segal, Williams, & Teasdale, 2002):

- An attitude of acceptance, letting go, and surrender (rather than trying to fix or change things).
- An inner experience of contentment, peace, and calmness (rather than anticipating danger or striving to achieve or accumulate).

- An awareness of the present moment (rather than focusing on the past or future).
- Attention that is focused and sustained (on Jesus' active, loving presence).
- An attitude of non-judgment towards thoughts and feelings (rather than trying to hold on to them or get rid of them).

As you learn to simply sit at Jesus' feet, you are working towards listening instead of talking, remaining still instead of moving, letting go instead of holding on to, accepting instead of fixing, and trusting instead of doubting. To do this, of course, requires quite a bit of effort, and is certainly no easy task. Practice, thus, is especially important. By spending time with Jesus in silence, you will be shifting from Martha's frantic activity to Mary's contemplative attitude so as to tap into the "contentment" system.

Now that you have read about the background of Mary and the contemplative life, continue with the following directions for ten minutes. Please consider using the corresponding audio recording, "Track 2," available at https://www.routledge.com/The-Compassion-Based-Workbook-for-Christian-Clients-Finding-Freedom-from/Knabb/p/book/9780815394365.

> Try to find a quiet environment, with no distractions. Sit in a comfortable chair, with your back straight and your eyes closed. Now, begin to imagine that you are sitting at Jesus' feet. There is nowhere else to go and nothing else to achieve or accomplish. Your only job is to sit at his feet, recognizing that he is the most important part of your current experience. In that you are with him, you are accessing a sense of safety, given he is your sovereign Lord and holds the world in his hands. In this state of silence, just focus on his presence, beginning to introduce the word, "rest." Whenever you seem to get distracted with activities, similar to Martha, just imagine sitting at Jesus' feet, reintroducing the word, "rest," as you find contentment, peace, and comfort in Jesus' presence.
>
> When the ten minutes come to a close, thank Jesus for the opportunity to spend time with him. Ask him to be with you throughout your day, and to help you slow down to notice his active, loving presence from moment to moment.

Safety with God: An Exercise

Although you may not currently feel safe in your relationship with God, I would like you to now spend ten minutes writing about what your life might be like if you were able to access the "contentment" system with him (Burroughs, 2010; Gilbert, 2010), turning to him during instances of shame and self-criticism to be soothed and comforted. Before doing so, read the following passage in the psalms (Psalm 91) to get a better sense of what confidently reaching for God might be like:

> Whoever dwells in the shelter of the Most High will rest in the shadow of the Almighty. I will say of the Lord, "He is my refuge and my fortress, my God, in whom I trust." Surely he will save you from the fowler's snare and from the deadly pestilence. He will cover you with his feathers, and under his wings you will find refuge; his faithfulness will be your shield and rampart. You will not fear the terror of night, nor the arrow that flies by day, nor the pestilence that stalks in the darkness, nor the plague that destroys at midday. A thousand may fall at your side, ten thousand at your right hand, but it will not come near you. You will only observe with your eyes and see the punishment of the wicked. If you say, "The Lord is my refuge," and you make the Most High your dwelling, no harm will overtake you, no disaster will come near your tent. For he will command his angels concerning you to guard you in all your ways; they will lift you up in their hands, so that you will not strike your foot against a stone. You will tread on the lion and the cobra; you will trample the great lion and the serpent.

> "Because he loves me," says the Lord, "I will rescue him; I will protect him, for he acknowledges my name. He will call on me, and I will answer him; I will be with him in trouble, I will deliver him and honor him. With long life I will satisfy him and show him my salvation."

In this passage, notice that the psalmist seems to be capturing the safety and protection that naturally flow from God. Although we are by no means sparred the inevitability of life's dangers, the psalmist appears confident that God will be there for him. What might it be like to rest in his loving arms, reminiscent of a child confidently falling asleep in the cradled embrace of a "stronger and wiser" parent (Mikulincer & Shaver, 2007), knowing that everything will be okay because he or she is under the care of a trusted other? What might your life be like if God is your source of contentment, peace, and tranquility, and you are able to spend time with him each day to access your "contentment" system (Burroughs, 2010; Gilbert, 2010)?

____

____

____

____

____

____

Developing "Contentment" with God: A Case Example

John grew up in a home filled with chronic physical abuse. His father was frequently violent, punching walls, throwing things, and verbally abusing the entire family. Residing in a middle-class house with his mother and older brother, John frequently hid in his room when he sensed his father was "escalating."

In his teenage years, he began to wonder if God exists, although he did not come to learn about the God of the Christian Bible until he was in his early 20s. As he started to attend a non-denominational church in the mid-west, he came to realize that God—at least as portrayed in the pages of the Bible—is infinitely loving, wise, and powerful, attributes he could not reconcile with his earthly father. John especially struggled to understand how God could be anything but punishing and violent towards his creation, given John was convinced he was deeply flawed and unlovable.

When he would attend sermons on God's grace and mercy, moreover, he would usually "check out," and noticed that he had a very difficult time staying engaged when his pastor would discuss God's active presence. Certainly, John saw that his deeper emotional experience of God (which he knew somehow connected to his experiences of his father) was inconsistent with what he was learning in his home church. Yet, he longed for the safety, comfort, and contentment that the Bible promised to those who put their trust in God, and desperately wanted to feel lovable in the eyes of God. This longing, of course, was completely foreign to him, but John was determined to find a way to fully consent—that is, surrender—to God, reminiscent of the perfect relationship between the Father and Son within the gospel of John.

Conclusion

In this chapter, you were introduced to attachment theory, including the development of secure and insecure attachments and the role that attachments play in accessing the "contentment" system (Gilbert, 2010). What is more, you learned about your attachment to God, including the related

God concept and image, and completed several exercises to better understand your relationship with God. As the story of Mary and Martha revealed, learning to sit at Jesus' feet is key in focusing your attention on him so as to experience the contentment that God can offer. Jesus' teaching on worry, too, captures the importance of looking to God, prioritizing the "contentment" system above the "danger" and "drive" systems when necessary (Burroughs, 2010; Gilbert, 2010).

In the next chapter, you will utilize this burgeoning lens to view God's compassion as an antidote to your shame and self-judgments. Building on your newfound awareness of the importance of your attachment to God, I will be reviewing both a psychological and a biblical view of compassion in order to pave the way for the remainder of the workbook—exercises designed to help you think, feel, behave, and attend and imagine with compassion. This compassion, to be sure, first comes from God, who freely responds to our needs with soothing comfort. In turn, you will be working on extending God's gift of compassion to yourself and others in order to live the life God has called you to live.

Notes

1 The link between attachment and compassion is foundational within compassion-focused therapy (Gilbert, 2010), one of the most popular compassion-based approaches in the contemporary literature. In this chapter, I review this connection—consistent with Gilbert (2010), Mikulincer and Shaver (2017) and others—then build on it with a summary of the God attachment literature.

2 John Bowlby referred to attachment figures as "stronger and wiser" (Mikulincer & Shaver, 2007).

References

Bartholomew, K., & Horowitz, L. (1991). Attachment styles among young adults: A test of a four-category model. *Journal of Personality and Social Psychology, 61*(2), 226–244.

Brennan, K., Clark, C., & Shaver, P. (1998). Self-report measurement of adult romantic attachment: An integrative overview. In J. Simpson & W. Rholes (Eds.), *Attachment theory and close relationships* (pp. 46–76). New York: The Guilford Press.

Bretherton, I. (1985). Attachment theory: Retrospect and prospect. *Monographs of the Society for Research in Child Development, 50*(1–2), 3–35.

Bretherton, I. (1992). The origins of attachment theory: John Bowlby and Mary Ainsworth. *Developmental Psychology, 28*(5), 759–775.

Buchheim, A., Heinrichs, M., George, C., Pokorny, D., Koops, E., Henningsen, P., O'Connor, M., & Gundel, H. (2009). Oxytocin enhances the experience of attachment security. *Psychoneuroendocrinology, 34*(9), 1417–1422.

Burroughs, J. (2010). *The rare jewel of Christian contentment.* Pensacola, FL: Chapel Library.

Cassian, J. (1997). *The conferences* (B. Ramsey, Trans.). New York: Paulist Press.

Clinton, T., & Sibcy, G. (2002). *Attachments: Why you love, feel, and act the way you do.* Brentwood, TN: Thomas Nelson Publishers.

Clinton, T., & Straub, J. (2010). *God attachment: Why you believe, act, and feel the way you do about God.* New York: Howard Books.

Colonnello, V., Petrocchi, N., & Heinrichs, M. (2017). The psychobiological foundation of prosocial relationships: The role of oxytocin in daily exchanges. In P. Gilbert (Ed.), *Compassion: Concepts, research and applications* (pp. 105–119). New York: Routledge.

Cutler, D. (2003). *Western mysticism: Augustine, Gregory and Bernard on contemplation and the contemplative life.* New York: Dover Publications, Inc.

Davis, E., Moriarty, G., & Mauch, J. (2013). God images and God concepts: Definitions, development, and dynamics. *Psychology of Religion and Spirituality, 5*(1), 51–60.

Ekman, P., & Ekman, E. (2017). Is global compassion achievable. In E. Seppala, E. Simon-Thomas, S. Brown, M. Worline, C. Cameron, & J. Doty (Eds.), *The Oxford handbook of science compassion* (pp. 41–52). New York: Oxford University Press.

Feeney, B., & Collins, N. (2004). Interpersonal safe haven and secure base caregiving processes in adulthood. In W. Rholes & J. Simpson (Eds.), *Adult attachment: Theory, research, and clinical implications* (pp. 300–338). New York: The Guilford Press.

Frenette, D. (2012). *The path of centering prayer: Deepening your experience of God*. Boulder, CO: Sounds True, Inc.

Garzon, F. (2008). A neuroscientific approach and the God image. *Journal of Spirituality in Mental Health, 9*(3/4), 139–155.

Gilbert, P. (1998). What is shame? Some core issues and controversies. In P. Gilbert & B. Andrews (Eds.), *Shame: Interpersonal behavior, psychopathology, and culture* (pp. 3–38). New York: Oxford University Press.

Gilbert, P. (2000). *Counselling for depression*. Thousand Oaks, CA: SAGE Publications.

Gilbert, P. (2010). *Compassion focused therapy: Distinctive features*. New York: Routledge.

Gilbert, P., & Irons, C. (2009). Shame, self-criticism, and self-compassion in adolescence. In N. Allen & L. Sheeber (Eds.), *Adolescent emotional development and the emergence of depressive disorders* (pp. 195–214). Cambridge: Cambridge University Press.

Gorsuch, R. (1968). The conceptualization of God as seen in adjective ratings. *Journal for the Scientific Study of Religion, 7*(1), 56–64.

Gross, C., & Hansen, N. (2000). Clarifying the experience of shame: The role of attachment style, gender, and investment in relatedness. *Personality and Individual Differences, 28*(5), 897–907.

Hall, T., Fujikawa, A., Halcrow, S., Hill, P., & Delaney, H. (2009). Attachment to God and implicit spirituality: Clarifying correspondence and compensation models. *Journal of Psychology and Theology, 37*(4), 227–242.

Harmless, W. (2004). *Desert Christians: An introduction to the literature of early monasticism*. New York: Oxford University Press.

Holbrook, C., Hahn-Holbrook, J., & Holt-Lunstad, J. (2015). Self-reported spirituality correlates with endogenous oxytocin. *Psychology of Religion and Spirituality, 7*(1), 46–50.

Homan, K. (2014). A mediation model linking attachment to God, self-compassion, and mental health. *Mental Health, Religion & Culture, 17*(10), 977–989.

Insel, T., & Young, L. (2000). The neurobiology of attachment. *Nature Reviews Neuroscience, 2*(2), 129–136.

Joeng, J., Turner, S., Kim, E., Choi, S., Lee, Y., & Kim, J. (2017). Insecure attachment and emotional distress: Fear of self-compassion and self-compassion as mediators. *Personality and Individual Differences, 112*, 6–11.

Karen, R. (1994). *Becoming attached: First relationships and how they shape our capacity to love*. New York: Oxford University Press.

Keener, C. (1999). *A commentary on the gospel of Matthew*. Grand Rapids, MI: William B. Eerdmans Publishing Company.

Knabb, J. (2016a). *Acceptance and commitment therapy for Christian clients: A faith-based workbook*. New York: Routledge.

Knabb, J. (2016b). *Faith-based ACT for Christian clients: An integrative treatment approach*. New York: Routledge.

Knabb, J., Frederick, T., & Cumming, G. (2017). Surrendering to God's providence: A three-part study on providence-focused therapy for recurrent worry (PFT-RW). *Psychology of Religion and Spirituality, 9*(2), 180–196.

Knabb, J., Vazquez, V., Wang, K., & Bates, T. (2018). "Unknowing" in the 21st century: Humble detachment for Christians with repetitive negative thinking. *Spirituality in Clinical Practice*. Advanced online publication.

Kolts, R. (2016). *CFT made simple: A clinician's guide to practicing compassion-focused therapy*. Oakland, CA: New Harbinger Publications, Inc.

Krause, S., Pokorny, D., Schury, K., Doyen-Waldecker, C., Hulbert, A., Karabatsiakis, A., Kolassa, I. T., Gündel, H., Waller, C., & Buchheim, A. (2017). Effects of the adult attachment projective picture system on oxytocin and cortisol levels in mothers. In A. Buchheim, C. George, H. Gundel, & R. Viviani (Eds.), *Neuroscience of human attachment* (pp. 155–166). Lausanne, Switzerland: Frontiers Media.

Lawrence, R. (1997). Measuring the image of God: The God Image Inventory and the God Image Scales. *Journal of Psychology and Theology, 25*(2), 214–226.

Martins, T., Canavarro, M., & Moreira, H. (2016). Adult attachment and dyadic adjustment: The mediating role of shame. *The Journal of Psychology, 150*(5), 560–575.

Mikulincer, M., & Shaver, P. (2004). Security-based self-representations in adulthood: Contents and processes. In W. Rholes & J. Simpson (Eds.), *Adult attachment: Theory, research, and clinical implications* (pp. 159–195). New York: The Guilford Press.

Mikulincer, M., & Shaver, P. (2007). *Attachment in adulthood: Structure, dynamics, and change*. New York: The Guilford Press.

Mikulincer, M., & Shaver, P. (2017). An attachment perspective on compassion and altruism. In P. Gilbert (Ed.), *Compassion: Concepts, research and applications* (pp. 187–202). New York: Routledge.
Mikulincer, M., Shaver, P., Gillath, O., & Nitzberg, R. (2005). Attachment, caregiving, and altruism: Boosting attachment security increases compassion and helping. *Journal of Personality and Social Psychology, 89*(5), 817–839.
Moriarty, G., Hoffman, L., & Grimes, C. (2006). Understanding the God image through attachment theory. *Journal of Spirituality in Mental Health, 9*(2), 43–56.
Neff, K. (2016). The self-compassion scale is a valid and theoretically coherent measure of self-compassion. *Mindfulness, 7*(1), 264–274.
Raque-Bogdan, T., Ericson, S., Jackson, J., Martin, H., & Bryan, N. (2011). Attachment and mental and physical health: Self-compassion and mattering as mediators. *Journal of Counseling Psychology, 58*(2), 272–278.
Rholes, W., & Simpson, J. (2004). Attachment theory: Basic concepts and contemporary questions. In W. Rholes & J. Simpson (Eds.), *Adult attachment: Theory, research, and clinical implications* (pp. 3–16). New York: The Guilford Press.
Schore, A. (1998). Early shame experiences and infant brain development. In P. Gilbert & B. Andrews (Eds.), *Shame: Interpersonal behavior, psychopathology, and culture* (pp. 57–77). New York: Oxford University Press.
Schore, A. (2000). Attachment and the regulation of the right brain. *Attachment & Human Development, 2*(1), 23–47.
Schore, J., & Schore, A. (2008). Modern attachment theory: The central role of affect regulation in development and treatment. *Clinical Social Work Journal, 36*, 9–20.
Segal, Z., Williams, J., & Teasdale, J. (2002). *Mindfulness-based cognitive therapy for depression: A new approach to preventing relapse*. New York: The Guilford Press.
Segal, Z., Williams, M., & Teasdale, J. (2012). *Mindfulness-based cognitive therapy for depression* (2nd ed.). New York: The Guilford Press.
Thomas, M., Moriarty, G., Davis, E., & Anderson, E. (2011). The effects of a manualized group-psychotherapy intervention on client God images and attachment to God: A pilot study. *Journal of Psychology and Theology, 39*, 44–58.
Wallin, D. (2007). *Attachment in psychotherapy*. New York: The Guilford Press.

CHAPTER 3

Compassion, "Contentment," and a Deeper Relationship with God for Shame and Negative Self-Judgments

Introduction

In the third chapter, you will further explore compassion, including definitions of compassion from psychological and Christian viewpoints, as well as the role that compassion plays in connecting to the "contentment" system and cultivating mental health (Germer, 2009; Gilbert, 2010). You will also review secular and Christian forms of meditation for developing compassion. Moreover, you will learn about compassion in the context of the Greek word, *eleos*, briefly revisiting God's merciful reply to Adam and Eve's original missteps in the creation story (Bonhoeffer, 1955, 1959) and examining Jesus' ministry of compassion.

In the chapter, I will be making a case for using Christian meditation as a way to (a) deepen your relationship with God, (b) cultivate a secure God attachment, and (c) access the "contentment" system (Burroughs, 2010; Gilbert, 2010) to better manage your shame and negative self-judgments. You will explore both *kataphatic* and *apophatic* forms of Christian meditation, which you will practice in subsequent chapters of this workbook.

Before transitioning to the actual coping skills in the remaining workbook chapters, I will be presenting a unified, integrative compassion-based approach: this workbook offers you (a) modified exercises from the compassion literature in clinical psychology so as to present a Christian-sensitive alternative (many of the current compassion definitions and skills build on Buddhist underpinnings), and (b) *kataphatic* and *apophatic* forms of meditation in the Christian tradition so you can move from shame, negative self-judgments, and repetitive negative thinking to an awareness of God's safety, mercy, compassion, and grace, cultivating a secure attachment with God along the way.

The goals of the skills-based workbook (adapted from Desmond, 2016; Germer, 2009; Gilbert, 2010; Jazaieri et al., 2013; Kabat-Zinn, 2013; Kristeller & Johnson, 2005; Knabb, 2016; Knabb, Frederick, & Cumming, 2017) are to (a) learn to gently and compassionately notice your shame and negative self-judgments with more distance, given God is actively loving you in each and every moment, (b) pivot from the "danger" to "contentment" system, because God is with you, reminiscent of Mary sitting at the feet of Jesus (Luke 10:38–42), (c) cultivate a deeper awareness of God's compassion and mercy, and (d) practice more compassion and mercy towards yourself and others.

A range of skills are presented (adapted from Germer, 2009; Gilbert, 2010; Jazaieri et al., 2013; Kabat-Zinn, 2013; Knabb, 2016; Knabb et al., 2017; Kolts, 2016; Thomas, Moriarty, Davis, & Anderson, 2011; Tirch, Schoendorff, & Silberstein, 2014) to develop compassion towards yourself and others—referred to as the "compassionate self" (Leahy, Tirch, & Napolitano, 2011) in clinical circles and the "new self" found in Christ (Colossians 3:1–17; Ephesians 4:24) in Christianity. The remaining chapters in the workbook will focus on four skill domains, including "thinking," "feeling," "behaving," and "attending and imagining" with compassion (Germer, 2009; Gilbert, 2010; Kolts, 2016). Mapped onto these skill-based domains, I will be integrating five bodies of Christian spiritual writings: desert spirituality (drawing from the *Sayings of the Desert Fathers*), Protestant spirituality (emphasizing Puritan theological writings such as the *Valley of Vision*), Orthodox spirituality (turning to the *Philokalia*), medieval spirituality (utilizing *The Cloud of Unknowing* and *The Imitation of Christ*, among other writings), and Ignatian spirituality (drawing from *Spiritual Exercises*). Throughout the chapter, exercises, examples from the Bible, and a case example will be used to deepen your awareness of the link between the goals and skills in this workbook.

Defining Compassion Within Psychology

In the 21st century, clinical psychology has commonly drawn from Buddhism to conceptualize compassion and related concepts. Although there is currently no unified definition within the field, compassion often has several ingredients, including thoughts, feelings, and behaviors (Jazaieri et al., 2013). Compassion can be directed towards ourselves or others, or we may receive compassion from other people (Jazaieri et al., 2013). As a process, compassion encompasses a cognitive understanding of suffering, an emotional reaction to suffering, a desire to respond to suffering, and behavioral action to address suffering (Jazaieri et al., 2013).

Self-compassion, in particular, has several key ingredients (Neff, 2003, p. 223):

- "Being kind and understanding toward oneself in instances of pain or failure rather than being harshly self-critical."
- "Perceiving one's experiences as part of the larger human experience rather than seeing them as isolating."
- "Holding painful thoughts and feelings in mindful awareness rather than over-identifying with them."

Here, you will see there is an element of kindness that is extended to yourself when you have fallen short of a standard, along with a sense that you are connected to others along the journey of life. As the third part of self-compassion, you are able to notice your inner pain without spending too much time equating your sense of self with unpleasant intrapsychic experiences. In other words, your pain is a part of your experience, but does not define who you are.

Defining Compassion Within Christianity

Although there is certainly some overlap, Christianity defines compassion a bit differently. For example, mercy and compassion are often used interchangeably within the Christian tradition (Erickson, 2013), with these two virtues commonly reflecting God's response to humankind. From a Christian viewpoint, we are in need of God's mercy and compassion, given our fallen nature (Erickson, 2013). In turn, because God regularly shows us mercy and compassion, we are to extend these virtues to others. Mercy and compassion, along with God's benevolence, grace, and persistence, naturally flow from his love (Erickson, 2013).

Mercy can also mean a willingness to withhold punishment, or forgive someone who deserves judgment for an offense (Douglas & Tenney, 2011). Within the gospels, mercy seems to capture the ability to assist someone who needs help and cannot help him- or herself, and is frequently used in the context of a pre-established relationship (Nicholson, 2013). At least two Greek words reflect the mercy referenced in the gospels, including *eleos* and *splanchnizomai*, with Jesus commonly responding to others' call for mercy (Nicholson, 2013). Consistent with a compassion definition from psychology, biblical mercy requires responsiveness to suffering so as to help the person in pain, sometimes with an additional element of forgiveness (Nicholson, 2013). Throughout the gospels, Jesus wanted his followers to extend the mercy he generously offered them to their relationship with others (Nicholson, 2013).

The Greek word, *eleos*, is used over 20 times in the Bible, and is translated as "compassion" or "mercy" (Strong, 2001). *Eleos* often involves kindness directed to those who are suffering, coupled with a motivation to respond to their needs, and can be extended from one human to another or from God to humans (Strong, 2001). Throughout his time on this planet, Jesus responded to those who asked for his mercy, and taught about the importance of showing mercy to others (Luke 10:25–37).

Interestingly, *eleos* is similar to the Greek word for olive oil, *elaion* (Coniaris, 1998). In biblical times, olive oil was utilized as a way to sooth wounds and bruises; as a result, asking Jesus for mercy and compassion is a way of asking him for soothing comfort, given that oil in Jesus' day was carefully spread onto the ailment to bring much-needed relief (Coniaris, 1998).

Finally, mercy can involve both compassion and empathy; therefore, when we ask God for mercy, we are asking him to be responsive to our pain and understand us from the inside out (Talbot, 2013).

To summarize, mercy and compassion, often used interchangeably within the Christian tradition, can have the following ingredients (adapted from Coniaris, 1998; Douglas & Tenney, 2011; Erickson, 2013; Nicholson, 2013; Strong, 2001; Talbot, 2013):

- Being emotionally impacted by the suffering of another.
- Understanding the suffering of another.
- Being responsive to the suffering of another.
- Showing kindness in the midst of the suffering of another.
- Extending forgiveness to someone who deserves judgment or punishment.
- Soothing the suffering of another.

Most importantly, mercy and compassion are often used to convey God's loving response to humankind; because of this, God is moved by our suffering, understands our suffering, forgives us in our suffering (which is sometimes self-inflicted), and responds to our suffering with kindness and soothing comfort. In the context of shame, God knows your pain, and is ready to respond to you in your time of need with his perfect love.

God Clothed Adam and Eve: A Biblical Example of Compassion

Remember, from a Christian viewpoint, shame is a signal that tells us we need to be clothed with God's compassion. If we revisit God's response to Adam and Eve's original mistake (Genesis 3:21), he "clothed them" in their fallen state. With this compassionate act, God accepted us as imperfect, fallen human beings (Bonhoeffer, 1959). Yet, God's gift of "garments of skin" by no means captures the end to the story. Rather, true forgiveness, compassion, and mercy come from Jesus' atonement (Bonhoeffer, 1955), revealed in the grand narrative of Scripture—creation, fall, redemption, and restoration (Wolters, 2005).

Whether we look to the first few pages of the Bible or read about Jesus' incarnation and atonement, a consistent theme involves God's loving, compassionate pursuit of humankind. In fact, God wants to ameliorate the shame we experience as a result of the fall by reconciling us to him. His responsiveness, to be sure, is best captured in his self-sacrificial act on the cross.

Jesus' Earthly Mission: A Biblical Example of Compassion

Shame is a signal that tells us we need to look no further than the cross in order to see how much God loves us and wants to respond to our suffering via reconciliation. Certainly, "God is love" (1 John 4:16) and the incarnation and atonement are evidence of God's unfailing love for his creation (Bonhoeffer, 1955). God has reconciled us to himself through his Son with this ultimate act of compassion (Bonhoeffer, 1955).

While on this planet, Jesus revealed God's "self-giving, compassionate love" for us (Grentz, 1994). A range of examples within the gospels capture Jesus' emphasis on displaying God's compassion for humankind (adapted from Grentz, 1994):

- Jesus came to this world to save us, rather than judge us (John 3:17).
- Jesus came to this world to give his own life for us (John 10:10–11).
- Jesus came to this world to offer healing and freedom to us (Luke 4:18–19).
- While in this world, Jesus was frequently moved by suffering (Matthew 14:14).
- While in this world, Jesus consistently responded to suffering (John 11).
- While in this world, Jesus cried for Jerusalem (Luke 19:41–44).
- While in this world, Jesus prayed for those who crucified him (Luke 23:34).

Overall, since Christians follow Christ, and Jesus' entire ministry was about displaying God's compassion for his creation, compassion is central to the Christian faith. What is more, because God offers us his compassion from moment to moment, we can extend his compassion to both ourselves and others. Still, psychology and Christianity may have somewhat different ways that compassion—including its source—emerges within the human predicament.

The "Compassionate Self" Versus the "New Self" Found in Christ

In compassion-focused therapy, the "compassionate self" is the ideal version of you that interacts with the world, capturing the wisdom, kindness, courage, and strength that you would like to regularly extend to yourself and others (Kolts, 2016). This compassionate version of you is flexible, in that you are able to adjust to the demands of life by practicing compassion from moment to moment (Kolts, 2016). Ultimately, the "compassionate self" in compassion-focused therapy is made up of four features (Gilbert, 2010):

1. Wisdom.
2. Strength and courage.
3. Kindness and warmth.
4. Motivation to respond to suffering with non-judgment.

These characteristics can be developed through practice, and serve as a proverbial road map for life. This map may be especially helpful when you are struggling with shame and self-criticism, in that painful thoughts and feelings can get in the way of applying compassion towards yourself and others.

For Christians, though, Jesus has given us a "new self" (which includes compassion), meaning we are called to live a virtuous life in a manner that reflects his loving behaviors. Although briefly mentioned in the first chapter, I would like to revisit Colossians 3 in order to draw a contrast between the "old self" and "new self" that Paul presents to the church of Colossae. In Colossians 3:1–17, Paul stated the following:

> Since, then, you have been raised with Christ, set your hearts on things above, where Christ is, seated at the right hand of God. Set your minds on things above, not on earthly things. For you died, and

> your life is now hidden with Christ in God. When Christ, who is your life, appears, then you also will appear with him in glory. Put to death, therefore, whatever belongs to your earthly nature: sexual immorality, impurity, lust, evil desires and greed, which is idolatry. Because of these, the wrath of God is coming. You used to walk in these ways, in the life you once lived. But now you must also rid yourselves of all such things as these: anger, rage, malice, slander, and filthy language from your lips. Do not lie to each other, since you have taken off your old self with its practices and have put on the new self, which is being renewed in knowledge in the image of its Creator. Here there is no Gentile or Jew, circumcised or uncircumcised, barbarian, Scythian, slave or free, but Christ is all, and is in all. Therefore, as God's chosen people, holy and dearly loved, clothe yourselves with compassion, kindness, humility, gentleness and patience. Bear with each other and forgive one another if any of you has a grievance against someone. Forgive as the Lord forgave you. And over all these virtues put on love, which binds them all together in perfect unity. Let the peace of Christ rule in your hearts, since as members of one body you were called to peace. And be thankful. Let the message of Christ dwell among you richly as you teach and admonish one another with all wisdom through psalms, hymns, and songs from the Spirit, singing to God with gratitude in your hearts. And whatever you do, whether in word or deed, do it all in the name of the Lord Jesus, giving thanks to God the Father through him.

Here, it is important to note that Paul was instructing his audience to focus on "things above," "where Christ is," rather than "earthly things." Unfortunately, we do not know what these "earthly things" may be, although he might be contrasting the Christian vices (e.g., anger, rage, malice, slander, filthy language) and virtues (e.g., compassion, kindness, humility, gentleness, patience) further along in the passage (Patzia, 1990). If this is the case, Paul is encouraging us to shift our attention from an old way of thinking and behaving to a new, Christ-like way of viewing the world and interacting in it. The vices mentioned relate to sexual and relational immorality, and the virtues are used in the context of optimal relational functioning (Patzia, 1990). In fact, the virtues listed are "godly qualities," and capture God's way of relating to humankind (Patzia, 1990). Finally, towards the end of this passage, Paul tells us to let Jesus' "peace rule in [our] hearts," which captures the reality that Christ offers his followers an "inner peace" that should guide daily living and be extended to others (Patzia, 1990). Ultimately, the "clothe yourselves" language in the context of the "old self" and "new self" paints a picture of someone taking off an old, soiled garment and putting on a new, clean article of clothing (Patzia, 1990). Thus, God is replacing your old garment of shame with a new garment that conveys his love for you.

In terms of the similarities and differences between the two, the "compassionate self" is personally generated, and cultivated on your own. On the other hand, the "new self" is found in Christ, and comes directly from him. What is more, the "new self" consists of a fixed set of Christian virtues, rather than personally constructed characteristics that we would like to cultivate. In order to begin to consider the role that your "new self" plays in extending compassion to yourself and others, I would like you to complete a short exercise.

The "New Self" Found in Christ: An Exercise

In this exercise, I would like you to imagine that your "old self" consists of all your experiences of shame and self-criticism that you have carried around with you—in the form of a dirty, soiled jacket—over the years. These experiences may involve sexual or relational struggles (consistent with Paul's references to several vices in Colossians 3), or other types of Christian vices or shortcomings you currently struggle with. In either case, this jacket is extremely heavy, because of multiple layers of filth, and smells, in that it has been through the rain, snow, and so on. Your jacket has holes in it, too, and is rather uncomfortable. Yet, it is seemingly all you know, given you have been wearing it for years on end. Although, prior to today, you have never considered that you can replace it with a new jacket, you are now ready to make a change.

You go to a local store, and see a brand new jacket in the window. This jacket represents your "new self" found in Christ, and captures the Christian virtues of compassion, kindness, humility, gentleness, and patience. Certainly, forgiveness is a part of this jacket experience, too. Now, imagine walking in the store, taking off the old jacket, and slowly trying on the new jacket. In this process, Jesus is the sales associate, and is assisting you as you replace the old jacket with the new one. As you try it on, you experience instant relief, basking in the love, compassion, kindness, humility, patience, and forgiveness that Jesus offers you. In return for this new jacket—which fits perfectly—Jesus asks you to extend these Christian virtues to others, given his peace dwells within you, by sharing your new jacket with those in need.

Now that you have completed this exercise, try to reflect on the experience by answering the following questions:

What was it like to take off the old jacket and put on the new jacket? What was it like to have Jesus help you? What thoughts and feelings came up as you made the transition? What might it be like to wear this new jacket around town, treating yourself and others with compassion, kindness, humility, gentleness, patience, love, and forgiveness? What might it be like to share the jacket with others?

Now that we have explored compassion from secular and Christian perspectives, I would like to compare and contrast mindfulness and loving-kindness (currently quite common in the clinical psychology literature) and Christian meditations as a vehicle through which we can cultivate compassion.

Compassion, "Contentment," Mindfulness and Loving-Kindness Meditations, and Shame

With mindfulness and loving-kindness meditations, the self is the source of compassion. Mindfulness meditation involves "nonattached awareness" (Germer, 2009), learning to notice the inner world (including psychological pain) with non-judgment, which has a calming impact on psychological functioning (Germer & Barnhofer, 2017). When we practice a focused form of mindfulness meditation, we are attempting to cultivate sustained attention without judgment, given we are repeatedly refocusing our wandering attention on a single point (e.g., the breath, one of the five senses) (Germer & Barnhofer, 2017). Over time, this can help us to ameliorate difficult inner experiences, such as self-criticism, given we are relating to them with more openness, kindness, and acceptance (Germer & Barnhofer, 2017; Neff, 2012). As we learn to approach shame and negative self-judgments with a kind, non-judgmental attitude, we are better able to approach life in a calm, deliberate manner (Gilbert, 2010). Mindfulness meditation, ultimately, is an indirect way of developing self-compassion.

On the other hand, in loving-kindness meditation, a deeper connection to humankind is emphasized (Kristeller & Johnson, 2005), helping us to directly generate compassion for ourselves and others. With loving-kindness meditation, we are extending love and goodwill towards ourselves and others, repeating statements such as "May I be safe," "May I be healthy," May I be at peace," "May my near and dear ones be safe," and so on (Stahl & Goldstein, 2010). Ultimately, these two types of Buddhist meditation can work effectively together—mindfulness meditation helps us to "deconstruct" our relationship to unpleasant inner experiences by learning to notice them with distance and curiosity, and loving-kindness allows us to "construct" positive experiences (e.g., compassion, kindness) (Germer & Barnhofer, 2017). Along the way, we are developing the ability to be kind, compassionate, and non-judgmental towards the inner word, which combines the two types of meditation (Baer, 2010).

With both mindfulness and loving-kindness meditations, we are attempting to access the "contentment" system (Gilbert, 2010), given that we are extending kindness to ourselves and others. In mindfulness practice, we are relating to the inner world with non-judgment and acceptance, cultivating an attitude of compassion and kindness towards shame and self-criticism. When practicing loving-kindness meditation, conversely, we are repeating statements about ourselves and others that conjure up feelings of compassion, warmth, well-being, and so forth. In both instances, we are attempting to develop contentment (Gilbert, 2010), given there is nowhere else to be and nothing else to do. This "mode of the mind" is often called the "being" mode, in that we are in the present moment (rather than in the past or the future) and letting go of efforts to somehow fix our thoughts and feelings (Segal, Williams, & Teasdale, 2012).

Compassion, "Contentment," and Christian Meditation for Shame

With Christian meditation, God is the source of compassion. As a result, time spent in solitude with him is crucial so as to deepen your intimacy with the author of life. Within these important moments, there are several types of meditation that can be helpful, including those that rely on words and images (*kataphatic*) and those that are wordless and imageless (*apophatic*).

Kataphatic meditation involves the following ingredients (adapted from Lane, 1998; Knabb & Frederick, 2017; Peterson, 1989):

- Utilizing words and images in your meditative practice with God.
- Utilizing thoughts, feelings, and sensations in your meditative practice with God.
- Utilizing the Bible in your meditative practice with God.
- Utilizing metaphors in your meditative practice with God.
- "Praying with your eyes open" in your meditative practice with God.

An example of *kataphatic* meditation comes from the Puritans, who advocated for meditating on God's attributes and his Word, the Bible. This type of meditation will be practiced in the fourth chapter of the workbook, and can help you shift your focus from repetitive negative thinking and self-criticism to God's attributes, actions, and promises in the Bible.

Conversely, *apophatic* meditation involves the following qualities (adapted from Lane, 1998; Knabb & Frederick, 2017; Peterson, 1989):

- Utilizing silence in your meditative practice with God.
- Letting go of your use of words and images in your meditative practice with God.

- Developing an attitude of surrender by letting go of control in your meditative practice with God.
- Developing an attitude of humility and detachment—"humble detachment"—in your meditative practice with God.
- "Praying with your eyes shut" in your meditative practice with God.

Popular forms of *apophatic* meditation include the Jesus Prayer and centering prayer (which comes from the instructions in *The Cloud of Unknowing*). These types of meditation will be practiced in subsequent workbook chapters.

In deepening your relationship with God, you are first getting to know about God by way of meditating on Scripture. Within the Bible, God has revealed his attributes, actions, and promises, given Christians believe the Bible is the Word of God (2 Timothy 3:16–17). In addition to *kataphatic* meditation, *apophatic* meditation can help you learn to experience God on a deeper level, given you are spending time with him in silence, beyond words and images. This communion with God is like first learning about a friend, followed by appreciating the time spent with him or her in silence. In other words, at a certain point, you no longer need to fill the time with words, and can just enjoy your friend without unnecessary noise. Certainly, once you know your friend, words are not always needed as you appreciate this companionship from moment to moment.

This understanding of the relationship between *kataphatic* and *apophatic* meditation is consistent with a recent study I completed among Christian college students (Knabb, Vazquez, Wang, & Bates, 2018). In this study, I explored the relationship between deeply held views of God's providence (i.e., God image), the Christian ability to surrender to him, and repetitive negative thinking. Results revealed that a positive view of God's providence was linked to the ability to surrender to him, which was linked to less repetitive negative thinking. As one of the more important findings of the study, the relationship between surrendering to God and less repetitive negative thinking was explained (i.e., mediated) by Christians' ability to "humbly detach."

In the Knabb et al. (2018) study, I defined "humble detachment" as follows:

> A detached, flexible, humble ability to (a) let go of the tendency to clutch or push away a preoccupation with inner experiences and the self, and (b) pivot from a preoccupation with the self and inner experiences to a more transcendent awareness of God's active, loving presence.
>
> (p. 3)

As we move from using words and images in our meditative practice with God to a wordless and imageless time spent with him, we are slowly learning to detach from our preoccupation with unpleasant inner experiences, especially self-criticism and repetitive negative thinking. In doing so, we are increasingly surrendering to God's active, loving presence. In this process, we are accessing the "contentment" system, in that we are simply sitting at Jesus' feet, like Mary in the gospel of Luke (10:38–42). With nowhere else to be and nothing else to do, we can find peace and contentment in the present moment with God. Rather than being preoccupied with shame and self-criticism, we are developing focused, sustained attention by looking towards our Creator, who defines us and sustains us in each passing second.

Christian Meditation: "Contentment" as the "Rare Jewel"

In *The Rare Jewel of Christian Contentment*, Puritan author Jeremiah Burroughs (2010) drew inspiration from the Apostle Paul's teaching on contentment in order to make a case for its importance in the Christian life. In his letter to the Philippians (4:11–13), Paul wrote the following:

> I have learned to be content whatever the circumstances. I know what it is to be in need, and I know what it is to have plenty. I have learned the secret of being content in any and every situation, whether well fed or hungry, whether living in plenty or in want. I can do all this through him who gives me strength.

Building on this teaching, Burroughs defined Christian contentment as follows:

> That sweet, inward, quiet, gracious frame of spirit, which freely submits to and delights in God's wise and fatherly disposal in every condition. This description is a box of precious ointment and very comforting and useful for troubled hearts in troubled times and conditions.
>
> (p. 3)

To attain Christian contentment, Burroughs recommended several suggestions (adapted from Burroughs, 2010), in no particular order:

- Practice relying on God's grace as the source of contentment (rather than outward possessions and circumstances).
- Practice making life decisions by asking whether or not God has called you to engage in the activity and whether or not it is consistent with biblical teachings.
- Practice surrendering to God's providential care by putting your faith in him.
- Practice meditating on (i.e., think deeply about) heavenly things, rather than being preoccupied with earthly matters.
- Practice interpreting life's negative circumstances with God's best intentions in mind.
- Do not spend too much time being preoccupied with the world.
- Do not spend too much time being preoccupied with your suffering.
- Do not pursue worldly happiness.
- Do not overly rely on worldly comforts.
- Do not compare yourself to other people.
- Do not set your goals too high.

Ultimately, Burroughs concluded that God's grace—which leads to a "gracious heart"—is a better source of contentment than "outward comfort." With God's grace, contentment ends up influencing your thoughts, feelings, and so forth, to the point that only God will satisfy the soul (Burroughs, 2010). What follows, therefore, is a brief review of Christian grace, which can help you to better understand its role in cultivating compassion, mercy, and forgiveness.

The Relationship Between Love, Mercy, Grace, and Shame

Although we have already discussed the overlap between compassion, mercy, and forgiveness, I would like to introduce another salient Christian term—grace—into the conversation in order to help you better understand how these concepts relate to each other in the context of shame. God's grace and mercy emanate from God's love for us, and God persistently pursues those he loves (Erickson, 2013). These three terms—love, mercy, and grace—reflect attributes of God, with God's love capturing the manifestation of his goodness expressed towards humans, God's grace involving his unmerited love for us in our fallen state (because of Jesus' redemptive work), and God's mercy encompassing his loving response by offering us comfort in our time of need (Sailhamer, 1998).

Whereas mercy can mean to withhold just punishment, grace typically captures God's undeserving kindness towards humans (Douglas & Tenney, 2011). In other words, mercy is to withhold what is inevitably due, and grace is to extend what is definitely not due. God's grace, therefore, is extremely important when we consider our ongoing struggles due to our fallen, broken nature.

In the context of shame, the fall of humankind led to our collective estrangement from God. Certainly, shame is a reminder that we are incomplete, that is, we are missing this vital union with our Creator (Bonhoeffer, 1955, 1959). Rather than continuing to turn from God because of the desire to conceal in the midst of shame, this painful inner experience can help us to learn to reach for God, given he offers us love, grace, and mercy from moment to moment by way of Jesus' redemptive work on the cross. After all, "It is finished" (John 19:30), meaning his redemptive plan has already been realized. In turn, we are a "new creation" in Christ (2 Corinthians 5:17), which suggests we are reconciled to God. To be sure, we are no longer isolated and alone, divorced from our "source of meaning and significance" (Roetzel, 2007, p. 82). Instead of being alone in our shame, "Christ brings his followers back to the glory associated with Adam before his fall into disobedience" (Hafemann, 2000, p. 244). Overall, we have merit in God's eyes, and he extends his forgiveness, kindness, and soothing comfort to us from minute to minute via the reconciling act of Jesus. In the end, God functions like the proverbial glue necessary to tightly bind together a shattered vase. Because of this, we can confidently apply God's love, compassion, mercy, grace, and forgiveness to ourselves, and, in turn, offer compassion to others.

Personal Experiences of God's Love, Compassion, Mercy, and Grace: An Exercise

In this exercise, you will be reflecting on several key experiences in your relationship with God. Consider instances in which you felt God's love, compassion, mercy, and grace. After doing so, please write about these events, before recollecting times that involved extending God's love, compassion, mercy, and grace to other people.

Begin by considering a time that involved feeling God's love (i.e., an "act of goodness" by God towards you; Sailhamer, 1998). How did God display a benevolent act towards you? What were the details? What was the setting? Who was involved? When did it happen? What do you remember thinking in this situation? Feeling? What did you do? How did this experience of God's love impact your relationship with him? How, if at all, did this experience impact your shame and negative self-judgments? Were you able to extend God's love towards yourself and others?

____

____

____

____

____

____

____

____

____

____

____

____

Now, consider a time that involved feeling God's compassion and mercy (i.e., God offering you help and comfort in response to your suffering; Sailhamer, 1998). How did God display this comforting responsiveness towards you? What were the details? What was the setting? Who was involved? When did it happen? What do you remember thinking in this situation? Feeling? What did you do? How did this experience of God's compassion and mercy impact your relationship with him? How, if at all, did this experience impact your shame and negative self-judgments? Were you able to extend God's compassion and mercy towards yourself and others?

____
____
____
____
____
____
____
____
____
____
____
____

Finally, consider a time that involved feeling God's grace (i.e., his "unmerited love" for you; Sailhamer, 1998). How did God display this grace towards you? What were the details? What was the setting? Who was involved? When did it happen? What do you remember thinking in this situation? Feeling? What did you do? How did this experience of God's grace impact your relationship with him? Were you able to extend God's grace towards yourself and others?

____
____
____
____
____
____
____
____
____
____
____
____

A Compassion-Based Approach: Next Steps

To prepare you for the next four chapters, I would like you to revisit the strategy, goals, skills, and sources utilized in this workbook. In the pages that follow, I provide a specific strategy to help you cultivate compassion for yourself and others, with four overarching goals and four skill domains. Although this information was already presented in the introduction, I would like you to review it one more time in anticipation of the next four chapters of the workbook.

A Compassion-Based Approach: The Strategy

In the next four chapters of this workbook, you will be utilizing (a) modified exercises from the compassion literature in clinical psychology, and (b) *kataphatic* and *apophatic* forms of meditation in the Christian tradition. In so doing, you will be working on moving from shame, negative self-judgments, and repetitive negative thinking to an awareness of God's safety, mercy, compassion, and grace, cultivating a secure attachment with him along the way.

A Compassion-Based Approach: The Goals

There are four main goals in this workbook (adapted from Desmond, 2016; Germer, 2009; Gilbert, 2010; Jazaieri et al., 2013; Kabat-Zinn, 2013; Knabb, 2016; Kristeller & Johnson, 2005):

1. Learn to gently and compassionately notice difficult inner experiences with more distance, given God is loving you in each and every moment.
2. Pivot from the "danger" to "contentment" system, in that God is with you, reminiscent of Mary sitting at the feet of Jesus (rather than Martha's anxious activity) (Luke 10:38–42).
3. Cultivate a deeper awareness of God's compassion and mercy.
4. With a deeper awareness of God's compassion and mercy, practice more compassion and mercy towards yourself and others.

A Compassion-Based Approach: The Skills

Anchored to the strategy and four goals, you will be learning and practicing skills within the following four domains (adapted from Germer, 2009; Gilbert, 2010; Jazaieri et al., 2013; Kabat-Zinn, 2013; Knabb, 2016; Kolts, 2016; Thomas et al., 2011; Tirch et al., 2014):

- Thinking
  - You will be learning strategies for thinking with compassion so as to ameliorate the repetitive negative thinking and self-criticism that can often accompany shame.
  - Strategy-wise, you will practice reciting a phrase to calm your mind, challenge your distorted thoughts about God, practice Christian *kataphatic* meditation, recite the Psalms, and practice *lectio divina* (i.e., "divine reading" of Scripture).
- Feeling
  - You will learn strategies for relating differently to difficult feelings (e.g., shame) and work on developing positive emotions (rather than just trying to ameliorate shame).
  - Strategy-wise, you will be practicing a Christian version of a loving-kindness meditation, as well as Christian *apophatic* meditation to reach out to God in love (rather than solely relying on knowledge). Finally, you will practice Christian *kataphatic* meditation via using words to conjure up feelings of compassion for yourself and others.
- Behaving
  - You will learn strategies for behaving with compassion and mercy, focusing on getting in touch with your values to serve as a guide for life. You will also work on shifting your focus from being preoccupied with yourself (due to shame) to being focused on others.
  - Strategy-wise, you will clarify a set of Christian virtues to guide your life, as well as an action plan to extend God's compassion and mercy to others (in terms of concrete behaviors).
- Attending and imagining
  - You will learn strategies for attending to difficult inner experiences with compassion.
  - Strategy-wise, you will learn about the role that the breath can play in allowing you to focus on Jesus' mercy and love, practice several meditations (e.g., the "body scan"), practice the

Jesus Prayer, and practice a form of Ignatian *kataphatic* meditation to cultivate compassion for yourself and others.
  - In addition, you will use the power of imagery to cultivate self- and other-compassion.
  - Strategy-wise, you will use visualization exercises to develop a deeper compassion for yourself and others, some of which come from the Christian tradition.

These skills will help you develop compassion for yourself and others, commonly called the "compassionate self" (Leahy et al., 2011) in clinical psychology and the "new self" found in Christ (Colossians 3:1–17; Ephesians 4:24) within the Christian faith.

A Compassion-Based Approach: Turning to Psychological Science

In the next four chapters (which correspond with the aforementioned four skill domains), I have drawn from several compassion-based approaches to help you with your shame and negative self-evaluations, including the following:

- Compassion-focused therapy (Gilbert, 2010).
- The mindful self-compassion program (Germer, 2009; Neff, 2011).
- Compassion cultivation training (Jazaieri et al., 2013).
- Mindfulness-based stress reduction (Kabat-Zinn, 2013).
- Acceptance and commitment therapy (Hayes, Strosahl, & Wilson, 2012; Knabb, 2016; Tirch, Schoendorff, & Silberstein, 2014).

Yet, because these approaches within the psychology literature are sometimes influenced by Buddhism, I will also be turning to the Christian tradition to help you with your shame and self-judgments.

A Compassion-Based Approach: Turning to the Christian Tradition[1]

The Christian faith has countless writings to draw from in order to better understand psychological functioning. In the next four chapters, I draw from five bodies of literature from the last 1,700 years, including the following:

- Desert spirituality
  - Desert spirituality includes the *Sayings of the Desert Fathers* and John Cassian's *The Conferences*. The former is a collection of sayings, writings, and experiences from Christians who moved to the deserts of Egypt, Syria, and Palestine in the first half of the first millennium in order to simultaneously reject the excessive materialism they observed in society and draw closer to God. Over the course of several centuries, they developed strategies for dealing with the harsh desert landscape, managing both the inner and outer world by regularly relying on God's comfort and care. *Apophatic* meditation, along with an awareness of the importance of living out Christian virtues, are key contributions within desert spirituality.
- Protestant spirituality
  - Protestant spirituality includes writings from the Puritans, a group of Protestants from England in the 1500s and 1600s. They believed in relying on the Bible to guide daily living. One especially important contribution is their development of Christian *kataphatic* meditation, rooted

in the Bible. The Puritans have a well-developed method, to be sure, for focusing the mind on God, which will be an important part of learning to rest in God's safety and comfort.

- Orthodox spirituality
    - Orthodox spirituality, embedded within the Eastern Orthodox Christian tradition, includes the writings and practices expressed in the *Philokalia*, which is a volume of contemplative works from the 4th to the 15th centuries. One important contribution from the *Philokalia* is the Jesus Prayer (an *apophatic* form of meditation), which you will be practicing within this workbook. With the Jesus Prayer, you will be learning to call upon Jesus for mercy, compassion, and empathy in the midst of your pain.
- Medieval spirituality
    - Medieval spirituality, spanning the 14th through 16th centuries, includes monastic writings from authors such as Theresa of Avila, John of the Cross, Thomas Kempis, and the anonymous author of *The Cloud of Unknowing*. Commonly, medieval contemplatives advocated for a wordless, imageless form of *apophatic* meditation so as to reach out to God in love, rather than knowledge. This emphasis on deepening your relationship with God—by way of love—is especially important when relating differently to shame and self-judgments.
- Ignatian spirituality
    - Ignatian spirituality includes writings from the Society of Jesus, or Jesuits. Founded by Ignatius Loyola in the 16th century, Ignatius' *Spiritual Exercises* is especially important for the purpose of this workbook. In this writing, Ignatius offered *kataphatic* meditations and other exercises that can be helpful for you in your struggles with shame and self-criticism.

Personal Goals for the Workbook: An Exercise

Now that you have reviewed the plan ahead, I would like you to come up with three personal goals as you transition to the skills-based chapters. These goals will help you as you move through the next four chapters, practicing skills along the way in order to address the shame and self-criticism you struggle with. In the mental health field, we typically set goals that are measurable, attainable, positive, and specific, meaning we want them to be goals that (a) you can measure (e.g., "I will exercise three days per week for 45 minutes per day to lose ten pounds"), (b) are realistic and achievable, (c) focus on what you will do (rather than will not do), and (d) are as precise as possible (rather than vague or overly general) (Chang, Scott, & Decker, 2013).

1. ______________________________
2. ______________________________
3. ______________________________

Compassion in Action: A Case Example

Before concluding this chapter, I would like to share with you the case of Sharon, a 19-year-old woman who struggled with chronic shame. Growing up, she was very close to her father, who was the "head of the household." Sharon lived with her father, mother, and two younger sisters. When she was 11 years old, her father had an affair with a co-worker, eventually divorcing Sharon's mother and remarrying. In the transition, Sharon ended up with a new stepmother and stepbrother.

In her adolescent years, Sharon felt unloved and neglected by her father, in that he moved over an hour away with his "new family" and rarely spent time with her or her siblings. As a result, she described a deep feeling of being "unwanted," given she believed her father "chose another family to raise." Sharon also struggled in her relationship with God, in that she believed God was absent from her life. Over time, she started to judge herself harshly, concluding that both her father and God were distant because she was incapable of being loved. Because of some sort of "defect" she believed she had yet to discover, she just "knew for sure" she was "broken."

Yet, she started to see a psychotherapist at the urging of her church pastor. In her clinical work, she began to explore the link between her self-criticism and shame and her relationship with God. Gradually, she started to feel supported by her therapist, and opened up about the shame she felt on a regular basis. As a topic she brought up regularly, her therapist helped her to see the connection between her estranged father and God, with Sharon deciding she wanted to deepen her relationship with God, even though she knew she may never fully reconcile with her earthly father.

In the year-long therapy experience, she practiced *kataphatic* and *apophatic* forms of Christian meditation in order to begin to feel content in her relationship with God as an antidote to the regular shame and negative self-judgments she experienced. As she learned to (a) meditate on God's attributes, actions, and promises in the Bible, and (b) sit in silence with God, she started to find a deeper peace, and cognitively and affectively experience God's closeness. In turn, she began to extend the love, compassion, mercy, and grace she felt from God to herself, and worked towards applying the compassion she felt from God towards her relationship with her father. Although it was by no means easy, she was slowly able to feel compassion for her father, given she realized he was in his own pain when he made the unfortunate decision to divorce her mother and stop contacting Sharon.

Conclusion

In the third chapter, you learned more about compassion, including definitions and the role that compassion plays in connecting to the "contentment" system (Burroughs, 2010; Gilbert, 2010). You also explored secular and Christian forms of meditation for cultivating compassion. Moreover, you revisited the integrative compassion-based approach in this workbook, including the goals, skills, and sources from clinical psychology and the Christian tradition.

As the next four chapters will reveal, you will be learning to use your thoughts, feelings, behaviors, and imagination and attention so as to cultivate compassion, drawing from a range of techniques and exercises. The ultimate goal, of course, is for you to be able to find rest in God, a term coined by Gregory the Great. Resting in God, to be sure, involves accessing your God-given "contentment" system (Gilbert, 2010), which is a "rare jewel" that can offer a deeper peace and comfort from God (Burroughs, 2010). The "contentment" system that God offers involves relying on his grace, focusing on God and "heavenly-mindedness" by surrendering to his perfect, providential care (Burroughs, 2010). To rest in the contentment that naturally emanates from God, you will be working on cultivating "tunnel vision," in that you will be shifting your focus from worldly concerns, self-criticism, repetitive negative thinking, and shame to God's attributes, actions, and promises.

Note

1 Consistent with Richard Foster's *Streams of Living Water* (2001), I have drawn from several "streams" of the Christian tradition. In so doing, my hope is to help you learn to recognize God's compassion, applying this compassion to yourself in terms of how you "think," "feel," "behave," and "attend and imagine" (Germer, 2009; Gilbert, 2010).

References

Baer, R. (2010). Self-compassion as a mechanism of change in mindfulness- and acceptance-based treatments. In R. Baer (Ed.), *Assessing mindfulness & acceptance processes in clients: Illuminating the theory & practice of change* (pp. 135–154). Oakland, CA: New Harbinger Publications, Inc.

Bonhoeffer, D. (1955). *Ethics*. New York: Touchstone.

Bonhoeffer, D. (1959). *Creation and fall*. New York: Touchstone.

Burroughs, J. (2010). *The rare jewel of Christian contentment*. Pensacola, FL: Chapel Library.

Chang, V., Scott, S., & Decker, C. (2013). *Developing helping skills: A step-by-step approach to competency* (2nd ed.). Belmont, CA: Brooks/Cole.

Coniaris, A. (1998). *Philokalia: The Bible of Orthodox spirituality*. Minneapolis, MN: Light & Life Publishing Company.

Desmond, T. (2016). *Self-compassion in psychotherapy: Mindfulness-based practices for healing and transformation*. New York: W. W. Norton & Company, Inc.

Douglas, J., & Tenney, M. (2011). *Zondervan illustrated Bible dictionary*. Grand Rapids, MI: Zondervan.

Erickson, M. (2013). *Christian theology* (3rd ed.). Grand Rapids, MI: Baker Academic.

Foster, R. (2001). *Streams of living water: Celebrating the great traditions of the Christian faith*. New York: Harper-Collins Publishers.

Germer, C. (2009). *The mindful path to self-compassion: Freeing yourself from destructive thoughts and emotions*. New York: The Guilford Press.

Germer, C., & Barnhofer, T. (2017). Mindfulness and compassion: Similarities and differences. In P. Gilbert (Ed.), *Compassion: Concepts, research and applications* (pp. 69–86). New York: Routledge.

Gilbert, P. (2010). *Compassion focused therapy: Distinctive features*. New York: Routledge.

Grentz, S. (1994). *Theology for the community of God*. Grand Rapids, MI: William B. Eerdmans Publishing Company.

Hafemann, S. (2000). *2 Corinthians*. Grand Rapids, MI: Zondervan.

Hayes, S., Strosahl, K., & Wilson, K. (2012). *Acceptance and commitment therapy: The process and practice of mindful change* (2nd ed.). New York: The Guilford Press.

Jazaieri, H., Jinpa, G., McGonigal, K., Rosenberg, E., Finkelstein, J., Simon-Thomas, E., Cullen, M., Doty, J., Gross, J., & Goldin, P. (2013). Enhancing compassion: A randomized controlled trial of a compassion cultivation training program. *Journal of Happiness Studies, 14*, 1113–1126.

Kabat-Zinn, J. (2013). *Full catastrophe living: Using the wisdom of your body and mind to face stress, pain, and illness*. New York: Bantam Books.

Knabb, J. (2016). *Faith-based ACT for Christian clients: An integrative treatment approach*. New York: Routledge.

Knabb, J., & Frederick, T. (2017). *Contemplative prayer for Christians with chronic worry: An eight-week program*. New York: Routledge.

Knabb, J., Frederick, T., & Cumming, G. (2017). Surrendering to God's providence: A three-part study on providence-focused therapy for recurrent worry (PFT-RW). *Psychology of Religion and Spirituality, 9*(2), 180–196.

Knabb, J., Vazquez, V., Wang, K., & Bates, T. (2018). "Unknowing" in the 21st century: Humble detachment for Christians with repetitive negative thinking. *Spirituality in Clinical Practice*. Advanced online publication.

Kolts, R. (2016). *CFT made simple: A clinician's guide to practicing compassion-focused therapy*. Oakland, CA: New Harbinger Publications, Inc.

Kristeller, J., & Johnson, T. (2005). Cultivating loving kindness: A two-stage model of the effects of meditation on empathy, compassion, and altruism. *Zygon, 40*(2), 391–407.

Lane, B. (1998). *The solace of fierce landscapes: Exploring desert and mountain spirituality*. New York: Oxford University Press.

Leahy, R., Tirch, D., & Napolitano, L. (2011). *Emotion regulation in psychotherapy: A practitioner's guide*. New York: The Guilford Press.

Neff, K. (2003). The development and validation of a scale to measure self-compassion. *Self and Identity, 2*, 223–250.

Neff, K. (2011). *Self-compassion: The proven power of being kind to yourself*. New York: HarperCollins.

Neff, K. (2012). The science of self-compassion. In C. Germer & R. Siegel (Eds.), *Wisdom and compassion in psychotherapy: Deepening mindfulness in clinical practice* (pp. 79–92). New York: The Guilford Press.

Nicholson, S. (2013). Mercy. In J. Green, J. Brown, & N. Perrin (Eds.), *Dictionary of Jesus and the gospels* (pp. 584–588). Downers Grove, IL: IVP Academic.

Patzia, A. (1990). *Ephesians, Colossians, Philemon*. Grand Rapids, MI: Baker Books.
Peterson, E. (1989). *The contemplative pastor: Returning to the art of spiritual direction*. Grand Rapids, MI: William B. Eerdmans Publishing Company.
Roetzel, C. (2007). *2 Corinthians*. Nashville, TN: Abingdon Press.
Sailhamer, J. (1998). *Christian theology*. Grand Rapids, MI: Zondervan.
Segal, Z., Williams, M., & Teasdale, J. (2012). *Mindfulness-based cognitive therapy for depression* (2nd ed.). New York: The Guilford Press.
Stahl, B., & Goldstein, E. (2010). *A mindfulness-based stress reduction workbook*. Oakland, CA: New Harbinger Publications, Inc.
Strong, J. (2001). *The Greek dictionary of the New Testament*. Nashville, TN: Thomas Nelson.
Talbot, J. (2013). *The Jesus prayer: A cry for mercy, a path of renewal*. Downers Grove, IL: InterVarsity Press.
Thomas, M., Moriarty, G., Davis, E., & Anderson, E. (2011). The effects of a manualized group-psychotherapy intervention on client God images and attachment to God: A pilot study. *Journal of Psychology and Theology, 39*(1), 44–58.
Tirch, D., Schoendorff, B., & Silberstein, L. (2014). *The ACT practitioner's guide to the science of compassion*. Oakland, CA: New Harbinger Publications, Inc.
Wolters, A. (2005). *Creation regained: Biblical basics for a reformational worldview* (2nd ed.). Grand Rapids, MI: William B. Eerdmans Publishing Company.

CHAPTER 4

Thinking with Compassion

Introduction

In this chapter, you will be working on thinking with compassion and mercy towards yourself and others. By doing this, the goal is for you to modify your God concept and image in order to access the "contentment" system (Burroughs, 2010; Gilbert, 2010) and experience a secure attachment with God, ameliorating your shame-proneness along the way. By working on thinking with compassion, you will be utilizing your God-given thinking process to experience a closer relationship with him as your Creator and sustainer.

Several modified compassion-based exercises from the psychology literature will be presented, including utilizing a "God image automatic thought record" to improve your God concept and God image, working towards closing the potential gap between the two in the process (Olson et al., 2016; Thomas, Moriarty, Davis, & Anderson, 2011). You will also be reciting a short passage in Scripture to calm your mind, reminiscent of a *mantra* (Germer, 2009; van den Brink & Koster, 2015).

From the Christian tradition, you will practice exercises to cultivate a deeper awareness of God's attributes in order to improve your God concept and God image, using *kataphatic* meditation within Protestant spirituality (prayers from the *Valley of Vision*, among other Puritan writings), reciting the Psalms within the desert spiritual tradition, and practicing *lectio divina* within medieval spirituality. The Puritan meditation exercise will include an audio file to help you think with compassion during a formal, ten-minute period of time. In addition, writing assignments (e.g., journaling), examples from the Bible, and a case example will be presented to deepen your understanding of the material. Throughout the chapter, compassion for yourself and others (originally emanating from God's love, compassion, mercy, grace, and forgiveness) will be emphasized as an antidote to your shame and negative self-judgments. As you think with compassion, you will be shifting from the "danger" to the "contentment" system (Gilbert, 2010), given you are learning to receive God's loving compassion and mercy in your time of need.

Thinking with Compassion: Psychological and Christian Perspectives

In order to think with compassion, we need to be able to differentiate "threat-based" from "compassionate" thinking (Kolts, 2016). See the two following lists in order to begin to identify the difference (adapted from Kolts, 2016; Leahy, 2003):

- "Threat-based" thinking
  - Viewing a situation solely as threatening.
  - Overly relying on labeling when you believe you are facing a threating situation.
  - Judging a situation with dichotomous, black-and-white language (e.g., "this is bad").

  - Ruminating about the past or worrying about the future.
  - Blaming yourself or someone else.

- "Compassionate" thinking

  - Generating a range of possible explanations for a situation.
  - Trying to understand a situation, rather than label it.
  - Making sense of a situation with language that is kind, gentle, and compassionate.
  - Focusing on the present moment.
  - Being non-judgmental towards yourself and empathic towards others.

When we overly rely on inflexible, dichotomous thinking, we can trigger the "danger" system, especially when it comes to shame and self-criticism. On the other hand, when we strive to employ thinking that is flexible, balanced, and compassionate, we are tapping into the "contentment" system (Gilbert, 2010).

In our thinking patterns from day to day, we often have three cognitive levels that can lead to shame: automatic thoughts, intermediate beliefs, and core beliefs (Beck, 1995). The first level, automatic thoughts, consists of passing thoughts that we may not even notice (e.g., "I'm not a good husband"), whereas intermediate beliefs involve basic attitudes (e.g., "It's horrible to be seen as useless"), rules (e.g., "I must be perfect"), and assumptions (e.g., "If I never make mistakes, people will love me") (Beck, 1995). At a third, core level, we have a deeper set of global, rigid, and ingrained beliefs, often involving thoughts about being unlovable or powerless (Beck, 1995). These core beliefs develop over time, based on formidable experiences in our family life or relationship with others.

In the context of shame and self-judgments, we may have passing thoughts all day long that involve criticism directed towards ourselves, with intermediate beliefs consisting of attitudes about our self-worth, assumptions about what we should do in order to earn the love of others, and rules about how we must succeed in life. If we "drill down" even further, core beliefs tend to fuel our intermediate beliefs, which influence our automatic thoughts. These core beliefs may involve a deeper, global view that we are flawed, inadequate, unlovable, broken, unattractive, bad, or defective (Beck, 1995), leading to recurrent experiences of shame and ongoing self-criticism.

From a Christian perspective, the way we believe God sees us—which should be grounded in a biblical viewpoint—is especially salient in our walk with him. Since Christians hold that the Bible is the Word of God (2 Timothy 3:16), several questions (adapted from Tan & Johnson, 2005) are important to ask when considering whether or not we have a positive God concept ("head knowledge") and God image ("heart knowledge") (Davis, Moriarty, & Mauch, 2013):

- What might the Bible state about this?
- What might God state about this?

Ultimately, when we explore whether or not a thought is consistent with healthy Christian living, turning to the Bible is foundational for followers of Jesus, given God has revealed himself to us within the pages of the Old and New Testaments.

As the next step, identifying and changing automatic thoughts and core beliefs—especially those that relate to shame and self-criticism—by writing them down on paper is key. Therefore, the following two exercises will allow you to recognize your automatic thoughts and core beliefs about how God views you, as well as challenge them with a biblically based understanding that is rooted in his compassion, mercy, grace, love, and forgiveness. From a Christian perspective, an accurate, biblically based understanding of how God sees you is especially important. Thus, you will be examining your automatic thoughts and core beliefs in the context of how you currently believe God views you, working towards ensuring these beliefs are firmly planted in a Christian view of God (i.e., a scriptural understanding). In doing so, you will be attempting to align your God concept and God image (Thomas et al., 2011), resulting in a deeper congruence between your "head" and "heart" knowledge about God (Davis et al., 2013; Olson et al., 2016).

In that our knowledge about God can have an impact on our deeper, emotional experience of him, the exercises in this chapter will help you think differently about God so as to feel differently about him (Hoffman, 2005). In other words, because our cognitively derived God concept and emotionally derived God image interact in an active, dynamic manner (Schaap-Jonker, 2008), engaging in activities that allow our thoughts and feelings to align by starting with our thinking can be an important first step. Still, given that the medium of thinking is by no means the only way to experience God's love, compassion, mercy, grace, and forgiveness, especially when considering that the relationship between our God concept and God image is a complex process (Hoffman, 2005), the remaining chapters in this workbook will help you to feel, behave, and attend and imagine with compassion in order to experience God on a deeper level. Along the way, my hope is that you will be simultaneously ameliorating your God concept and God image, so they match up in an authentic manner. After all, thinking and feeling walk hand in hand on the roads of life.

What is more, developing a secure attachment to God involves cultivating a positive view of both yourself and God, believing you are worthy of his love and he is capable and willing to love you in your time of need (Bartholomew & Horowitz, 1991; Clinton & Straub, 2010). By examining your thoughts about how God views you, you will be working towards internalizing a biblically accurate perspective that God is responsive to your needs and has your best intentions in mind. This positive view of your "self-in-relationship-with-God" emanates directly from him, given he created you and comprises the other half of this vital, life-giving union.

Certainly, the Bible is filled with a plethora of examples of the importance of focusing on how God sees you, rather than being preoccupied with what other people think of you or how they treat you (Isaiah 51:12; Psalm 27:1, 56:10–11, 118:5–9; Romans 8:31; Hebrews 13:6). This shift in focus is also important when considering how you view yourself. A range of biblical figures, such as Moses, David, and Peter, were called by God to fulfill his purposes, yet struggled with doubt and feelings of inadequacy. Still, God's view of them (rather than how other people viewed them or how they viewed themselves) was paramount. As a result, these next two exercises will help you see that the God of the Bible loves you and wants what is best for you. In fact, God is extending his compassion, mercy, and grace to you in this very moment, which means you can learn to rest in his active presence by replacing your own distorted view of God with a biblically accurate perspective.

The God Image Automatic Thought Record: An Exercise

To begin this exercise (adapted from Moriarty, 2012), please review the list of common thinking errors in your relationship with God. In particular, these are automatic, inaccurate thoughts (adapted from Leahy, 2003) about how you may believe God views you, which, in turn, can result in personal experiences of shame and self-criticism. Most importantly, these erroneous forms of thinking are personally constructed, rather than emanating from the God of the Bible.

- Mind reading: you are convinced God believes something negative about you without evidence from the Bible.
- Fortune telling: you are convinced that God will do something negative to you in the future (or allow something negative to happen) without evidence from the Bible.
- Catastrophizing: you are convinced that God has caused (or allowed) a "worst case scenario" to happen to you without evidence from the Bible.
- Discounting the positives: you dismiss God's view of you, found in the Bible, and replace it with your own negating understanding of how God sees you.

- Negative filter: you dwell on all the ways you believe God sees you in a negative manner, and ignore God's positive, loving view of you from the Bible.
- Black-and-white thinking: you believe God sees you in only "bad," judgmental terms, rather than believing God loves you in your fallen state and offers you compassion, mercy, grace, and forgiveness.
- Personalizing: when something negative happens in life, you assume that God sees the worst in you, and, as a result, is punishing you for what you have done or who you are.
- Emotional reasoning: you allow your feelings about how you believe God sees you to get in the way of what the Bible says about how God sees you.

Next, please review the following "A-B-C" model (adapted from Leahy, 2003), which suggests that we experience an activating event in life ("A"), followed by an interpretation (i.e., an automatic thought or belief) of the event ("B"), which leads to a corresponding emotional consequence ("C"):

- Activating event: something happens in life (e.g., "I lost my job today").
- Belief: an interpretation is made about the event (e.g., "I lost my job because I'm a terrible sales manager").
- Emotional consequence: after making an interpretation, a corresponding emotion is experienced (e.g., "Because I'm a terrible sales manager, I feel depressed").

Notice that the event does not directly lead to the depressed mood; instead, the interpretation of what the job loss means results in the negative emotional experience. The "A-B-C" model can help you better understand the influential role that your thoughts, beliefs, and interpretations have in shaping your emotional world, including your experience of shame.

In your daily life, you may struggle with inaccurate, personally constructed thoughts about how God views you. These thoughts might come from your own understanding of God, influenced by prior experiences with parents, caregivers, or other important people in your life. Consequently, when you experience a negative event, and struggle with a corresponding feeling of shame, your automatic thoughts about how God sees you may be playing a role in the process. If this is the case, you might have a difficult time receiving God's compassion and mercy from moment to moment. In fact, you may have a hard time trusting that God loves you and wants to respond to your needs in the here-and-now. This possible gap between the God of the Bible (your God concept, which develops based on Christian teachings from church, mentors, and so on) and your own deeply embedded, emotionally charged view of God (your God image, which develops based on relationships in your family growing up) can lead to significant shame and self-criticism (Davis et al., 2013).

In this first exercise, you will be challenging your distorted image of God so you are better able to experience the God of the Bible as loving, compassionate, and merciful. With a healthy view of God's attributes, grounded in Scripture, you will be in a better position to surrender to his providential care in the midst of shame and self-criticism. To be sure, fixing this potential discrepancy between your God concept (positive or negative) and God image (positive or negative) requires a deliberate, sustained effort to do so (Olson et al., 2016; Thomas et al., 2011). Along the way, you may find that both your God concept and God image change (given you will be accurately thinking about God's attributes, actions, and promises in Scripture).

In the space that follows (adapted from Moriarty, 2012), please record a specific situation that involves believing you have disappointed God, your automatic thought about how God sees you (which comes from your own personally constructed thoughts and beliefs), the type of thinking error you have engaged in (referencing the previous list), and the way God actually sees you (based on the Bible). You will be completing this exercise once per day for the next week, whenever you experience shame.

Day of the Week	*Situation*	*Automatic Thought*	*Type of Thinking Error*	*How God Actually Sees You*
Monday				
Tuesday				
Wednesday				
Thursday				
Friday				
Saturday				
Sunday				

Identifying and Challenging Your Core Beliefs: An Exercise

Now that you have practiced identifying and replacing automatic thoughts about how God views you by differentiating the God of the Bible from your own personally constructed thoughts, you will be tracking more deeply held beliefs about how God sees you over the next week. As a Christian, what is most important is how God actually views you, at your core, rather than relying on your own beliefs. Therefore, you will be writing down your core beliefs based on how you believe God sees you (e.g., "I'm flawed," "I'm unlovable," "I'm defective," "I'm unattractive"), then identifying a passage in the Bible that refutes the negative belief by revealing how God actually views you.

Over time, you will be practicing viewing yourself—at your core—the way God sees you, rather than unilaterally deciding who you are, apart from him. Worth mentioning, one way to know that you are likely being influenced by an arbitrarily constructed negative core belief about how God views you is to notice when you are experiencing shame. Given that your automatic thoughts and core beliefs are connected to your feelings (remember the aforementioned "A-B-C" model), with the things you think to yourself commonly influencing how you end up emotionally experiencing the world, asking yourself what you are thinking on a deeper level when you are feeling shame is important in this exercise. Shame, after all, is a signal (Bonhoeffer, 1955, 1959) that tells you to reach for him, given you are incomplete without God's loving, merciful act of reconciliation.

In the space that follows, please record your belief about how God views you at least three times per day (in the left column). Then, record a passage in the Bible that helps you dispute your distorted core belief (in the right column). Negative core beliefs about how you believe God views you (with overarching themes of being helpless, unlovable, or worthless) may include the following (adapted from Beck, 2011):

- I can't do anything right in the eyes of God.
- God thinks I'm a complete and total failure.
- God believes I'm less valuable than other people.
- God thinks I'm unlovable.
- I'm ugly, broken, and flawed in God's eyes.
- God has abandoned me or is ignoring me because I'm so defective.
- I'm such a sinful person in God's eyes that he won't forgive me.
- Jesus died for other people's sins, not mine, because I'm unworthy of his love, compassion, mercy, grace, and forgiveness.

Of course, these core beliefs about how God views you do not capture his love, compassion, mercy, grace, and forgiveness. Therefore, turning to the Bible can help you to challenge them on an ongoing basis in order to close the gap between your God concept ("head" knowledge) and God image ("heart" knowledge) (Davis et al., 2013; Olson et al., 2016; Thomas et al., 2011).

Passages you may wish to focus on—which capture your inherent worth in God's eyes—include the following:

- You were "created in God's image" (Genesis 1:27).
- God values your heart (not your "outward appearance") (1 Samuel 16:7).
- You were "fearfully and wonderfully made" by God (Psalm 139:13–14).
- You are a "new creation" in Christ (2 Corinthians 5:17).
- When you feel weak, God's grace is enough for you (2 Corinthians 12:9).
- You have strength because of Jesus' power (Philippians 4:13).
- You are called to "put on the new self" in order to be righteous and holy (Ephesians 4:24).
- God loves you to the point of sacrificing Jesus for you (John 3:16).

By focusing on God's view of you, you are learning to shift from the "danger" to "contentment" system (Gilbert, 2010), resting in God's proverbial arms in the process.

Day of the Week	*Core Belief that is Distorted, Inconsistent with the Bible, and Comes from You*	*Core Belief that is Compassionate, Consistent with the Bible, and Comes from God*
Monday Morning		
Monday Mid-Day		
Monday Evening		
Tuesday Morning		
Tuesday Mid-Day		
Tuesday Evening		
Wednesday Morning		
Wednesday Mid-Day		
Wednesday Evening		
Thursday Morning		
Thursday Mid-Day		
Thursday Evening		
Friday Morning		
Friday Mid-Day		
Friday Evening		
Saturday Morning		
Saturday Mid-Day		
Saturday Evening		
Sunday Morning		
Sunday Mid-Day		
Sunday Evening		

Thinking and the "Limited Capacity Channel": An Exercise

In addition to identifying and challenging automatic thoughts and core beliefs (both of which can lead to shame), there is a more practical, pragmatic aspect of what we choose to focus on. Specifically, recognizing that you can only focus on a limited number of things at any given moment is an important realization when attempting to combat shame and self-criticism. Because of this, some authors have pointed out that we can "take up cognitive space in the mind" by shifting our focus from repetitive negative thinking to something else (Segal, Williams, & Teasdale, 2012). This "something else" can certainly be more helpful styles of thinking (e.g., automatic thoughts, core beliefs), or focusing on another experience altogether.

For Christians, there are a wide variety of activities that can "take up cognitive space in the mind," crowding out the ruminations, worries, and self-critical thoughts that leave us stuck in experiences of shame. Think of this psychological phenomenon like you would a crowded restaurant with a maximum capacity of 100 people. Once 100 people are seated for dinner, there is no room for anyone else to dine at the establishment. In a similar vein, when our attention is fully devoted to one thought, task, or activity, we do not have space for anything else, like the 101st dinner guest.

In the space that follows, see if you can come up with at least five things you can do to occupy your mind with positive activities that are firmly grounded in the Christian tradition, such as singing worship music, reading your Bible, or praying. Remember, the idea is to focus your entire attention on these Christian tasks, spending quality time with God in the process. When this happens, you are practicing filling your restaurant to its maximum capacity so that the 101st guest (which symbolizes self-criticism) cannot enter to ruin the evening spent dining with friends.

1. ____________________
2. ____________________
3. ____________________
4. ____________________
5. ____________________

Thinking and Metacognitive Awareness

Beyond disputing and replacing self-critical thoughts and focusing your attention on more positive activities, learning to notice the patterns of the mind with distance and flexibility is key. Within clinical psychology, we call this ability to notice our thinking "metacognitive awareness" (Herbert & Forman, 2011). When we are able to think about our thinking, we are taking a step back in order to see our thoughts as passing events, rather than automatically capturing reality.

Characteristics of metacognitive awareness include the following (adapted from Herbert & Forman, 2011):

- Being aware of your thought process.
- Being detached from your thought process with distance and flexibility.
- Being able to let go of unhelpful thinking patterns, rather than getting into a "tug-of-war" with them by trying to clutch them or push them away.
- Treating thoughts as passing inner events, rather than automatically assuming they constitute objective reality.
- Relating to thoughts as impermanent, instead of a fixed state.
- Seeing thoughts as benign, rather than dangerous.

This type of awareness is especially important in the process of learning to think with compassion, kindness, mercy, and grace. By recognizing that we are engaging in a negative, "threat-based" thinking style (Kolts, 2016), we can begin to gently notice the inner workings of the mind, reminiscent of sitting on the bank of a stream and watching the leaves float by on the surface of the water (Hayes, Strosahl, & Wilson, 2012).

Cognitive Fusion: Getting "Hooked" by Repetitive Negative Thinking

Unfortunately, when we struggle to maintain "metacognitive awareness," we can get stuck "looking *from* our thoughts," rather than "looking *at* our thoughts" (Harris, 2009, p. 97, italics added). When we look from our thoughts, we assume they are true and accurate, and have a hard time being able to take a step back to simply notice them with a calm curiosity. If we are fused with our thinking, we may end up doing the following (adapted from Harris, 2009):

- Holding on to inflexible, rigid rules as a guide for life.
- Overly relying on "good reasons" for avoiding life.
- Struggling with judging our inner (e.g., thoughts, feelings) or outer (e.g., environment) world.
- Being preoccupied with the past or future.
- Believing a negative, personally generated description of ourselves.

Fusion is similar to the famous saying, "We can't see the forest for the trees." Sometimes, we can get so focused on the trees in the forest (i.e., our particular thoughts) that we can lose sight of the fact that we are in an actual forest (i.e., our general thinking patterns). Reminiscent of a camera, shifting the focus from "zooming in" (focusing on this or that particular thought) to "zooming out" (seeing the larger patterns of our mind) is crucial. When we do so, we can begin to see that the "I'm worthless" thought (or any other negative thought) is actually part of a broader pattern of self-critical thinking, and this newly discovered, predictable pattern can be viewed from a safe distance without getting caught up in every isolated thought. From this safe vantage point, we can shift from the "danger" to the "contentment" system (Gilbert, 2010), recognizing that we do not need to fight our thinking process.

In the context of repetitive negative thinking—whether ruminating about the past, worrying about the future, or criticizing ourselves—we can begin to notice the "forest," rather than remaining fixated on the "trees." When this happens, we are able to non-judgmentally examine, with a compassionate, kind curiosity, our own proverbial "forest," and let go of the tendency to focus on each and every "tree." What is more, when considering our God image and attachment style with God, we can learn to step back, recognizing that our view of our "self-in-relationship-with-God" may be based on painful relationships in family life, rather than the reality of who God actually is in this very moment. One way to do so is through "defusion" strategies, which come from acceptance and commitment therapy (ACT).

Defusion: Watching Your Thinking

Rather than getting entangled with negative thinking patterns—especially in the context of shame and self-criticism—we can start to watch our thinking from a safe distance, reminiscent of going to the zoo and watching wildlife in its natural habitat with a curious, non-judgmental attentiveness. When we are able to just notice our thinking, the following processes may begin to take shape (adapted from Harris, 2009):

- We just notice our thinking.
- We are non-judgmental towards our thinking.
- We ask whether or not a thought is helpful, rather than automatically assume it is true.
- We watch our thinking from a safe psychological distance, recognizing that it cannot harm us in any way.

In relation to shame and self-criticism, defusion can help us to be kind, compassionate, and non-judgmental towards our thinking, rather than automatically assume our self-judgments are true and accurate depictions of who we are. In this next exercise, you will have the opportunity to notice your thinking, with Jesus by your side, and learn to be more compassionate, loving, and merciful towards your inner world because Jesus is with you.

Watching Your Thinking with Jesus: An Exercise

In this exercise (adapted from Hayes et al., 2012; Knabb, 2016), imagine that you are sitting with Jesus on the shore of the Sea of Galilee, watching the choppy waters in the distance. Visualize spending this important time with your Lord and Savior, sinking your feet into the warm sand as you look out towards the vast blue space in front of you. Off in the distance, you see white clouds hovering above the hillside, with a cool breeze gently brushing up against your face. As you sit with him, you are able to safely watch what goes on in the water, without worrying about getting swept away. With Jesus by your side, you notice a few waves on the lake, with birds soaring over the water. The sun is shining as you absorb the scenery with a calm, peaceful demeanor.

Now, try to imagine that the waves of the water and the birds in the air represent your self-critical thoughts. Rather than trying to control them or make them go away, your job is to just notice them as you sit with Jesus. Because he is by your side—and in complete control of the lake, the birds, the clouds, the sun, and the breeze—there is nothing you need to be doing, other than noticing what is happening with him. In other words, you are watching your thoughts with a calm, curious, non-judgmental attentiveness, reminiscent of observing nature.

Begin to notice the thoughts that are passing through your mind, just like you are watching this biblical landscape in Israel. However, rather than getting into a "tug-of-war" match with them, your job is to just notice your self-critical thoughts, like you are watching the lake, the birds, and the surrounding terrain. Spend about ten minutes just noticing the proverbial landscape of your mind, recognizing that Jesus is with you in this very moment. There is nothing you need to be doing, other than spending time with him, in that he is in complete control and has your best intentions in mind. In this time, you are shifting from the "danger" to "contentment" system (Gilbert, 2010)—there is nothing you need to protect yourself from, and nothing you need to pursue. You are just watching your inner world, like you would the Sea of Galilee—there is no need to try to control God's creation in any way. Rather, your job is to simply watch, given you are in awe of God's creation. Over and over again, just notice the inner workings of your mind, with Jesus by your side.

When you are done, spend a minute or two reflecting on the exercise. What was it like to just notice your thoughts, like you would observe your surroundings while sitting on the shore of the Sea of Galilee with Jesus? Were you able to apply the same calm, curious, non-judgmental attentiveness to your inner world that you would apply to your experience of watching nature with

Jesus? What, if anything, got in the way of doing so? Moving forward, how can you extend this approach to your self-critical thoughts? What role will Jesus play in the process?

Thinking with Compassion: A Journaling Exercise

As the next exercise in this chapter, spend ten minutes journaling about what your life might be like in your relationship with both God and others if you were able to think with compassion, extending God's love, mercy, grace, and forgiveness to yourself and others from moment to moment. Thinking with compassion, viewed through this lens, involves the following ingredients:

- Being kind to yourself, rather than judgmental.
- Being understanding towards yourself, not critical.
- Accepting yourself as created in God's image, with dignity and worth, rather than worthless, useless, or unlovable.
- Viewing yourself as a "new creation in Christ" (2 Corinthians 5:17), "putting on the new self" (Ephesians 4:24) on a regular basis, instead of remaining preoccupied with who you were before you gave your life to Christ.

What thoughts might you have if you were able to think with compassion? How about feelings? How might your behavior be different? What, specifically, might you be doing differently? How might your relationship with God be different? How might your relationship with others look different?

Regrettably, rather than thinking with compassion, we can end up fixated on all sorts of topics that are unhelpful in our quest to be more compassionate, kind, and loving towards ourselves and others. In this next section, you will learn about the reality of mind wandering, including some distinctly Christian strategies for refocusing your mind on God's active, loving presence.

Mind Wandering: Psychological and Christian Perspectives

We all get distracted throughout the day. In fact, recent research has revealed that 50% of a sample of adults reported their mind was wandering when they were supposed to be focusing on a specific task (Killingsworth & Gilbert, 2010). Unfortunately, mind wandering can lead to repetitive negative thinking and self-criticism, which can result in a long-term battle with shame. Interestingly, we also meditate all day long (Hall, 2016), with meditation broadly defined as thinking deeply about a given topic. Yet, what we choose to meditate on can either help us to feel God's love, compassion, mercy, grace, and forgiveness, or result in repetitive negative thinking, self-criticism, and shame.

Next, you will be learning to calm and focus your mind with a Christian *mantra*, practicing Christian meditation to fill up the "limited capacity channel" of the mind (Segal et al., 2012) with God's attributes, actions, and promises. In doing so, you will be working towards thinking with compassion, instead of relying on personally constructed self-criticisms, self-evaluations, and self-judgments. Remember, the Apostle Paul instructed us to think about what is true, noble, right, pure, lovely, admirable, excellent, and praiseworthy (Philippians 4:8); doing so, though, will require a major shift in your thinking habits.

Calming and Focusing the Mind with a Christian *Mantra*: The Antidote to Mind Wandering

When you notice that your mind is wandering, especially towards negative self-judgments, gently reciting a *mantra* can be a way to calm your mind and shift your focus. This strategy can be particularly helpful when you are stuck in repetitive negative thinking. Although *mantras* have historically been associated with Eastern religions, they can be pragmatic in that you are calming your racing thoughts by focusing on the meaning of a short phrase (Germer, 2009). Over time, you are learning to turn from negative, self-critical thoughts to encouraging, uplifting words.

Within the Christian tradition, there are all kinds of short phrases—typically rooted in the Bible—that can help you to refocus your mind on God. One such *mantra*—*Maranatha*, the Aramaic word for "Come, O Lord" (Fee, 1987)—is found at the end of Paul's letter to the Corinthians (1 Corinthians 16:22). This specific *mantra* is "a very, very simple device that is meant to bring you in all simplicity into the presence of the Lord" (Main, 2001, p. 39).

When applying this *mantra* to self-criticism, the idea is to first notice that you are stuck in this type of thinking process. Once you have done so, shifting your focus from negative self-judgments to "Come, O Lord" can help you focus your attention on God's loving presence. In turn, gently repeating the phrase so as to cultivate sustained attention for a brief period of time can allow you to fill up the "limited capacity channel" (Segal et al., 2012) with Jesus' active, loving presence.

This practice can take place formally, devoting ten minutes at a time, or informally throughout your day. If the former, you may want to find a quiet environment, sitting in a chair with your eyes closed. Once you have done this, begin to introduce the phrase, "Come, O Lord," pivoting back to these words whenever you notice your mind drifting towards negative thinking. If the latter, you may want to simply introduce the phrase throughout your day when you notice your mind has wandered towards repetitive negative thinking. In either case, the short phrase—which was likely an early Christian prayer (Douglas & Tenney, 2011)—can help you develop focused, sustained attention on Jesus, rather than getting sidetracked by self-criticism. As you ask Jesus to be present, you are petitioning him for his love, compassion, mercy, grace, and forgiveness. In doing so, you are accessing the "contentment" system, in that he is all you need in this very moment (Burroughs, 2010; Gilbert, 2010). As another example of focusing the mind, next, you will be learning about *kataphatic* meditation within the Puritan tradition.

Kataphatic Meditation Within Protestant Spirituality: Refocusing a Wandering Mind

In the Old Testament, the Hebrew word, *hagah,* is often used for meditation, whereas the Greek word, *melatao,* is sometimes used in the New Testament (Strong, 2001a, 2001b). Among the Puritans, a group of Protestants from England in the 1500s and 1600s who believed strongly in turning to God's Word, the Bible, to guide life, meditation was defined in several different ways:

- "[Meditation] is the steadfast and earnest bending of the mind on some spiritual and heavenly matter, discoursing on it with ourselves, until we bring it to some profitable point, both for the settling of our judgments, and the bettering of our hearts and lives" (Ball, 2016, p. 25).
- "Meditation is the soul's retiring of itself, that by a serious and solemn thinking upon God, the heart may be raised up to heavenly affections" (Watson, 2012, Chapter 2, Section 1, para. 1).

In terms of a more contemporary definition, I define Puritan meditation as follows:

- A focused, sustained cognitive process within Puritan Christianity, shifting from earthly- to heavenly-minded thinking in order to cultivate a corresponding feeling state for Christ-like behavioral action.

Puritan meditation can be occasional, meaning you might say very brief meditations throughout the day; or, Puritan meditation can be deliberate, which involves a more formal practice in solitude and for a set amount of time (Beeke & Jones, 2012).

There are a variety of reasons to use Puritan meditation in your daily life, including, but not limited to, the following (adapted from Ball, 2016; Hall, 2016):

- It is rooted in Scripture (e.g., Psalm 1:2).
- It can help you shift your focus from negative thoughts to God.
- It can help you cultivate a deeper awareness of God's active, loving presence.
- It can help your mind to find rest.
- It can help you develop focused, sustained attention, which can ameliorate repetitive negative thinking.
- It can help you meditate on the right things, given you are always meditating on something.

Puritan meditation can help you gain a deeper awareness of God's active, loving presence, especially when meditating on his love, compassion, mercy, grace, and forgiveness. In this process, you are learning to access the "contentment" system by finding comfort in him (Burroughs, 2010; Gilbert, 2010). In addition, meditating on God's providential care can help you begin the process of learning to trust in him when you are stuck in repetitive cycles of thinking, shifting from "earthly-mindedness" to "heavenly-mindedness." In other words, as you learn to meditate on God, you are turning from rumination, worry, and self-criticism so you can untangle yourself from repetitive thinking cycles that get in the way of the life God has called you to live. In order to prepare you to engage in Puritan meditation, I have drawn from several Puritan writings so as to present an eight-step process in a straightforward manner.

Puritan Meditation: An Eight-Step Process

I have organized the instructions from a variety of Puritan writings (adapted from Ball, 2016; Baxter, 2015; Beeke & Jones, 2012; Hall, 2016; Watson, 2012) into eight steps for you to practice in a ten-minute timespan. When practicing, find a quiet space, free from distractions, and sit up straight in a supportive chair with your eyes closed.

1. Choose a biblical topic to focus all your attention on.
2. Say a short prayer to God, asking him for guidance during the next ten minutes.
3. Shift your focus from "earthly-mindedness" to "heavenly-mindedness," letting go of rumination, worry, and self-criticism and shifting towards a single point of focus—a short passage in Scripture that reveals the biblical topic.
4. Repeat the passage in Scripture with focused, sustained attention.
5. Begin to move from your "brain" to your "heart," focusing on the feeling that corresponds with the biblical topic and short passage in Scripture.
6. Deeply experience the feeling that corresponds with the biblical topic and passage in Scripture.
7. As you conclude the meditation, make a commitment to act on what you have just focused all your attention on by extending compassion to others in a Christ-like manner.
8. Say a short prayer to God, thanking him for revealing himself to you via the biblical topic and short passage in Scripture.

Puritan Meditation: An Exercise

Each day this week, you will be meditating on God's compassion (adapted from Ball, 2016; Baxter, 2015; Beeke & Jones, 2012; Hall, 2016; Watson, 2012). Try to find a quiet place, free from distractions, and meditate for ten minutes. Close your eyes and sit up straight as you meditate on the pre-selected Bible verse. Please consider using the corresponding audio recording, "Track 3," available at https://www.routledge.com/The-Compassion-Based-Workbook-for-Christian-Clients-Finding-Freedom-from/Knabb/p/book/9780815394365.

1. For the next ten minutes, you will be focusing on the Bible verse, "The Lord is full of compassion and mercy" (James 5:11).
2. Say a short prayer to God, asking him for guidance during the next ten minutes.
3. Shift your focus from "earthly-mindedness" to "heavenly-mindedness," letting go of rumination, worry, and self-criticism and pivoting towards the "The Lord is full of compassion and mercy" Bible verse.
4. Repeat this passage in Scripture with focused, sustained attention.
5. Begin to move from your "brain" to your "heart," focusing on feeling God's love for you.
6. Deeply feel the compassion and mercy of God that correspond with his infinite goodness.
7. As you conclude the meditation, make a commitment to act on this deeper awareness of God's compassion and mercy by extending compassion to others in a Christ-like manner.
8. Say a short prayer to God, thanking him for revealing his compassion and mercy to you.

In the space that follows, please record your efforts over the next week.[1]

Day/Date	*Practice (Yes/No)*	*Comments*
Wednesday Date: ________	*Kataphatic* Meditation:	
Thursday Date: ________	*Kataphatic* Meditation:	
Friday Date: ________	*Kataphatic* Meditation:	
Saturday Date: ________	*Kataphatic* Meditation:	
Sunday Date: ________	*Kataphatic* Meditation:	
Monday Date: ________	*Kataphatic* Meditation:	
Tuesday Date: ________	*Kataphatic* Meditation:	

The Valley of Vision: An Exercise

In addition to the above Puritan writings, *The Valley of Vision* is a famous collection of Puritan meditations and prayers, elucidating their passion for God in the form of short, heartfelt writings that span a range of Christian topics. In this next exercise (adapted from Thomas et al., 2011), you will be reading one such meditation—"God All-Sufficient"—which powerfully captures God's mercy, grace, and loving-kindness. Slowly read through the meditative prayer, allowing the words to sink in as you work towards thinking deeply with compassion:

> King of glory, divine majesty, every perfection adorns thy nature and sustains thy throne; the heavens and the earth are thine, the world is thine and its fullness. Thy power created the universe from nothing; thy wisdom has managed all its multiple concerns, presiding over nations, families, individuals. Thy goodness is boundless; all creatures wait on thee, are supplied by thee, are satisfied in thee. How precious are the thoughts of thy mercy and grace! How excellent thy loving-kindness that draws men to thee! Teach us to place our happiness in thee, the blessed God, never seeking life among the dead things of earth, or asking for that which satisfies the deluded; but may we prize the light of thy smile, implore the joy of thy salvation, find our heaven in thee. Thou hast attended to our happiness more than we can do; though we are fallen creatures thou hast not neglected us. In love and pity thou hast provided us a Savior; apply his redemption to our hearts, by justifying our persons, and sanctifying our natures. We confess our transgressions, have mercy on us. We are weary, give us rest, ignorant, make us wise unto salvation, helpless let thy strength be made perfect in our weakness, poor and needy, bless us with Christ's unsearchable riches, perplexed and tempted, let us travel on unchecked, undismayed, knowing that thou hast said, 'I will never leave thee nor forsake thee.' Blessed be thy name!
>
> (Bennett, 1975, p. 214)

After reading this powerful meditation, reflect on the central theme—in spite of our fallen nature, filled with shortcomings, weariness, and helplessness, God remains in control. In fact, from moment to moment, he offers us his love, mercy, and grace, and we can access our God-given "contentment" system because he is enough (Burroughs, 2010; Gilbert, 2010). Above all else, he generously offers us redemption by way of Jesus' perfect work on the cross, which restores our connection with him and helps us to experience a secure attachment with our Creator (Knabb & Emerson, 2013). As you "try on" the themes of this devotional, journal for five minutes on what your life would be like if you were to regularly look to God for love, mercy, and grace, shifting from being preoccupied with your own fallen nature to his perfect attributes, actions, and promises.

Reciting the Psalms Within Desert Spirituality: Filling the Mind with God's Promises

Jesus used Scripture when he was in the wilderness for 40 days (Matthew 4:1–11), citing Deuteronomy as a way to combat the Devil's temptations. Likewise, the early desert Christians used the Psalms as a strategy for shifting their focus from compulsive, distracting thoughts to God's promises in the Bible (Burton-Christie, 1993). For these desert dwellers, thoughts came from either God, the Devil, or themselves (Cassian, 1997). In either case, Moses, one of the early desert Christians, noted, "it is, indeed, impossible for the mind not to be troubled by thoughts, but accepting them or rejecting them is possible for everyone who makes an effort . . . Therefore we practice the frequent reading of and constant meditation on Scripture, so that we may be open to a spiritual point of view" (Cassian, 1997, p. 56).

As you learn to think with compassion, reciting the Psalms is a way to keep your mind focused on God's promises, rather than automatically accepting self-critical thoughts as true and accurate. If, as the early desert Christians taught, the mind is constantly generating thoughts, we have a choice about whether or not we will focus on such thoughts or shift our attention to thoughts that help us adopt a "spiritual point of view."

Reciting the Psalms: An Exercise

In this exercise, read Psalm 145 slowly in order to practice focusing your mind on God's promises. When you notice that your mind has shifted towards self-critical thoughts, simply return to the text.

Along the way, notice all the trustworthy descriptions of God (e.g., powerful, loving, good, compassionate) and ponder them as an alternative to your own personally constructed self-judgments. To conclude the exercise, select one sentence to meditate on throughout your day (e.g., "The Lord is good to all; he has compassion on all he has made"). Whenever you notice your mind has wandered to negative thinking (which can lead to shame), return to the passage by quietly reciting it in your mind for a few minutes at a time.

> I will exalt you, my God the King; I will praise your name for ever and ever. Every day I will praise you and extol your name for ever and ever. Great is the Lord and most worthy of praise; his greatness no one can fathom. One generation commends your works to another; they tell of your mighty acts. They speak of the glorious splendor of your majesty—and I will meditate on your wonderful works. They tell of the power of your awesome works—and I will proclaim your great deeds. They celebrate your abundant goodness and joyfully sing of your righteousness. The Lord is gracious and compassionate, slow to anger and rich in love. The Lord is good to all; he has compassion on all he has made. All your works praise you, Lord; your faithful people extol you. They tell of the glory of your kingdom and speak of your might, so that all people may know of your mighty acts and the glorious splendor of your kingdom. Your kingdom is an everlasting kingdom, and your dominion endures through all generations. The Lord is trustworthy in all he promises and faithful in all he does. The Lord upholds all who fall and lifts up all who are bowed down. The eyes of all look to you, and you give them their food at the proper time. You open your hand and satisfy the desires of every living thing. The Lord is righteous in all his ways and faithful in all he does. The Lord is near to all who call on him, to all who call on him in truth. He fulfills the desires of those who fear him; he hears their cry and saves them. The Lord watches over all who love him, but all the wicked he will destroy. My mouth will speak in praise of the Lord. Let every creature praise his holy name for ever and ever.

Lectio Divina Within Medieval Spirituality: Divine Reading for Self-Criticism

In addition to reading the Psalms, *lectio divina* is a time-honored Christian approach to interacting with the Bible that involves a deeper reflection upon Scripture. Popular in monasteries in the Middle Ages, *lectio divina* has four major steps, which can be easily remembered because they all start with "R" (adapted from Benner, 2010; Knabb, 2016):

- Read (*lectio*): read a selected verse within the Bible, slowly absorbing the chosen section of Scripture.
- Reflect (*meditation*): reflect on the verse, striving to better understand what God is revealing to you in this very moment.
- Respond (*oratio*): respond to the verse, thanking God for his active, loving presence in the here-and-now.
- Rest (*contemplation*): in solitude and silence, rest in God, setting aside all words and images by surrendering to his loving care in the present moment.

In the context of shame and self-criticism, *lectio divina* can help you focus on God's Word, the Bible, shifting from negative self-judgments towards God's loving presence. Along the way, you are filling the "limited capacity channel" (Segal et al., 2012) with Scripture, which explicates God's compassion for you in spite of your shortcomings (Romans 5:8). In addition, as you find rest in God, you are learning to access the "contentment" system (Burroughs, 2010; Gilbert, 2010).

Divine Reading: An Exercise

In this exercise (adapted from Benner, 2010; Knabb, 2016), you will be selecting your own passage in Scripture, spending the next ten minutes slowly moving through the four stages of *lectio divina*. Try to choose a short verse on God's compassion so that you can absorb it, reminiscent of taking a small (rather than large) bite out of a savory plate of food. As you engage in each step, record your reactions below:

		Reactions
Verse in the Bible		
	Read	
	Reflect	
	Respond	
	Rest	

"Father, Forgive Them": Jesus' Example of Thinking with Compassion Towards Others[2]

Before concluding this chapter, you will be working on extending compassion to others, consistent with Jesus' loving response towards 1st-century Jews and Romans while on the cross (Morris, 1988). As Jesus was dying on a lonely wooden cross, he powerfully declared, "Father, forgive them, for they do not know what they are doing" (Luke 23:34). With this prayer to his Father, Jesus painted a picture of forgiveness and redemption (Green, 1997). What is more, in his petition to God, he modeled the importance of praying for our enemies (Green, 1997; Luke 6:28). In spite of the fact that he was in tremendous pain, he practiced integrity, demonstrating forgiveness for the very people who were taking his life from him (Carroll, 2012).

As Jesus' prayer in Luke reveals, God has compassion for you, which means you can extend this God-given compassion towards yourself. In turn, an important next step is to offer others the compassion and mercy that God has generously provided.

In the next ten minutes, try to think about someone who has mistreated you over the years by criticizing and judging you, resulting in a corresponding feeling of shame. Now, imagine what it might have been like for Jesus to hang on two wooden beams, with both Jews and Romans watching him suffer and die. In the midst of this pain, though, he cried out to his Father, asking God to forgive the very people who were causing him agony. Try to deeply reflect on Jesus' willingness to forgive those who were executing him.

Now, try your best to forgive the person who has caused you pain. Begin to introduce the phrase, "Father, forgive [him or her]," gently repeating the phrase over and over again as you allow it to sink in with compassion, mercy, and forgiveness. Just as Jesus has forgiven you, see if you can generously extend his merciful compassion towards the person who wronged you (Ephesians 4:32). When you notice thoughts of protest arising (e.g., "But he doesn't deserve to be forgiven"), simply return to the phrase, "Father, forgive [him or her]." Continue this process for about ten minutes, and carry Jesus' prayer with you throughout your day, exercising an attitude of compassion and mercy towards those who have wronged you.

Thinking with Compassion: A Case Example

Celeste, an African American woman in her 40s, started to struggle with repetitive negative thinking when she was about 10 years old. Around this time, her mother died, resulting in recurrent ruminations about the past, worries about the future, and negative self-judgments. As she moved into her adolescent years, she especially struggled with revisiting past arguments with her mother before she died, concluding that she could have prevented her mother's death if she was a "good kid." In that her mother died in an automobile accident, Celeste believed her mother crashed because she was "too stressed out" from parenting.

In the years after her mother died, Celeste also worried about the future, wondering if she would ever be loved again. Gradually, she started to judge herself, believing she was deeply flawed and broken. Without a mother to love her, she reasoned, she lacked worth, and did not deserve to be happy.

Fast forward to her adult years, and she continued to struggle with self-doubt and self-criticism. On a deeper level, she also concluded that God did not love her, given he "took away [her] mother" and "didn't bless [her] with a spouse." As a single woman, she felt a tremendous sense of shame, which led to isolation and withdrawal from others.

On one particular summer afternoon, she decided to call a local Christian psychologist to get help. In the first session, she explained that she felt God's distance and judgment, and doubted that she could ever be loved. She described a childhood filled with self-judgment, guilt, shame, and a preoccupation with her mother's tragic death, openly doubting her ability to be in an intimate, lasting relationship.

Over the course of the next few months, she worked with her therapist on recognizing that God loved her, and was offering his compassion and mercy from moment to moment. She was especially drawn towards the Psalms, which she believed captured the "ups and downs" of an intimate relationship with God. As she learned to shift her focus from repetitive negative thinking to God's promises in the Bible, she was able to feel a sense of compassion for herself and contentment in her time spent with him. Gradually, she started to see herself as an imperfect, yet lovable, human being, and realized that her mother's accident was by no means her fault.

Instead of blaming herself, she recognized that she was a 10-year-old in pain at the time of her mother's death, someone who deeply needed a parent's love. She also was able to acknowledge that she longed for God's love, and began to recognize the connection between her self-critical thinking and feelings of shame. With her therapist's help, she practiced a variety of strategies to notice when her mind wandered, then gently pivot towards God's promises in the Bible. Although she continued to struggle with self-criticism and shame, she was able to increasingly "take a step back" in order to watch her thinking habits with Jesus, who she eventually realized was sitting by her side the whole time.

Conclusion

In this chapter, you practiced thinking with compassion and mercy towards yourself and others. You were able to work on disputing and replacing distorted thoughts and beliefs about how God sees you, striving to modify your God image in the process, and recite a Christian *mantra* as a way to calm and focus your mind. Drawing from the Christian tradition, you practiced *kataphatic* meditation within Protestant spirituality, recited the Psalms within the desert spiritual tradition, and learned *lectio divina* within medieval spirituality. In addition to striving towards shifting your focus to God's attributes, actions, and promises, you were able to practice extending Jesus' compassion towards someone else. In doing so, you have started the lifelong process of refocusing your thinking on God and "heavenly-mindedness" whenever your wandering mind has drifted. In the next chapter, you will be learning to feel with compassion, given that God created you with a range of emotions, which are by no means the enemy. Instead, your emotions are a gift, helping you to deepen your relationship with God and others.

Notes

1 This form is adapted from Segal et al. (2012).
2 In Everett Worthington's (2003) popular *REACH* model of forgiveness, he presents a five-step solution, which includes remembering the pain ("R"), empathizing with the person who hurt us ("E"), forgiving the offending person as an "altruistic gift" (in that we have hurt others, too) ("A"), making a verbal commitment to forgive in front of loved ones (for them to hold us accountable) ("C"), and maintaining an attitude of forgiveness by holding on to it on a daily basis ("H"). This exercise is influenced by the second and third steps in his model.

References

Ball, J. (2016). *A treatise of divine meditation*. Crossville, TN: Puritan Publications.
Bartholomew, K., & Horowitz, L. (1991). Attachment styles among young adults: A test of a four-category model. *Journal of Personality and Social Psychology*, *61*(2), 226–244.
Baxter, R. (2015). *The Saints' everlasting rest*. Louisville, KY: GLH Publishing.
Beck, J. (1995). *Cognitive therapy: Basics and beyond*. New York: The Guilford Press.
Beck, J. (2011). *Cognitive therapy for challenging problems: What to do when the basics don't work*. New York: The Guilford Press.
Beeke, J., & Jones, M. (2012). *A Puritan theology: Doctrine for life*. Grand Rapids, MI: Reformation Heritage Books.
Benner, D. (2010). *Opening to God: Lectio divina and life as prayer*. Downers Grove, IL: InterVarsity Press.
Bennett, A. (Ed.). (1975). *The valley of vision: A collection of Puritan prayers & devotions*. Carlisle, PA: The Banner of Truth Trust.
Bonhoeffer, D. (1955). *Ethics*. New York: Touchstone.
Bonhoeffer, D. (1959). *Creation and fall*. New York: Touchstone.
Burroughs, J. (2010). *The rare jewel of Christian contentment*. Pensacola, FL: Chapel Library.
Burton-Christie, D. (1993). *The word in the desert: Scripture and the quest for holiness in early Christian monasticism*. New York: Oxford University Press.
Carroll, J. (2012). *Luke: A commentary*. Louisville, KY: Westminster John Knox Press.
Cassian, J. (1997). *The conferences* (B. Ramsey, Trans.). New York: Paulist Press.
Clinton, T., & Straub, J. (2010). *God attachment: Why you believe, act, and feel the way you do about God*. New York: Howard Books.
Davis, E., Moriarty, G., & Mauch, J. (2013). God images and God concepts: Definitions, development, and dynamics. *Psychology of Religion and Spirituality*, *5*(1), 51–60.
Douglas, J., & Tenney, M. (2011). *Zondervan illustrated Bible dictionary*. Grand Rapids, MI: Zondervan.
Fee, G. (1987). *The first epistle to the Corinthians*. Grand Rapids, MI: William B. Eerdmans Publishing Company.
Germer, C. (2009). *The mindful path to self-compassion: Freeing yourself from destructive thoughts and emotions*. New York: The Guilford Press.
Gilbert, P. (2010). *Compassion focused therapy: Distinctive features*. New York: Routledge.
Green, J. (1997). *The gospel of Luke*. Grand Rapids, MI: William B. Eerdmans Publishing Company.
Hall, J. (2016). *The art of divine meditation*. Titus Books.
Harris, R. (2009). *ACT made simple: An easy-to-read primer on acceptance and commitment therapy*. Oakland, CA: New Harbinger Publications, Inc.
Hayes, S., Strosahl, K., & Wilson, K. (2012). *Acceptance and commitment therapy: The process and practice of mindful change* (2nd ed.). New York: The Guilford Press.

Herbert, J., & Forman, E. (2011). The evolution of cognitive behavior therapy: The rise of psychological acceptance and mindfulness. In J. Herbert & E. Forman (Eds.), *Acceptance and mindfulness in cognitive behavior therapy: Understanding and applying the new therapies* (pp. 3–25). Hoboken, NJ: John Wiley & Sons, Inc.

Hoffman, L. (2005). A developmental perspective on the God image. In R. Cox, B. Ervin-Cox, & L. Hoffman (Eds.), *Spirituality and psychological health* (pp. 129–150). Colorado Springs, CO: Colorado School of Professional Psychology Press.

Killingsworth, M., & Gilbert, D. (2010). A wandering mind is an unhappy mind. *Science, 330*(6006), 932.

Knabb, J. (2016). *Acceptance and commitment therapy for Christian clients: A faith-based workbook.* New York: Routledge.

Knabb, J., & Emerson, M. (2013). 'I will be your God and you will be my people': Attachment theory and the grand narrative of scripture. *Pastoral Psychology, 62*(6), 827–841.

Kolts, R. (2016). *CFT made simple: A clinician's guide to practicing compassion-focused therapy.* Oakland, CA: New Harbinger Publications, Inc.

Leahy, R. (2003). *Cognitive therapy techniques: A practitioner's guide.* New York: The Guilford Press.

Main, J. (2001). *Christian meditation: The Gethsemani talks.* London: Medio Media Publishing.

Moriarty, G. (2012). *Pastoral care of depression: Helping clients heal their relationship with God.* New York: Routledge.

Morris, L. (1988). *Luke.* Grand Rapids, MI: Wm. B. Eerdmans Publishing Co.

Olson, T., Tisdale, T., Davis, E., Park, E., Nam, J., Moriarty, G., Davis, D., Thomas, M., Cuthbert, A., & Hays, L. (2016). God image narrative therapy: A mixed-methods investigation of a controlled group-based spiritual intervention. *Spirituality in Clinical Practice, 3*(2), 77–91.

Schaap-Jonker, H. (2008). *Before the face of God: An interdisciplinary study of the meaning of the sermon and the hearer's God image, personality and affective state.* Piscataway, NJ: Transaction Publishers.

Segal, Z., Williams, M., & Teasdale, J. (2012). *Mindfulness-based cognitive therapy for depression* (2nd ed.). New York: The Guilford Press.

Strong, J. (2001a). *The new Strong's expanded dictionary of the words in the Hebrew Bible.* Nashville, TN: Thomas Nelson.

Strong, J. (2001b). *The new Strong's expanded dictionary of the words in the Greek New Testament.* Nashville, TN: Thomas Nelson.

Tan, S., & Johnson, W. (2005). Spiritually-oriented cognitive-behavioral-therapy. In L. Sperry & E. Shafranske (Eds.), *Spiritually-oriented psychotherapy* (pp. 77–103). Washington, DC: American Psychological Association.

Thomas, M., Moriarty, G., Davis, E., & Anderson, E. (2011). The effects of a manualized group-psychotherapy intervention on client God images and attachment to God: A pilot study. *Journal of Psychology and Theology, 39*(1), 44–58.

van den Brink, E., & Koster, F. (2015). *Mindfulness-based compassionate living: A new training programme to deepen mindfulness with heartfulness.* New York: Routledge.

Watson, T. (2012). *A treatise concerning meditation* [Kindle version]. Charleston, SC: Waxkeep Publishing. Retrieved from Amazon.com

Worthington, E. (2003). *Forgiving and reconciling: Bridges to wholeness and hope.* Downers Grove, IL: InterVarsity Press.

CHAPTER 5

Feeling with Compassion

Introduction

In the fifth chapter, you will be learning to feel with compassion and mercy towards yourself and others. In doing so, the goal is to cultivate a deeper emotional experience of God's compassion in order to improve your God image (especially your "heart knowledge" about his providential care [Davis et al., 2013]) and ameliorate your shame. Along the way, you will be working towards accessing your God-given "contentment" system (Burroughs, 2010; Gilbert, 2010) and developing a secure attachment to God so as to find rest in his presence.

Modified compassion-based approaches and exercises from the psychology literature are included in this chapter, such as relating differently to your difficult inner experiences by "befriending" your feelings (Germer, 2009; van den Brink & Koster, 2015), developing positive emotions (Bannink, 2012; Germer, 2009; Van Dijk, 2012), and "developing your inner compassionate self" (Gilbert, 2010). Loving-kindness exercises, quite popular in the current clinical literature (Baer, 2014), will be modified for you, highlighting that God is the author of love, compassion, mercy, and kindness.

In addition, as a Christian, you will imagine receiving a letter from God (Kempis, 2015; Thomas et al., 2011), rather than from your "compassionate" to "vulnerable" self (Kolts, 2016), and sing worship music (Germer, 2009; Thomas et al., 2011) that focuses on God's love, mercy, and compassion.

From the Christian tradition, you will learn about medieval spirituality and *apophatic* meditation (as revealed in the instructions from *The Cloud of Unknowing*), including the use of your will (as opposed to your memory or intellect; Beasley-Topliffe, 2003) to reach out to God in love (rather than knowledge) during moments of shame and self-criticism. In this practice, the *Cloud* author advocated for self-forgetfulness, placing everything (including focusing on yourself) beneath a "cloud of forgetting" as you faithfully and lovingly reach out to God. This exercise will include an audio recording for you to use. Throughout the fifth chapter, you will complete written exercises (e.g., journaling), learn from examples in the Bible, and read about a case example so as to actively strive towards feeling with compassion.

Accepting Painful Feelings: Perspectives from Psychology and Christianity

Making peace with difficult feelings by "befriending" them can help us to be more compassionate towards our inner world (Germer, 2009). When we learn to relate to painful emotions by allowing them to simply be, as they are, we let go of the tendency to get into a "tug-of-war" match with them—holding on to the "good" feelings and pushing away the "bad" ones. A range of words can be utilized to capture a more nurturing, supportive attitude towards our inner experiences, such as empathy, kindness, and forgiveness (Germer, 2009).

Interestingly, the writer of Hebrews (4:14–16) explained that Jesus is the "Great High Priest," who understands our pain and wants us to approach him when we need his grace:

> Therefore, since we have a great high priest who has ascended into heaven, Jesus the Son of God, let us hold firmly to the faith we profess. For we do not have a high priest who is unable to empathize with our weaknesses, but we have one who has been tempted in every way, just as we are—yet he did not sin. Let us then approach God's throne of grace with confidence, so that we may receive mercy and find grace to help us in our time of need.

Here, we can see that Jesus understands what we are going through, given he was "tempted in every way" while living as a human being on this planet. In this passage, the Greek word, *synpatheo*, is used for "empathize," meaning to "suffer along with" (Guthrie, 1983, p. 122). In addition, the Greek word, *astheneia*, is utilized for "weaknesses," reflecting "any form of felt need" (Guthrie, 1983, p. 122).

Therefore, in addition to unilaterally making peace with our emotions, we have an ally in Jesus, who empathizes with our most difficult human experiences and suffers with us. In fact, he wants us to reach for him with confidence, where he sits on his throne and offers us mercy and grace when we need him the most (Guthrie, 1983). Stated differently, he offers his responsiveness in the midst of our suffering, accompanied by his loving, freely given favor towards us (even when we have fallen short of his perfect standards). This availability, responsiveness, and merit resembles the secure attachment style that is described in the psychology literature (Bartholomew & Horowitz, 1991).

When we are securely attached, we believe we are worthy of love, and those closest to us are available, willing to accept us, and capable of responding to our needs (Bartholomew & Horowitz, 1991). With secure attachments, moreover, we are more likely to express painful feelings, recognizing that others will be responsive in the midst of our pain. This leads to the ability to accept our most difficult emotional states, given we know we are not alone. In turn, we are able to access the "contentment" system for soothing comfort from a trusted other (Gilbert, 2010).

Returning to the fourth chapter of Hebrews, Jesus accepts us because of his loving grace, and encourages us to reach for him in our state of suffering. His responsiveness, to be sure, is naturally embedded within his loving relationship with us. Because of this, we can be confident that he understands our predicament. After all, he has experienced the human condition, too.

As Germer (2009) revealed, "The compassionate way is to befriend painful emotions—to stop fighting them" (p. 106). In the context of Hebrews, the following words seem to capture Jesus' consistent, unwavering qualities in his willingness to respond to our emotional pain:

- Empathic
- Receptive
- Merciful
- Gracious

As a result, when you are struggling with shame (or any related emotions), gently reminding yourself that Jesus is with you, calling you towards him and offering his empathy, receptivity, mercy, and grace, is especially important. By doing so, you will be learning to "befriend" your emotions in the process (Germer, 2009), rather than fighting with them, which distracts you from the life God has called you to live.

As another way to understand the importance of our emotions, the "two-sided coin" metaphor in the acceptance and commitment therapy (ACT) literature can help us to recognize the utility of our emotions (Greco, Barnett, Blomquist, & Gevers, 2008; Knabb & Meador, 2016), especially in the context of our most important relationship—with God. One side of the coin captures the human experience of shame, which is ubiquitous and paralyzing. To be sure, shame is a signal, pointing to our separation from God because of the fall (Bonhoeffer, 1955, 1959; Knabb & Meador, 2016).

Yet, the other side of the coin reflects our values, including what is most important to us in life. For Christians, we value deepening our relationship with God, reflected in our unwavering longing to restore this devastating rupture. Phrased differently, one side of the coin symbolizes our emotions, and the other side consists of our values. Both sides make up the coin; thus, we cannot have one without the other.

In consideration of the human predicament, shame tells us that something is not quite right—we are separated from God, which is a truly painful experience. Although shame is difficult to endure, it can actually serve a useful purpose if it points us to God and tells us to reach for him over and over again. In the context of "befriending" your emotions (Germer, 2009), rather than functioning as an enemy you need to battle, shame can help you boldly approach God's throne of grace so as to receive the proverbial glue that is necessary to bind the broken pottery. In other words, God's grace is readily available, with shame serving as the catalyst towards this two-step process: (a) we experience the pain of our separation from God; and (b) we reach for him, given our pain serves as a useful signal.

In support of this two-step process, the lament Psalms capture the utility of our emotions in helping us make sense of our relationship with God and return to him when we notice we have wandered away. In these biblical writings, the psalmists typically offered some sort of plea to God, then thanked God for listening to their experience (Brueggemann, 1984). See Psalm 22 for an example of the psalmist's interaction with God in the midst of pain. As you read through the 22nd Psalm, notice the writer's emotional turmoil (especially shame), including his willingness to share his inner experiences with God. In addition, observe his ability to thank God in the midst of pain, praising God in spite of his current suffering.

> My God, my God, why have you forsaken me? Why are you so far from saving me, so far from my cries of anguish? My God, I cry out by day, but you do not answer, by night, but I find no rest. Yet you are enthroned as the Holy One; you are the one Israel praises. In you our ancestors put their trust; they trusted and you delivered them. To you they cried out and were saved; in you they trusted and were not put to shame. But I am a worm and not a man, scorned by everyone, despised by the people. All who see me mock me; they hurl insults, shaking their heads. "He trusts in the Lord," they say, "let the Lord rescue him. Let him deliver him, since he delights in him." Yet you brought me out of the womb; you made me trust in you, even at my mother's breast. From birth I was cast on you; from my mother's womb you have been my God. Do not be far from me, for trouble is near and there is no one to help. Many bulls surround me; strong bulls of Bashan encircle me. Roaring lions that tear their prey open their mouths wide against me. I am poured out like water, and all my bones are out of joint. My heart has turned to wax; it has melted within me. My mouth is dried up like a potsherd, and my tongue sticks to the roof of my mouth; you lay me in the dust of death. Dogs surround me, a pack of villains encircles me; they pierce my hands and my feet. All my bones are on display; people stare and gloat over me. They divide my clothes among them and cast lots for my garment. But you, Lord, do not be far from me. You are my strength; come quickly to help me. Deliver me from the sword, my precious life from the power of the dogs. Rescue me from the mouth of the lions; save me from the horns of the wild oxen. I will declare your name to my people; in the assembly I will praise you. You who fear the Lord, praise him! All you descendants of Jacob, honor him! Revere him, all you descendants of Israel! For he has not despised or scorned the suffering of the afflicted one; he has not hidden his face from him but has listened to his cry for help. From you comes the theme of my praise in the great assembly; before those who fear you I will fulfill my vows. The poor will eat and be satisfied; those who seek the Lord will praise him—may your hearts live forever! All the ends of the earth will remember and turn to the Lord and all the families of the nations will bow down before him, for dominion belongs to the Lord and he rules over the nations. All the rich of the earth will feast and worship; all who go down to the dust will kneel before him—those who cannot keep themselves alive. Posterity will serve him; future generations will be told about the Lord. They will proclaim his righteousness, declaring to a people yet unborn: He has done it!

Now that you have considered the importance of seeing your emotions as both your "friend" (Germer, 2009) and helpful in your relationship with God, I would like you to explore several strategies for accepting your pain, from both psychological and Christian viewpoints. Within psychology, there are pragmatic reasons for accepting (rather than fighting against) your most difficult emotions, such as being able to live your life without being stuck on the sidelines, futilely waiting for your distressing emotions to go away.

For Christians, though, your emotions are God-given; thus, they can help you make sense of your relationship with God (Allender & Longman, 1994), especially in the context of your efforts to reach for him in your time of need. What is more, since God is sovereign, his providential care extends to your emotional world. If this is the case, he has a reason for your inner experiences, with his infinite goodness, power, and wisdom guiding your daily occurrences. This understanding of God's active role in your pain, though, is by no means easy to grasp, given that pain (including emotional distress) is commonly viewed as something we need to get rid of. Yet, we can also find tremendous comfort when we surrender to God's providential care, which will be explored in the next section.

Strategies for Accepting Emotional Pain: Psychological and Christian Perspectives

In clinical psychology, emotional pain is often accepted for pragmatic purposes. In other words, the alternative to accepting emotional pain—avoidance—does not tend to work in the long run and ends up getting in the way of living the life we want (Hayes, Strosahl, & Wilson, 2012). Thus, mindfulness meditation, for example, is utilized to non-judgmentally accept difficult inner experiences, moving from trying to get rid of them to making peace with them. As an empirically supported treatment for a range of disorders, acceptance and commitment therapy (ACT) advocates for making room for inner pain, living in the present moment (rather than the past or future), and living out a set of well-defined values (Harris, 2009).

With Christianity, however, pain is accepted, first and foremost, because we trust in God's providential care. From a biblical perspective, providence involves "God's benevolent and wise superintendence of His creation," and includes his "wisdom, power, justice, goodness, and mercy" (Blount, 2003, p. 1340). In fact, a range of Christian authors throughout the centuries have written on the importance of surrendering to God's providence as the antidote to our suffering. In that God is infinitely loving, powerful, and wise, we can trust that he has our best intentions in mind from moment to moment, even when life does not go our way, and that he is extending his compassion and mercy along the way. To be sure, we follow a Suffering Servant (Isaiah 53), which means suffering, hardship, and pain are inevitable in this life. What is more, God uses adversity to help us grow, improve, and depend on him in this life (Isaiah 48:10; Hebrews 12:5; James 1:2–4; Romans 5:3–4, 8:28; 1 Peter 5:1–11). In the midst of our suffering, trusting in God's providence is key in order to boldly face our struggles (which include shame) by faithfully surrendering to his will.

Worth mentioning, in the last two decades, the God image literature has explored God's providence as a psychological construct (Lawrence, 1997). In other words, beyond a cognitive understanding of God's providence, we have a deeper, more experiential image of whether or not God guides us, intervenes for us, and provides for us (Lawrence, 1997). As a result, to surrender to God's loving care means we are trusting his infinite wisdom, power, and goodness on a more intimate level, reconciling our "head knowledge" from Scripture with our "heart knowledge" based on experience (Davis et al., 2013).

Nevertheless, within Ignatian spirituality, several Jesuit authors from the 1600s advocated for yielding to God's providential care in response to a wide variety of adversities, including minor annoyances in daily living (e.g., stubbing a toe), natural disasters (e.g., an earthquake), family discord (e.g., an argument with a spouse), loss of income (e.g., getting laid off from a job), and unpleasant inner experiences (e.g., anxiety) (Saint-Jure & Colombiere, 1980). Similar to trusting a surgeon to remove a tumor, we can put our faith in God when we are suffering, knowing that "in all things God works for the good of those who love him" (Romans 8:28). Although, at first glance, we may attribute the cause of our psychological pain to ourselves or someone else, God's providence is centrally involved, with God sanctifying us along the way (Saint-Jure & Colombiere, 1980). Trusting in his providence in the midst of psychological pain, therefore, can help us to make peace with ongoing emotional struggles such as shame.

In addition, within Protestant spirituality, the Puritans wrote extensively on the role of God's providence in daily living (Beeke & Jones, 2012). In particular, they argued that God is active, present, and sovereign over every aspect of his creation, including the environment and our physical, psychological, and social functioning (Beeke & Jones, 2012). In his sovereign control, God exercises loving care by sustaining us from moment to moment (Beeke & Jones, 2012). John Flavel, a popular 17th-century Puritan writer, argued that God's "afflictive providences," which can include physical and psychological pain, can actually benefit us (Flavel, 2017). In support of this notion, he used examples such as a headache that distracts someone from being overwhelmed with lust, as well as the Apostle Paul's famous example of the "thorn in [his] flesh" (2 Corinthians 12:7; Flavel, 2017). In Flavel's writings, he advocated for a "both/and" approach to effectively respond to suffering, arguing that both "quiet submission and patience under the afflicting hand of God" and taking action in the face of "beneficial afflictions" are necessary (Cosby, 2012, Chapter 5). In other words, seeing our suffering as a vehicle through which God helps us grow is especially salient.

In the context of shame, we can begin to make peace with the experience, especially if it is a catalyst towards a deeper relationship with God, resembling a child scraping his or her knee and running into the outstretched arms of a loving parent. Ultimately, within Protestant spirituality, responding to psychological pain may involve a passive (e.g., making peace with pain and suffering by accepting it as we patiently wait on God) or active (e.g., praying to God and reading the Bible as strategies to actively face pain and suffering) strategy (Cosby, 2012). Whether we take action or patiently endure, Flavel (2017) offered the following: "Under all providences maintain a contented heart with what the Lord allots you, be it more or less of the things of this world. This grace must run parallel with all providences" (p. 151). Consistent with this recommendation, we can learn to make peace with painful emotions, allowing shame to serve as a signal for accessing the "contentment" system in our time of need (Gilbert, 2010).

As another example within Protestant spirituality, the 20th-century Evangelical mystical writer Frank Laubach wrote a series of letters that were first published in the 1930s. Since then, they have been reproduced over and over again in the form of *Letters by a Modern Mystic*. In one such letter, dated January 30, 1930, he wrote the following (Laubach, 2007):

> For the past few days I have been experimenting in a more complete surrender than ever before. I am taking, by deliberate act of will, enough time from each hour to give God much thought. Yesterday and today I have made a new adventure, which is not easy to express. I am feeling God in each movement, by an act of will—willing that He shall direct these fingers that now strike this typewriter—willing that He shall pour through my steps as I walk—willing that He shall direct my words as I speak, and my very jaws as I eat!

In this particular letter, he went on to discuss two important goals in his efforts to surrender his entire being to God, including to (a) "be like Jesus" and (b) "respond to God as a violin responds to the bow of the master" (Laubach, 2007).

When considering shame, striving to emulate Jesus and allow him to direct us in all our experiences is paramount. Worded differently, being malleable in his hands is especially important in the context of our inner world. By surrendering our emotional experiences to him with a trusting openness, we are allowing God to guide us and do what is best for us from moment to moment. Drawing inspiration from Laubach's (2007) letter, the most important questions are as follows: "How can I feel God in this moment as I experience this particular emotion?" "What is God revealing to me through this emotion?" If we return to Bonhoeffer (1955, 1959), God may be using our experience of shame as a gage, letting us know we are incomplete without him and need to return to him as the center of our existence for nurturance, sustenance, and contentment.

In a similar vein, within medieval spirituality, Thomas Kempis advocated for trusting in God's care by learning to rest in his comfort, no matter what the situation. In particular, in *The Imitation of Christ*, Kempis (2009) said the following:

> Give me, Lord Jesus, special grace to rest in You above all creatures, above all health and beauty, above all glory and honor, above all dignity and power, above all wisdom and prudence, above all riches and skills, above all gladness of body and soul, above all fame and praise, above all sweetness and consolation, above all hope and promise, above all merit and desire, above all gifts and rewards that You may give or send, except Yourself, and above all joy and mirth that man's heart or man can conceive or feel, and above all angels or archangels and all the company of heavenly spirits as well, above all things visible and invisible, above all things that are not Yourself. You, Lord God, are most good, most high, most mighty, most sufficient and most full of goodness, most sweet, most consoling, most fair, most loving, most noble, and most glorious above all things. In You all goodness is together, perfectly and fully—has been and will be. Therefore, whatever You give me, beside Yourself, is little and insufficient to me, for my heart cannot rest, or be fully brought to peace, so that it may ascend above all gifts and above all manner of created things, save in You.
>
> (p. 101)

In this powerful writing, Kempis advocated for finding contentment in God, above and beyond everything else in this world. When we learn to access our God-given "contentment" system (Gilbert, 2010), we are cultivating a secure attachment to God, in that we are trusting that God's infinite goodness, power, and wisdom extend to our emotional world. In other words, we are putting our faith in our relationship with him, confidently waiting for his responsiveness in our moment of need. Over time, we are developing a deeply held view of God's providential care in the form of a healthy God image (Lawrence, 1997).

These writings are highly relevant to our current conversation about feeling with compassion, given God's role in your daily emotional functioning. If, as the aforementioned Christians have revealed, God's sovereignty extends to your thoughts, feelings, and behaviors from minute to minute, he is certainly present as you struggle with shame.

In light of the aforementioned review, the following points are important to consider in preparation for learning a range of strategies for effectively surrendering to God's providential care so as to make peace with your most painful emotions:

- God is active in this very moment, exercising perfect control over both larger and smaller aspects of daily living.
- Because of God's infinite wisdom, power, and goodness, you can trust that life's most painful occurrences have a divine purpose.
- Even your inner world is known and guided by God.
- God has a plan and purpose for your psychological pain.

In terms of research support, I recently conducted a study on strategies for surrendering to God's providence (Knabb, Frederick, & Cumming, 2017). In the first part of the study, I found empirical support for the link between deeply held views of God's providence (a type of God image) and being able to surrender to God during instances of adversity among both college students and a community church sample. Within the second part of the study, I tested an eight-week Christian meditation program, using both *apophatic* and *kataphatic* meditation, for surrendering to God's providence as a strategy for chronic worry. After eight weeks, there was a significant improvement in God image, as well as the ability to surrender to God. Although the second part was only a pilot study with 13 participants, it offers preliminary support for the use of Christian meditation for simultaneously improving God image (i.e., deeply held views of his providential care) and reducing psychiatric symptoms.

As noted in the third chapter, in a separate study, I found that "humble detachment" helps to explain the link between the Christian ability to surrender to God's providence and repetitive negative thinking (Knabb, Vazquez, Wang, & Bates, 2018). Again, "humble detachment" involves the following ingredients (Knabb et al., 2018):

- Relinquishing the tendency to hold on to or push away painful inner experiences.
- Letting go of a preoccupation with the self.
- Shifting from being focused on inner experiences and the self to an awareness of God's presence.

Christian detachment may help you in your struggles with painful emotions (such as shame), given that you are working on surrendering your inner world to God (including a preoccupation with the self) in order to focus on him. In doing so, you are learning to gently shift your attention, acknowledging your inner pain before deciding to intentionally gaze upon God. To cultivate Christian detachment, especially in the context of shame, Christian meditation can be a useful strategy. Although *apophatic* meditation will be presented in a subsequent section of this chapter, for now, I would like you to practice a three-step strategy from Ignatian spirituality for surrendering to God's providential care (adapted from Saint-Jure & Colombiere, 1980; Knabb & Frederick, 2017).

Accepting Pain: An Exercise

In this exercise, you will be working on viewing your pain differently, recognizing that God's providential care extends to your inner world from moment to moment. Rather than fighting against your most difficult emotions, practicing yielding to God's providence can help you exercise compassion during instances of inner distress.

See if you can cultivate an attitude of surrender towards your feelings by recognizing that God is loving you in the here-and-now. In other words, as you slowly move through this exercise, attempt to access the "contentment" system (Gilbert, 2010) by placing your trust, hope, and love in God. Strive to run into his outstretched arms, consistent with a child naturally reaching for a safe, trustworthy parent. This process of repeatedly surrendering your inner world to God can help you develop a more compassionate reply to your most painful emotions, given you are trusting that God is active and present in these experiences. Please follow the following three steps, drawn from *Trustful Surrender to Divine Providence* (adapted from Saint-Jure & Colombiere, 1980):

- Spend a few minutes meditating on (i.e., thinking deeply about) the role that God's providence plays in life in general, as well as the smaller, particular occurrences from day to day and minute to minute. In other words, every event, whether on a global or microscopic level, is controlled by God. As he orchestrates the world's events with his very hands, God does so with a perfect combination of love, wisdom, and power, which means you can trust in his caring guidance within the realm of your own psychological experiences.
- Next, take a few moments to place your hope in God's providence, feeling God's loving protection in both the present moment and future. As life unfolds, God has your best intentions in

mind, which means you can have hope that your life will work out according to his perfect will. Even your current suffering is part of his divine plan. Feel his care as you place your hope in him.

- To conclude, reach out to God in love, reminiscent of a child running into the arms of a trustworthy parent. Conjure up a deep feeling of gratitude for God, thanking him for guiding your life based on his perfect plan. Because he is infinitely loving, you can rest assured that he is intimately involved in your psychological experiences, similar to a caring parent who is right behind his or her child, helping the toddler learn to walk.

After you have slowly walked through these three steps, spend a few minutes reflecting on this exercise in the space below. What was it like to attempt to place your hope in God's providential care, even in the midst of your current emotional pain? What, if anything, seemed to get in the way of running into God's proverbial arms to be comforted via the "contentment" system (Gilbert, 2010)? How can you continue to practice resting in God's outstretched arms in the midst of your pain, receiving his soothing comfort, rather than striving to make the pain go away?

Now that this exercise has concluded, I would like you to practice talking directly to God about your emotional pain, attempting to deepen your relationship with him by verbalizing your inner distress in a five-step process. As you do this, my hope is that you will be relating to your emotional pain with more compassion and accessing your "contentment" system along the way (Gilbert, 2010), given God is with you in the process and offering you a deeper attachment bond because of the work of Jesus on the cross.

Writing a Lament to God: An Exercise[1]

In this brief exercise, you will work on accepting your pain by offering it to God. In particular, you will write a lament to God, utilizing the lament Psalms (e.g., Psalm 22) as a guide. As the lament Psalms reveal, the writers often wrestled with their emotional pain, crying out to God in the midst of their psychological turmoil. In two major steps (with five smaller steps), the psalmists typically offered a plea to God, then praised him for hearing their cry (adapted from Brueggemann, 1984).

In the space that follows, first describe the situation you are in, explaining the details in the form of a complaint to God. In this first step, converse with God like you know him in a personal, intimate way. Then, ask for God's help in responding to your predicament, followed by expressing your emotional pain to him. After doing so, share your gratitude with God, and let him know you believe he has heard your pain (adapted from Brueggemann, 1984; Knabb, 2016a).

Share Your Complaint with God

Ask for God's Help

Express Your Emotional Pain to God

Share Your Gratitude with God

Thank God for Hearing Your Lament

In this exercise, the goal is to recognize that your emotions (including shame) are important in your relationship with God and can help you to deepen your interactions with him. To repeatedly present your suffering to God, then praise him for hearing your situation, can allow you to deepen your trust in him. Along the way, you are working towards cultivating a healthy God attachment, with his providential care extending to your personal situation. In addition, you are developing a more intimate attachment bond with him, given you are learning to see (on an emotional level) that God values you, hears your pain, and responds to your needs.

Although the previous exercises were intended to assist you in being soothed and comforted by God via surrendering your inner world to him, the next section will focus on developing positive emotions. In doing so, you will be working towards experiencing a different feeling in the midst of your shame.

Developing Positive Emotions: Perspectives from Psychology and Christianity

Sometimes, it is necessary for us to make peace with our most difficult feelings, including shame. In fact, painful emotions serve as a signal, letting us know what the problem is so as to take steps to remedy the situation (Germer, 2009). As a central theme in this workbook, for example, shame helps us know that we are incomplete without God (Bonhoeffer, 1955, 1959) and need to reach for him in the midst of our isolation.

At other times, though, we can actively work towards developing positive emotions, such as hope, joy, love, gratitude, and contentment (Gilbert, 2010; Germer, 2009). For example, one way to develop the positive emotion of gratitude in the psychology literature involves actually thinking with gratitude, as revealed in the following exercise:

> Make an effort to think about . . . particular supportive relationships, sacrifices or contributions that others have made for you, facts about your life such as your advantages and opportunities, or even gratitude for life itself, and the world that we live in.
>
> (Sheldon & Lyubomirsky, 2006, p. 76)

Gratitude can involve directing grace and gratefulness towards God, other people, nature, and so on, capturing our ability to see value in life occurrences (Emmons & McCullough, 2003).

When it comes to expressing gratitude, research has revealed that doing so can have a positive impact on well-being (Emmons & McCullough, 2003), and increasing our frequency of prayer (on a daily basis) can improve our sense of gratitude (Lambert, Fincham, Braithwaite, Graham, & Beach, 2009). These studies elucidate that improving gratitude can have a positive impact on our psychological functioning.

Turning from the psychology literature to the Christian tradition, in one of the most popular passages in the New Testament, the Apostle Paul revealed that the "fruit of the Spirit is love, joy, peace, [patience], kindness, goodness, faithfulness, gentleness and self-control" (Galatians 5:22–23). Certainly, these spiritual qualities and virtues have a corresponding emotional experience, with God as the source (Cole, 1989). Among this list, joy involves grace, hope, and celebration in the midst of suffering, regardless of the environmental surround (George, 1994). What is more, peace captures the well-being that naturally emanates from a deeper, more intimate union with God (George, 1994). Moving to the next virtue on Paul's list, patience comes from God, who has repeatedly exercised "long-temperedness" with humankind; as a result, we need to be patient with others (George, 1994). As one more example, kindness typically involves a "beneficent disposition toward others" (Witherington, 1998, p. 401).

Just prior to his list of Christian virtues, which are to be lived out in the context of being other-focused in community, Paul offered a list of vices that are considered "acts of the flesh" (Galatians 5:19–21). The contrast between the two is as follows (adapted from Witherington, 1998):

- Hatred or joy and love.
- Discord or peace.
- Anger and jealousy or patience.
- Rage or kindness.

Notice the stark difference between hatred and anger and love and kindness. Within the context of shame, we may end up criticizing ourselves or blaming others in response to this painful emotion (Gilbert & Irons, 2009). Yet, for Christians, God (i.e., the Spirit) is the source of the "fruit," and we are to extend these salient virtues to others. Before doing so, though, we need to experience God's love, joy, peace, patience, and kindness in our own lives, with this "fruit" organically emanating from God's presence.

Within Protestant spirituality, the Puritan author Francis Rous argued that putting on the "oil of gladness" (Psalm 45:7; Hebrews 1:9), which flows from God, is central to Christian happiness (Rous, 2016). Rous defined the "oil of gladness" as follows:

> The very substance of the Spirit in us, is a kind of *heavenly oil*, which makes *glad*, not so much the face as the very heart of man. It has in it a taste and relish of the Deity, and therefore above all other, this is the true *oil of gladness*. The heart anointed with this, as it finds a light to guide it, and a virtue moving it to good, and freeing it from the slavery of sin, so also it feels in itself a blessed rest, an heavenly Sabbath, a joy glorious and unspeakable, an harmony and peace with God, which passes all understanding.
>
> (p. 113, italics added)

In *The Art of Happiness*, Rous made the argument that "true happiness" comes from the source of perfect happiness—God. If this is the case, the world, on its own, cannot make us happy, and our typical pursuits of happiness—our reputation, our possessions and wealth, our knowledge and intelligence—are futile endeavors (Rous, 2016). Rather, we must be intentional in our hunt for godly happiness, which includes "watchfulness" (Rous, 2016).

Of watchfulness, Rous (2016) explained the following:

> [Watchfulness] ought to stand as on the top of a tower, to spy a far off as well as near at hand. Even to shout out against the remote occasions of such motions, and to sound the bell to the soul, that she shut out the messengers of the enemies of her peace, and lovingly admit the friends of her happiness.
>
> (pp. 167–168)

Stated differently, we need to be aware of our inner world, and regularly question the source of our thoughts and feelings. In the context of shame and self-judgments, we must ask whether or not the source is God.

For Rous, watchfulness involves a few key ingredients (adapted from Rous, 2016):

- When we notice a thought or feeling, we need to understand its source. Is this thought or feeling from God?
- If the thought or feeling is from God, we need to welcome it, reminiscent of inviting a good friend into our home.
- In this special time with God, we need to ask what God is revealing to us and surrender our entire being to him.

- If the thought or feeling is not from God, we need to ensure it does not distract us from him.
- Finally, we need to be aware of our watchfulness, meaning we must ensure we are staying attentive towards our thoughts and feelings throughout the day.

"Watchfulness" and the "Oil of Gladness": An Exercise

In this exercise (adapted from Allender & Longman, 1994; Rous, 2016), imagine you are in a watchtower, and can see the entire city that you have been entrusted to guard. Your job is to control the main gate, welcoming in your friends and keeping out your enemies. Throughout the day, you must be vigilant, given that a wide variety of people come and go on a regular basis.

Now, begin to extend this role to your inner world. Your job is to watch your feelings (including shame) for the next ten minutes. Whenever a feeling comes up, your task is to welcome it in, reminiscent of a friend who has traveled to the gate in order to gain entry. More specifically, when an emotion arises, try to imagine that God is knocking on the gate (rather than an enemy), revealing himself to you in the same way that a friend would as he or she enthusiastically asks for entry in order to spend time with you.

As a next step, invite God in, allowing him to be with you as you accept this feeling as a gift, like you would a close friend. Your job, in this moment, is to welcome the emotion, recognizing that God is active and moving within this inner experience. Because God is sovereign, he is in control of your pain. In addition, because he is infinitely wise and loving, he has your best intentions in mind.

Try to view this painful feeling as a catalyst towards receiving God's love, mercy, grace, and forgiveness. As you experience the feeling, God is bringing with him the anointment necessary to sooth and comfort you in your time of need. Over and over again, your emotional pain reveals your need for him; in turn, you are accessing the "contentment" system in order to rest in his loving arms (Gilbert, 2010).

Finally, as you welcome in this feeling (with God by your side), simply bask in this moment with him. As you do this, apply the "oil of gladness" to your emotional experience, imagining that God has brought with him a comforting ointment for your psychological wounds. In this time, just appreciate the peace that comes from God's "oil of gladness" and let go of your own understanding. Imagine that God has brought with him the "oil of gladness" to share with you as you yield to his active, loving presence. Because God's providence extends to your emotional pain, you can trust—in this very moment—that he is guiding you and offering you his perfect safety.

Now that you have concluded the exercise, spend a few minutes journaling about your experience. What was it like to welcome this emotion as you spent time with God? Were you able to try on the "oil of gladness" as you experienced God's presence in your emotional pain? What, if anything, got in the way of doing so?

____

____

____

____

____

____

Before transitioning to the role that loving-kindness meditations can play in your efforts to ameliorate shame, I would like to briefly return to Frank Laubach's letters in order to present a simple strategy for maintaining an awareness of God's active, loving presence throughout your day.

In doing so, you will be striving to feel God's love from moment to moment, especially when you experience shame and self-criticism.

The "Game of Minutes": An Exercise

Returning to Frank Laubach's (2007) writings, in his lifetime, he developed a simple "game of minutes," which can help us to connect to God in the present moment. The game is ideal for people struggling with all sorts of ailments, given the emphasis is on remembering God from moment to moment (Laubach, 2007). In the process, we are learning to feel with compassion because God is right by our side. In other words, the world comes to life when we know that we are experiencing each passing moment with him. Undoubtedly, we can more confidently feel our way into our experiences, recognizing that the author of life is walking along by our side.

In preparation for this "game of minutes," Laubach (2007) noted that there are several "prices to pay" (i.e., sacrifices to consider), including applying a gentle pressure on the will to repeatedly return to God, persevering in spite of frustrations that come from falling short of the goal, and surrendering our entire being to God. On the other hand, we benefit in a variety of ways, such as cultivating a deeper friendship with Jesus, developing focused attention on God, resting in a more fulfilling contentment in that God is with us, and ameliorating a range of emotional struggles because we are learning to love like God loves (Laubach, 2007).

The "game of minutes," Laubach (2007) explained, simply requires us to remember God at least one time each minute of the day. The medium through which we remember God can involve praying, singing a song to God, talking directly to God, surrendering our pain to God, feeling God's presence, reading a passage in Scripture, showing compassion towards others by helping them, and spending time with God in nature (Laubach, 2007).

To start, try to spend an hour remembering God every ten minutes. You can use the examples noted above, or come up with your own. Record your answers, including the emotional impact of remembering God every ten-minute block of time. Once you have done so, build on this experience by extending this "game" to two hours in length. The following table allows you to record your efforts from minute to minute.

Time	*Strategy for Remembering God*	*Impact on Your Emotions*
10-minute mark		
20-minute mark		
30-minute mark		
40-minute mark		
50-minute mark		
60-minute mark		

Ultimately, the goal of this exercise is to deepen your friendship with God, cultivating a secure attachment with him along the way. In addition, in your efforts to remain aware of his presence, you are improving your God image, especially a deeper, affect-laden view of his loving presence. Finally, you are working towards accessing the "contentment" system (Gilbert, 2010), given you are maintaining an awareness of his availability from minute to minute.

Now that you have practiced surrendering your pain to God and developing positive emotions, we will be shifting the focus towards loving-kindness meditations, connecting to your "true self," receiving a letter from God, singing worship music to God, practicing *apophatic* meditation, and weeping with Jesus as a way to develop compassion for others. In doing so, you will be practicing a plethora of strategies for feeling with compassion.

Compassion and "Loving-Kindness": A Brief Review

"Loving-kindness" meditation (the Pali term, *metta*) comes from the Buddhist tradition, and is utilized to cultivate universal kindness (Hofmann, Grossman, & Hinton, 2011). In contemporary clinical psychology, this practice has been employed to develop compassion for ourselves and others, as well as connectedness to humanity (Hofmann et al., 2011; Siegel, 2010). Within this form of meditation, we slowly and silently repeat certain phrases, such as "may I be happy, may I be peaceful, may I be free from suffering," "may I be safe," and "may I be kind to myself," although there is built-in flexibility to change the wording if we are struggling with a certain issue and need to let go of ruminations and worries (Germer & Neff, 2013, p. 862; Siegel, 2010, p. 84). In this formal time, we may move from focusing on ourselves and loved ones to individuals we are not getting along with or the universe as a whole in order to develop compassion and other positive feelings (Hofmann et al., 2011). A recent review of two dozen studies on loving-kindness found it to be effective in increasing positive emotions (Zeng, Chiu, Wang, Oei, & Leung, 2015). Ultimately, within the Buddhist tradition, loving-kindness is meant to increase friendliness, compassion, joy, calmness, and wisdom (Zeng et al., 2015).

For Christians, though, compassion is generated by God, who has revealed himself throughout the pages of the Bible. As a result, developing the "compassionate self" (Gilbert, 2010) in the Christian life involves turning to God as the source of love, compassion, mercy, grace, and forgiveness. Certainly, the source of the "fruit of the Spirit" is God, with the fruit (love is the ultimate virtue among the nine listed) emerging when we surrender to God and allow him to work in our life (Fung, 1988).

What follows is a brief review of Christianity's version of the "compassionate self," the "true self" found in Christ. Jesus was able to model this "true self' (and reject the "false self") with his temptations in the desert (Matthew 4:1–11; Pennington, 2000), which can provide guidance for 21st-century Christians in order to pivot from shame to freedom in Christ. What is more, the Christian "true self" is a vehicle through which God can reveal the "fruit of the Spirit," with love as the driving force and compassion organically emanating from love (Grenz, 1994).

The "True Self" and "Compassionate Self": Jesus in the Desert[2]

Almost two decades ago, the late Trappist monk Basil Pennington (2000) argued that Christians often create a "false self," which comes from overly focusing on our accomplishments, reputation, and material possessions. Pennington pointed to Jesus' interactions with the Devil in the wilderness (see Matthew 4:1–11) to highlight how this "false self" can develop in the Christian life. In the desert, Jesus was hungry and thirsty for over a month, with the Devil telling Jesus to turn stones into bread, pointing to what Jesus could accomplish. Yet, Jesus replied that he would steadfastly rely on God, not "live on bread alone."

Turning to Jesus' second temptation, the Devil told Jesus to throw himself off a high ledge, possibly so onlookers would be able to see angels save him, and, in turn, know that Jesus is God. However, Jesus responded that he would not put "God to the test," illuminating that the "true self" is not wrapped up in our reputation and what other people think of us.

As the third temptation, the Devil offered Jesus the entire world if Jesus would simply worship the Devil. Jesus, though, stated that he would only follow God, revealing that his identity was based on what his Father thought of him, not his possessions.

Consistently, Jesus rejected the "false self," locating his "true self" in God and God alone. Although by no means an easy task, as followers of Jesus, we are to let go of this "false self" that relies on our short-lived accomplishments, temporary reputation, and impermanent possessions. Instead of turning away from God and creating a "false self," we are to surrender to him, allowing God to work through us as a conduit for the "fruit of the Spirit" (Galatians 5:22–23).

In describing the distinction between the "true self" and "false self," the late Trappist monk Thomas Merton (1961) said the following:

> The only true joy on earth is to escape from the prison of our own false self, and enter by love into union with the Life Who dwells and sings within the essence of every creature and in the core of our own souls. In His love we possess all things and enjoy fruition of them, finding Him in them all. And thus as we go about the world, everything we meet and everything we see and hear and touch, far from defiling, purifies us and plants in us something more of contemplation and of heaven.
>
> (p. 25)

As we learn to surrender the "false self" to God, we are simultaneously allowing him to work within us so as to serve as a vehicle for the "fruit of the Spirit" (Arico, 2015). In fact, this list of "fruit" fittingly captures loving God, others, and ourselves: love, joy, and peace are about loving God; patience, kindness, and goodness are about loving others; and faithfulness, gentleness, and self-control are about loving ourselves (Arico, 2015). For the "fruit" to naturally emerge, we must relinquish the grip we have on our "false self," meaning we need to surrender this pseudo-self to God by letting go. In doing so, we are learning to love like God loves, cultivating compassion in the process. After all, God's compassion naturally flows from his love, revealed via the Father's generous offering of the Son (John 3:16).

Within the compassion literature in clinical psychology, the "compassionate self" is the ideal version of you—kind, wise, and caring (Kolts, 2016). With loving-kindness meditations, we are attempting to further develop a more compassionate, ideal version of ourselves by increasing friendliness, compassion, joy, calmness, and wisdom (Zeng et al., 2015). Over time, we are able to access this compassionate inner self more frequently, leading to the application of compassion towards ourselves and others.

Within the Christian tradition, the "true self" is similar to the "compassionate self" in that we are more compassionate and kind, reminiscent of Jesus. Beyond these qualities, the "true self" serves as a medium through which God can display the "fruit of the Spirit," including love, joy, peace, patience, kindness, goodness, faithfulness, gentleness, and self-control (Galatians 5:22–23). Leading the way, love is at the core of the "true self," with God as the source of love (1 John 4:8). When we let go of the "false self," we are able to yield to Jesus' loving action, as the Apostle Paul famously declared: "I have been crucified with Christ and I no longer live, but Christ lives in me" (Galatians 2:20; Merton, 1961). In this process, a "new self" emerges that is united with God, resting in his love, joy, and peace (Pennington, 1988).

In the next few exercises, you will have the opportunity to let go of your "false self," shifting towards an awareness of God's active, loving presence as your "true self." Along the way, love is the vehicle through which this deeper awareness can emerge. Over time, connecting to your "true self" can help you in your struggles with shame and self-criticism, given you are letting go of unilateral efforts to define who you are. Instead, you are learning to look towards Jesus as the author of your identity, allowing him to reveal himself through you by way of the "fruit of the Spirit."

Shifting from the "False" to the "True" Self: An Exercise[3]

To begin, close your eyes, and get into a comfortable position in a supportive chair. After sitting in silence for a minute, begin to recognize a recent situation that involved turning to the "false self" to define who you are, especially in the form of your accomplishments, reputation, or material possessions. In silence, spend ten minutes noticing the thoughts and images that make up your "false self."

Next, try to imagine letting go of these ingredients of the "false self," including your accomplishments, reputation, and material possessions. In other words, relinquish the grip you have on them in defining who you are. What is more, surrender your tendency to criticize yourself when you come up short in your pursuit of one or more of these three areas, giving your negative self-evaluations to God. Reminiscent of Jesus stating he would rely on God's Word to get him through his temptations in the wilderness, try to shift your focus to God, who defines you and offers you his love, compassion, mercy, grace, and forgiveness in the midst of your trials. With this pivot, see if you can deeply feel God's love for you, recognizing that he is active and present within your inner world. In other words, beneath your "false self," which you have constructed apart from him, God is patiently waiting for you, defining you based on his love for you and Jesus' redemptive, reconciling work on the cross.

When you are done, spend a few minutes reflecting on your thoughts, memories, and feelings in the space below, documenting aspects of the "false self" that you may be relying on in your daily functioning. In addition, consistent with Jesus' reliance on God's Word (i.e., Deuteronomy) when tempted in the wilderness (Matthew 4:1–11), select several passages in the Bible to draw from when the "false self" emerges. Upon selecting key verses in the Bible, try to utilize those that emphasize God's love, compassion, mercy, grace, and forgiveness so as to connect to a deeper experience of God's love for you.

Loving-Kindness with God: An Exercise

In loving-kindness meditations, you are learning to repeat short phrases in an attempt to cultivate compassion for yourself and others. As a Christian, though, God is the begetter of compassion;

thus, in this exercise (adapted from Germer, 2009), you will be repeating short phrases that capture God's compassion for you and others.

Try to spend ten minutes repeating the following three phrases, surrendering to God's providential care in the process. Sit up straight in a supportive chair, closing your eyes and resting in God in silence and solitude. In this time, you are learning to access the "contentment" system (Burroughs, 2010; Gilbert, 2010), because God is all you need.

- God, may your perfect love flow through me.
- God, may your perfect joy flow through me.
- God, may your perfect peace flow through me.

Over and over again, gently repeat the three phrases, functioning as a conduit for the "fruit of the Spirit" (especially love, joy, and peace, which come directly from God) to manifest in your life. As you repeat these powerful phrases, try to imagine that God is sitting with you, loving you in this very moment and offering you love, joy, and peace as the seconds pass by. When your mind drifts to something else (e.g., a thought, an image), non-judgmentally return to the statements with a gentle attentiveness.

Once you have completed the ten-minute exercise, try to reflect on your emotional experience by writing about your time spent with God. Were you able to feel God's love, joy, and peace on a deeper level, which he offers to you in each passing moment? If not, what might have gotten in the way? How can you extend God's perfect love, joy, and peace to others, compassionately responding to their suffering in the process?

____
____
____
____
____
____

In addition to loving-kindness meditations, there are a variety of other ways to cultivate compassion for yourself, accessing the "contentment" system and developing a deeper attachment bond with God in your efforts. Next, you will be envisioning you have received a letter directly from God and singing worship music, before transitioning to *apophatic* meditation as a way to reach for God in love, rather than knowledge.

Receiving a Letter from God: An Exercise

In this next exercise (adapted from Kempis, 2015; Thomas et al., 2011), you will imagine that you are receiving a letter directly from God. Upon receiving the envelope, you quickly open it to view its contents. Inside the envelope, you see a hand-written letter from Jesus, addressed directly to you. Spend several minutes slowly reading through the letter, absorbing the words by deeply feeling Jesus' loving grace. The letter, drawn directly from Kempis' (2015) medieval spiritual classic, *The Imitation of Christ*, reads as follows:

> My friend, I am good and "a strong refuge when trouble comes" (Nahum 1:7). Come to me whenever it is not well with you. When you are too slow to call to me in prayer, this causes a lack in heavenly comfort. Before you earnestly seek me, you first seek after many other means of comfort. You refresh

yourself with outward things. So you find that all these earthly things have not helped you at all. You must learn that I am the only one you can trust to deliver you. There is no strong help, no helpful counsel, or no lasting remedy but me. But now, as you recover courage following your storm, grow strong in the light of my mercies. For, I the Lord, say that I restore all things, not only as they were at the beginning, but more abundantly and stacked higher than they once were. "I am the Lord, the God of all the peoples of the world. Is anything too hard for me?" (Jeremiah 32:27). Where is your faith? Stand firm with perseverance. Be patient and strong. Comfort will come to you at the right time. Wait for me. Yes, wait. I will come and heal you. When temptation troubles you and unfounded fears terrify you, remember this: "Don't worry about tomorrow, for tomorrow will bring its own worries. Today's trouble is enough for today" (Matthew 6:34). It is futile and useless to be disturbed or wrought up about future things which may never come.

(Chapter 55, Section 1, para. 1)

After reading this passage, spend a minute reflecting on Jesus' promises. In your struggles, Jesus is active and present, offering you comfort and mercy in your time of need. Instead of turning to the "danger" or "drive" system, rest in Jesus' presence by accessing the "contentment" system (Gilbert, 2010). Try to surrender your emotional pain to Jesus, trusting in his providential care. Feel his compassion and comfort, extended to you in this very moment. Rest in the security of his sovereign, benevolent care.

In response to Jesus' letter, singing to him can help you feel with compassion. In the next exercise, imagine responding to Jesus' promises by praising him through the medium of a song. As you do so, strive to feel his active, loving presence.

Worshiping God by Singing to Him: An Exercise[4]

In the 19th century, in response to the tragic death of his four daughters, Horatio Spafford wrote, "It is Well with My Soul." In this famous Christian hymn, Spafford captured the ups and downs of life, including the peace, security, and contentment that is found in Jesus. Although suffering is inevitable, we can tap into the God-given "contentment" system (Gilbert, 2010) so as to reach for God as our perfect, unfailing attachment figure. In fact, God's providential care—consistent with being held in the arms of a loving father—is active and present in this very moment, in spite of your struggles with self-criticism. Instead of accessing the "danger" or "drive" system (Gilbert, 2010), turning to God is key so as to find comfort in the midst of your shame, inadequacy, powerlessness, and isolation. Remember, in reaching for God, you are attempting to ameliorate a faulty God image, replacing this distorted image with a deeper "heart knowledge" of God's providential care (Davis et al., 2013).

In this exercise, slowly sing "It is Well with My Soul" to God, striving to feel God's compassion for you in the midst of your emotional pain.

When peace, like a river, attendeth my way,
When sorrows like sea billows roll;
Whatever my lot, Thou has taught me to say,
It is well, it is well, with my soul.

It is well, with my soul,
It is well, with my soul,
It is well, it is well, with my soul.

Though Satan should buffet, though trials should come,
Let this blest assurance control,

That Christ has regarded my helpless estate,
And hath shed His own blood for my soul.

My sin, oh, the bliss of this glorious thought!
My sin, not in part but the whole,
Is nailed to the cross, and I bear it no more,
Praise the Lord, praise the Lord, O my soul!
For me, be it Christ, be it Christ hence to live:
If Jordan above me shall roll,
No pang shall be mine, for in death as in life
Thou wilt whisper Thy peace to my soul.

But, Lord, 'tis for Thee, for Thy coming we wait,
The sky, not the grave, is our goal;
Oh trump of the angel! Oh voice of the Lord!
Blessèd hope, blessèd rest of my soul!

And Lord, haste the day when my faith shall be sight,
The clouds be rolled back as a scroll;
The trump shall resound, and the Lord shall descend,
Even so, it is well with my soul.

Next, journal for five minutes about your reactions to singing this song to God. Possible questions include the following: (a) What helped the songwriter to repeatedly state, "It is well with my soul?" (b) What role did God play in his ability to experience a deeper contentment in the depths of his soul, in spite of tremendous loss? (c) How can you extend his message of hope, based on Jesus' love, compassion, mercy, grace, and forgiveness, to your own struggles with shame and self-criticism? and (d) What role can God play in your efforts?

____
____
____
____
____
____
____
____
____
____

The Cloud of Unknowing: Reaching for God in Love

The Cloud of Unknowing was written over 500 years ago. In this famous contemplative writing, the anonymous author advocated for the use of both knowledge and love to connect to God, consistent with the Christian tradition. Reading God's Word and meditating on biblical themes are especially salient steps in preparing us for contemplative meditation (Bangley, 2006, p. 49).

In the last chapter, you practiced Puritan meditation, consistent with the *kataphatic* tradition. Just like slowly getting to know a trustworthy friend, you have been thinking deeply about God's attributes and actions so as to cultivate self- and other-compassion. Now, you will be practicing finding rest in God in silence and solitude, reminiscent of taking your friendship to a deeper level by enjoying the moment without using words to fill the air.

Within the pages of *The Cloud of Unknowing*, the author offered instructions for *apophatic* meditation. Located within medieval spirituality, contemplative writers such as Theresa of Avila, John of the Cross, and the *Cloud* author have brought attention to God's ineffability, meaning that, at a certain point, words fail to fully capture God's greatness. This experience is like hiking to the top of a mountain, looking out onto the horizon, and struggling to find the right words to describe your memorable experience. In the Bible, this is consistent with God telling Moses, "I am who I am" (Exodus 3:4). Returning to the example of growing your relationship with a good friend, since you already know this person on a deeper level, you do not need to think *about* him or her when you are spending time together.

In the *Cloud* author's instructions, reaching out to God in love (rather than knowledge) is especially important. The author suggested that this reaching for God in love leads to an awareness of a dense cloud separating us from God, reminiscent of Moses approaching God in a "dark cloud" when God revealed the Ten Commandments to him (Exodus 20:21). When we let go of our knowledge about God during contemplative meditation, we are able to experience his love from moment to moment.

The *Cloud* author explained further:

> If you want to enter, live, and work in this cloud of unknowing, you will need a cloud of forgetting between you and the things of this earth. Consider the problem carefully and you will understand that you are farthest from God when you do not ignore for a moment the creatures and circumstances of the physical world. Attempt to blank out everything but God.
>
> (Bangley, 2006, p. 11)

Through formal practice, we can work towards looking up to God in love, letting go of earthly preoccupations so as to find him in the midst of a "dark, dense cloud." Simultaneously, we are gently placing all of our earthly preoccupations and distractions, including our shame and self-criticisms, beneath a "cloud of forgetting."

Slowly, we are learning to surrender everything to God's providential care in that he is infinitely loving, wise, and powerful. As we strive to let go of our preoccupation with thoughts and feelings, we are pivoting from human knowledge (which is often flawed) to a loving awareness of God's fatherly care. In this process, we are accessing the "contentment" system (Gilbert, 2010), given there is nothing else to do when we are experiencing God's loving embrace. Rather than using the "danger" or "drive" system (Gilbert, 2010), we are basking in the contentment of God's perfect presence.

To keep your focus on God (rather than getting distracted by thoughts and feelings), you will be utilizing a one-syllable word—"Love"—to cultivate sustained attention, as the *Cloud* author revealed:

> You may wish to reach out to God with one simple word that expresses your desire . . . Once you have selected the word you prefer, permanently bind this word to your heart. This word becomes your shield and spear in combat and in peace. Use this word to beat upon the cloudy darkness above you and to force every stray thought down under a cloud of forgetting. If a nagging thought pesters you, strike it with this word.
>
> (Bangley, 2006, p. 14)

Your chosen word—"Love"—functions as a "shield and spear" to help you repeatedly pivot from self-critical thinking to an awareness of God's active, loving presence. "Love" is an especially salient word, moreover, because "God is love" (1 John 4:8). In the process, you are gently placing everything other than God beneath the "cloud of forgetting." Over time, you may be able to relate differently to your negative self-evaluations, given you are developing focused, sustained attention on God and surrendering to his loving care via detachment. Consequently, you are deepening your attachment bond with God, ameliorating a distorted God image in the process.

Memory, Intellect, and the Will: Knowledge Versus Love

Among medieval spiritual authors, such as the *Cloud* writer, John of the Cross, and Theresa of Avila, the self is composed of the intellect (reason), memory, and will, with preference for relating to God in love (an act of the will), rather than overly utilizing the intellect, during contemplative meditation (Beasley-Topliffe, 2003; Johnston, 1973; Knabb et al., 2018). As a result, the *Cloud* author is arguing for a different type of encounter with an ineffable God, relying on love (by way of the will), instead of overly leaning on the intellect and reason (which are certainly important for knowing *about* God), during formal meditative practice.

This shift from knowledge and memory to love may seem quite foreign to you. Yet, in our most important human relationships, I believe we get a fitting glimpse of this dynamic. Consistent with the metaphor for getting to know a friend (mentioned above), we initially rely on our knowledge and memory to deepen our relationship with someone we have recently met. Still, at a certain point, we learn to enjoy each passing moment, without constantly relying on knowledge about this person or prior memories. Instead, we have a direct experience, which is not fully captured with words.

In the exercise that follows, you will be practicing using your will (via love) to reach for God, letting go of the human tendency to overly rely on thoughts and memories. In this effort, you are working towards surrendering your self-critical thoughts about yourself, as well as your distorted thoughts about God. With letting go, you are learning to rest in God's presence, reminiscent of Mary sitting at Jesus' feet (Luke 10:38–42).

Reaching for God in Love: An Exercise[5]

The following exercise can be practiced daily to learn to reach for God in love (rather than knowledge) whenever you find you are struggling with shame and self-criticism. To begin, find a quiet environment in order to spend the next ten minutes in solitude. Sit up straight in a supportive chair, closing your eyes in the process. Please consider using the corresponding audio recording, "Track 4," available at https://www.routledge.com/The-Compassion-Based-Workbook-for-Christian-Clients-Finding-Freedom-from/Knabb/p/book/9780815394365.

1. Briefly pray to God, asking him to be with you as you surrender your inner world to him during this formal practice.
2. Begin to gently recite your chosen word, "Love," in your mind, reaching out to God in love, rather than your own arbitrarily constructed knowledge. This word helps you to focus all your attention on God via an act of the will, rather than thinking about him or remembering him.
3. Gently and non-judgmentally place all other thoughts beneath a "cloud of forgetting," consistently returning to your chosen word, "Love," when you notice you are thinking about "earthly things" (e.g., self-judgments, distorted thoughts about God).
4. When the formal practice is over, thank God for extending his providential, fatherly care to you in this time spent with him.

In the space that follows, please record your efforts over the next week.[6]

Day/Date	*Practice (Yes/No)*	*Comments*
Wednesday Date: ________	*Apophatic* Meditation:	
Thursday Date: ________	*Apophatic* Meditation:	
Friday Date: ________	*Apophatic* Meditation:	
Saturday Date: ________	*Apophatic* Meditation:	
Sunday Date: ________	*Apophatic* Meditation:	
Monday Date: ________	*Apophatic* Meditation:	
Tuesday Date: ________	*Apophatic* Meditation:	

Weeping with Jesus: An Exercise

Before concluding this chapter, I would like you to practice extending compassion to others (adapted from Germer, 2009). When entering Jerusalem, Jesus wept, stating: "If you, even you, had only known on this day what would bring you peace—but now it is hidden from your eyes" (Luke 19:42). In this passage, Jesus "wailed" for "lost opportunity" (Morris, 1988, p. 306), experiencing a deep sadness for Jerusalem (Bock, 1996). During this powerful moment, Jesus "represented the compassionate heart of God" in being moved to tears (MacArthur, 1985).

In 1 John 4:7, the author encouraged us to love each other, with love emanating directly from God. John went on to state the following (4:8–12):

> This is how God showed his love among us: He sent his one and only Son into the world that we might live through him. This is love: not that we loved God, but that he loved us and sent his Son as an atoning sacrifice for our sins. Dear friends, since God so loved us, we also ought to love one another. No one has ever seen God; but if we love one another, God lives in us and his love is made complete in us.

Here, we see the importance of extending God's compassionate, merciful love to others because of the fact that God has generously offered it to us.

Several passages later, John noted, "If anyone acknowledges that Jesus is the Son of God, God lives in them and they in God. And so we know and rely on the love God has for us" (1 John 4:15–16). Because God lives in you, he is the source of your love, which should be abundantly offered to others.

In this exercise, you will be developing loving compassion for another person, reminiscent of Jesus' aforementioned emotional experience and John's instructions. Rather than using loving-kindness meditations (e.g., "may you be safe," "may you be happy," "may you be healthy," "may you be at ease" [Germer, 2009, p. 174]), though, you will be extending God's love to others, recognizing that he has graciously offered it to you first.

Closing your eyes, try to think about someone who you are currently struggling with. This might be a person who has hurt you, or someone you frequently argue with (e.g., a spouse, a coworker, a family member). Now, consider that this person needs Jesus' love, compassion, mercy, grace, and forgiveness, just like you. In fact, he or she may be struggling to receive the peace that Jesus offers, reminiscent of Jerusalem. As you think about this person—with a clear image of him or her in your mind—begin to gently repeat the following words in your mind:

- "May you experience the peace that Jesus offers."
- "May you experience the love that Jesus offers."

As you repeat these two sentences over and over again, try to allow yourself to be moved with loving compassion, consistent with Jesus' emotional experience as he entered Jerusalem. Imagine that the person you are thinking about is struggling, and needs Jesus' peace and love, just like you do.

After spending ten minutes repeating these phrases and feeling for this person, thank God for the peace and love that he has extend to you.

Feeling with Compassion: A Case Example

Juan, a Mexican American male in his late 50s, reluctantly scheduled an appointment to see a psychotherapist, recognizing that his anger was getting "out of control." In the initial meeting, he explained to the therapist that he grew up in an abusive household. In particular, his father was verbally abusive, often shaming him by calling him "ugly" and "stupid" when he would make mistakes around the house. Over time, he became increasingly resentful towards his father, promising himself he would never let anyone "disrespect" him again.

In his 20s, he met his wife, who he described as the "love of [his] live." Yet, from time to time, he would get angry with her when she pointed out something he was doing wrong or an area in life he needed to improve. When she would do so, he instantly experienced anger, yelling at her to "get away from [him]." Unfortunately, his frequent angry outbursts (which never turned into violence or verbal abuse) led to increased distance between them, impairing his ability to trust her and lean on her during difficult times.

In therapy, Juan worked to better understand his anger, which was a reaction to a deeper experience of shame. For Juan, his earlier experiences with his father led to the emotional conclusion that people are unsafe, and will eventually be critical, judgmental, and shaming towards him. Because his wife "meant the world to [him]," he experienced a deep sense of shame whenever she gave him feedback about perceived shortcomings.

In his relationship with God, moreover, Juan felt a deep sense of rejection, doubting that God loved him and wanted what was best for him. Although his pastor frequently taught about God's love and mercy from the pulpit on Sunday mornings, Juan experienced a chasm between what the Bible said about God and his deeper, emotional experience of God's availability and love. From Juan's perspective, God could never love him, given he was "ugly" and "stupid," just like his father said he was.

Gradually, Juan started to feel God's compassion, especially when he would spend time in solitude with God. In the silence of the spare bedroom of his suburban home, Juan practiced *apophatic* meditation, reaching for God in love (rather than relying on his knowledge of God, which was often distorted). Over and over again, Juan placed his self-critical thoughts and distorted thoughts about God beneath a "cloud of forgetting," shifting towards loving God via an act of the will.

Although the process unfolded slowly, he started to trust—on a deeper level—that God's providential care extended to him from moment to moment. In fact, Juan started to feel God's love, which helped him with his shame. In addition, as he practiced letting go and resting in God's presence, he found that the anger he previously expressed turned to a more vulnerable experience of sadness and fear, emotions that surprised him.

With his wife, he realized he could express these newly discovered emotions, reaching for her in a more tender manner. Reminiscent of Jesus' emotional expression (e.g., Luke 19:42) in the gospels, he began to work on showing his wife his softer side, giving himself permission to share his deeper experiences with her. Along the way, he found he was able to reach for God as the proverbial glue—drawing upon God's readily available love, compassion, mercy, grace, and forgiveness—whenever he felt broken, flawed, or unlovable.

Conclusion

In the fifth chapter, you practiced feeling with compassion and mercy towards yourself and others. In the process, the goal was to experience God's compassion on a deeper level in order access your "contentment" system (Burroughs, 2010; Gilbert, 2010), improve your God image (especially your "heart knowledge" about his providential care [Davis et al., 2013]), and ameliorate your shame.

A range of exercises were practiced, such as "befriending" your emotions (Germer, 2009; van den Brink & Koster, 2015), cultivating positive emotions (Bannink, 2012; Germer, 2009; Van Dijk, 2012), and connecting to your "true self" (Pennington, 2000). You also had the opportunity to practice a Christian version of loving-kindness exercises, and imagine receiving a letter from God (Kempis, 2015; Thomas et al., 2011). Finally, you practiced *apophatic* meditation, and strived to extend Jesus' love and peace to someone you are currently struggling with.

Thus far, you have worked on thinking and feeling with compassion, drawing upon God's love, compassion, mercy, grace, and forgiveness and modifying your God image and attachment style with him along the way. In the next chapter, you will be building on this momentum by working towards behaving with compassion, drawing from a set of well-defined values to guide your life.

Notes

1 This exercise is adapted from Knabb (2016a) and influenced by Dworsky et al. (2013).
2 This section is based on Pennington (2000) and adapted from Knabb (2016b).
3 This exercise is adapted from Pennington (2000) and Knabb (2016a).
4 This exercise is adapted from Knabb and Frederick (2017) and Thomas et al. (2011).
5 These instructions are adapted from *The Cloud of Unknowing* (Bangley, 2006) and Pennington (1982).
6 This form is adapted from Segal, Williams, and Teasdale (2012).

References

Allender, D., & Longman, T. (1994). *The cry of the soul: How our emotions reveal our deepest questions about God*. Colorado Springs, CO: NavPress.

Arico, C. (2015). *A taste of silence: Centering prayer and the contemplative journey*. Brooklyn, NY: Lantern Books.

Baer, R. (2014). Introduction to the core practices and exercises. In R. Baer (Ed.), *Mindfulness-based treatment approaches: Clinician's guide to evidence base and applications* (pp. 5–28). New York: Elsevier.

Bangley, B. (Ed.). (2006). *The cloud of unknowing: Contemporary English edition*. Brewster, MA: Paraclete Press.

Bannink, F. (2012). *Practicing positive CBT: From reducing distress to building success*. Mainden, MA: John Wiley & Sons Ltd.
Bartholomew, K., & Horowitz, L. (1991). Attachment styles among young adults: A test of a four-category model. *Journal of Personality and Social Psychology, 61*(2), 226–244.
Beasley-Topliffe, K. (2003). *The upper room dictionary of Christian spiritual formation*. Nashville, TN: Upper Room Books.
Beeke, J., & Jones, M. (2012). *A Puritan theology: Doctrine for life*. Grand Rapids, MI: Reformation Heritage Books.
Blount, D. (2003). Providence. In C. Brand, C. Draper, & A. England (Eds.), *Holman illustrated Bible dictionary* (pp. 1340–1342). Nashville, TN: Holman Reference.
Bock, D. (1996). *Luke 9:51–24:53*. Grand Rapids, MI: Baker Academic.
Bonhoeffer, D. (1955). *Ethics*. New York: Touchstone.
Bonhoeffer, D. (1959). *Creation and fall*. New York: Touchstone.
Brueggemann, W. (1984). *The message of the Psalms: A theological commentary*. Minneapolis, MN: Augsburg Publishing House.
Burroughs, J. (2010). *The rare jewel of Christian contentment*. Pensacola, FL: Chapel Library.
Cole, A. (1989). *The epistle of Paul to the Galatians: An introduction and commentary*. Grand Rapids, MI: William B. Eerdmans Publishing Company.
Cosby, B. (2012). *Suffering and sovereignty* [Kindle version]. Grand Rapids, MI: Reformation Heritage Books. Retrieved from Amazon.com
Davis, E., Moriarty, G., & Mauch, J. (2013). God images and God concepts: Definitions, development, and dynamics. *Psychology of Religion and Spirituality, 5*(1), 51–60.
Dworsky, C., Pargament, K., Gibbel, M., Krumrei, E., Faigin, C., Haugen, M., Desai, K., Lauricella, S., Lynn, Q., & Warner, H. (2013). Winding road: Preliminary support for a spiritually integrated intervention addressing college students' spiritual struggles. *Research in the Social Scientific Study of Religion, 24*, 309–339.
Emmons, R., & McCullough, M. (2003). Count blessings versus burdens: An experimental investigation of gratitude and subjective well-being in daily life. *Journal of Personality and Social Psychology, 84*(2), 377–389.
Flavel, J. (2017). *The mystery of providence*. Zeeland, MI: Reformed Church Publications.
Fung, R. (1988). *The epistle to the Galatians*. Grand Rapids, MI: Wm. B. Eerdmans Publishing Co.
George, T. (1994). *Galatians: An exegetical and theological exposition of holy scripture*. Nashville, TN: Broadman & Holman Publishers.
Germer, C. (2009). *The mindful path to self-compassion: Freeing yourself from destructive thoughts and emotions*. New York: The Guilford Press.
Germer, C., & Neff, K. (2013). Self-compassion in clinical practice. *Journal of Clinical Psychology, 69*(8), 856–867.
Gilbert, P. (2010). *Compassion focused therapy: Distinctive features*. New York: Routledge.
Gilbert, P., & Irons, C. (2009). Shame, self-criticism, and self-compassion in adolescence. In N. Allen & L. Sheeber (Eds.), *Adolescent emotional development and the emergence of depressive disorders* (pp. 195–214). Cambridge: Cambridge University Press.
Greco, L., Barnett, E., Blomquist, K., & Gevers, A. (2008). Acceptance, body image, and health in adolescence. In L. Greco & S. Hayes (Eds.), *Acceptance & mindfulness treatments for children & adolescents* (pp. 187–216). Oakland, CA: New Harbinger Publications, Inc.
Grenz, S. (1994). *Theology for the community of God*. Grand Rapids, MI: William B. Eerdmans Publishing Company.
Guthrie, D. (1983). *The epistle to the Hebrews: An introduction and commentary*. Grand Rapids, MI: William B. Eerdmans Publishing Company.
Harris, R. (2009). *ACT made simple: An easy-to-read primer on acceptance and commitment therapy*. Oakland, CA: New Harbinger Publications, Inc.
Hayes, S., Strosahl, K., & Wilson, K. (2012). *Acceptance and commitment therapy: The process and practice of mindful change* (2nd ed.). New York: The Guilford Press.
Hofmann, S., Grossman, P., & Hinton, D. (2011). Loving-kindness and compassion meditation: Potential for psychological interventions. *Clinical Psychology Review, 31*(7), 1126–1132.
Johnston, W. (Ed.). (1973). *The cloud of unknowing*. New York: Doubleday.
Kempis, T. (2009). *The imitation of Christ* (H. Gardiner, Trans.). New York: Doubleday Religion.
Kempis, T. (2015). *The imitation of Christ* [Kindle version] (J. Watkins, Trans.). Franklin, TN: Worthy Inspired. Retrieved from Amazon.com
Knabb, J. (2016a). *Acceptance and commitment therapy for Christian clients: A faith-based workbook*. New York: Routledge.
Knabb, J. (2016b). *Faith-based ACT for Christian clients: An integrative treatment approach*. New York: Routledge.

Knabb, J., & Frederick, T. (2017). *Contemplative prayer for Christians with chronic worry: An eight-week program.* New York: Routledge.

Knabb, J., & Meador, K. (2016). A theological lens for integrating ACT with conceptions of health, healing, and human flourishing. In J. Nieuwsma, R. Walser, & S. Hayes (Eds.), *ACT for clergy and pastoral counselors: Using acceptance and commitment therapy to bridge psychological and spiritual care.* Oakland, CA: New Harbinger Publications, Inc.

Knabb, J., Frederick, T., & Cumming, G. (2017). Surrendering to God's providence: A three-part study on providence-focused therapy for recurrent worry (PFT-RW). *Psychology of Religion and Spirituality, 9*(2), 180–196.

Knabb, J., Vazquez, V., Wang, K., & Bates, T. (2018). "Unknowing" in the 21st century: Humble detachment for Christians with repetitive negative thinking. *Spirituality in Clinical Practice.* Advanced online publication.

Kolts, R. (2016). *CFT made simple: A clinician's guide to practicing compassion-focused therapy.* Oakland, CA: New Harbinger Publications, Inc.

Lambert, N., Fincham, F., Braithwaite, S., Graham, S., & Beach, S. (2009). Can prayer increase gratitude? *Psychology of Religion and Spirituality, 1*(3), 139–149.

Laubach, F. (2007). *Letters by a modern mystic* [Kindle edition]. Colorado Springs, CO: Purposeful Design Publications. Retrieved from Amazon.com

Lawrence, R. (1997). Measuring the image of God: The God image inventory and the God image scales. *Journal of Psychology and Theology, 25*(2), 214–226.

MacArthur, J. (1985). *The MacArthur New Testament commentary.* Chicago, IL: Moody Press.

Merton, T. (1961). *New seeds of contemplation.* New York: New Directions Publishing Corporation.

Morris, L. (1988). *Luke.* Grand Rapids, MI: William B. Eerdmans Publishing Company.

Pennington, B. (1982). *Centering prayer: Renewing an ancient Christian prayer form.* New York: Doubleday.

Pennington, B. (1988). *Centered living: The way of centering prayer.* New York: Doubleday.

Pennington, B. (2000). *True self/false self: Unmasking the spirit within.* New York: The Crossroad Publishing Company.

Rous, F. (2016). *The art of happiness.* Crossville, TN: Puritan Publications.

Saint-Jure, J., & Colombiere, C. (1980). *Trustful surrender to divine providence: The secret to peace and happiness.* Charlotte, NC: TAN Books.

Segal, Z., Williams, M., & Teasdale, J. (2012). *Mindfulness-based cognitive therapy for depression* (2nd ed.). New York: The Guilford Press.

Sheldon, K., & Lyubomirsky, S. (2006). How to increase and sustain positive emotion: The effects of expressing gratitude and visualizing best possible selves. *The Journal of Positive Psychology, 1*(2), 73–82.

Siegel, R. (2010). *The mindfulness solution: Everyday practices for everyday problems.* New York: The Guilford Press.

Thomas, M., Moriarty, G., Davis, E., & Anderson, E. (2011). The effects of a manualized group-psychotherapy intervention on client God images and attachment to God: A pilot study. *Journal of Psychology and Theology, 39*(1), 44–58.

van den Brink, E., & Koster, F. (2015). *Mindfulness-based compassionate living: A new training programme to deepen mindfulness with heartfulness.* New York: Routledge.

Van Dijk, S. (2012). *DBT made simple: A step-by-step guide to dialectical behavior therapy.* Oakland, CA: New Harbinger Publications, Inc.

Witherington, B. (1998). *Grace in Galatia: A commentary on St. Paul's letter to the Galatians.* Grand Rapids, MI: William B. Eerdmans Publishing Company.

Zeng, X., Chiu, C., Wang, R., Oei, T., & Leung, F. (2015). The effects of loving-kindness meditation on positive emotions: A meta-analytic review. *Frontiers in Psychology, 6*, 1693.

CHAPTER 6

Behaving with Compassion

Introduction

In the sixth chapter, you will be working on behaving with compassion and mercy towards yourself and others. In the process, the main goal is to live out a set of Christian virtues, reminiscent of Jesus' loving compassion. In that you have practiced thinking and feeling with compassion, the next step is to express this newfound compassion in concrete, behavioral steps as you love others like Jesus does.

Modified compassion-based exercises in the psychology literature involve getting in touch with your values to practice compassion for yourself and others, drawing from the acceptance and commitment therapy (ACT) literature (Hayes et al., 2012; Tirch et al., 2014). As a Christian, though, you will be tapping into biblical virtues—consistent with Jesus' famous teachings on loving others, forgiveness, servanthood, and self-sacrifice, among others (e.g., Matthew 5–7)—which are vitally important for healthy Christian living (Knabb, 2016a). In addition, you will be working towards shifting from being self-focused to being selfless in your interpersonal interactions, consistent with the contemporary compassion literature (Germer, 2009; Tirch et al., 2014), the faith integration literature (Welsh & Knabb, 2009), and medieval spirituality (Kempis' *The Imitation of Christ* and the *Cloud* author's instructions refer to this as self-forgetfulness). Ultimately, sometimes "being" is important, especially when it comes to relating differently to the inner world, and sometimes "doing" is necessary (Segal, Williams, & Teasdale, 2012), living out a set of virtues to guide life. Stated differently, sitting at Jesus' feet is often what is best (like Mary in Luke's gospel), whereas Martha's service is important at other junctures in life (Knabb, 2016a).

Exercises for helping you get in touch with biblical virtues will be offered, along with strategies to compassionately balance "being" and "doing" (Segal et al., 2012) in your Christian walk so as to buffer against the negative effects of shame and self-judgments. As another modified example from the compassion literature, treating your body with compassion (Germer, 2009; Linehan, 2015; Kabat-Zinn, 2013) will be adjusted to focus on viewing your body as God's temple (1 Corinthians 6:19). By treating your physical self with more compassion, you will be working to ameliorate your shame and negative self-judgments. To offer one final example, early desert Christians commonly attempted to respond to tempting, compulsive thoughts by living out a set of Christian virtues. In fact, seven clearly defined virtues were utilized to respond to seven distinct thoughts that distracted desert monks from their relationship with God. Reminiscent of ACT (Tirch et al., 2014), these virtues will be explored as a behavioral strategy for you to cultivate self- and other-compassion, living out moral principles in the service of others in daily living. Throughout the chapter, exercises, a guided meditation (with an audio file), writing exercises (e.g., journaling), biblical examples, and a case example will be presented to highlight behavioral strategies for you to develop self- and other-compassion.

The Proverbial Map: Living Life Based on a Set of Values

Within acceptance and commitment therapy (ACT), clients learn how to be more accepting (and less judgmental) towards their inner experiences, such as thoughts, feelings, and sensations;

in doing so, the goal is to pursue a set of values to guide life (Hayes et al., 2012). In other words, rather than letting our thoughts and feelings—which come and go and change from moment to moment—guide what we choose to do in life, a set of personally chosen values can function as a proverbial map for life. These values, rather than unstable inner experiences, can help us to live with intentionality and compassion. Examples of values include being creative, forgiving, healthy, loving, kind, and humble (Harris, 2013). Compassion, of course, can also be a value, given we are striving to treat ourselves and others with kindness and love.

Within ACT, values are defined with the following characteristics (adapted from Harris, 2009; Hayes et al., 2012; Tirch et al., 2014):

- Values are principles for living.
- Values are global (rather than isolated or fragmented).
- Values are consistent (instead of fluctuating and changing on a regular basis).
- Values exist in the here-and-now (instead of the past or future).
- Values are concrete, behavioral patterns of action (rather than abstract rules for living or goals that can be completed).
- Values are personally chosen by each person (instead of dictated by someone else).
- Values contribute to a life of purpose and meaning (but are not necessarily synonymous with "happiness" or "pleasure").

In the last two chapters, you worked on thinking and feeling with compassion. In ACT, thinking with compassion involves seeing our thoughts with a bit more distance, ameliorating the tendency to automatically assume they are true. In this process, we are letting go of the propensity to allow our thoughts to bully us around, choosing, instead, to pivot towards valued living on the roads of life. What is more, with our feelings, we are relating to them with more compassion and non-judgment, rather than shaming ourselves for them and allowing them to get in the way of living the life we want.

When we are living out compassion as a value, we are striving to relate to our suffering in a different manner (Tirch et al., 2014), connecting to a range of compassion-based qualities, such as kindness, wisdom, warmth, patience, and perseverance (Kolts, 2016). Along the way, values function like a compass, helping us to head in an intentional direction (Hayes et al., 2012). Instead of treating our most cherished values like goals—somehow finishing them and crossing them off a list—we can always head in a valued direction, reminiscent of traveling East or West (Hayes et al., 2012).

Once we have identified a set of values to guide life, we can prioritize them and apply them to a range of life domains, such as family life, work life, religious life, and so on (Hayes et al., 2012). In turn, we must be committed to act upon them, rather than sitting back and merely thinking about our values in an abstract, distant manner (Hayes et al., 2012). For Christians, Jesus perfectly modeled healthy living, revealing himself to us throughout the pages of the Bible. To be sure, Jesus' life was all about action, from the incarnation, to healing and ministering to people, to training his disciples (who would eventually become apostles), to dying on a cross for humankind, to ascending to heaven. When Jesus declared, "Come, follow me" (Matthew 4:19), and "Whoever wants to be my disciple must deny themselves and take up their cross and follow me" (Matthew 16:24), he required action. As Christians faithfully follow Jesus, a set of biblical virtues is necessary (rather than arbitrarily generated values), described in the next section.

The Christian Version of Values: Biblical Virtues

Within the Christian tradition, virtues are a set of moral behaviors that lead to a purposeful life (Harrington & Keenan, 2002). Revealed throughout the pages of the Bible, Christianity has typically pointed to seven key virtues in forming a pattern for daily living, including four cardinal virtues (wisdom, justice, self-control, and courage) and three theological virtues (faith, hope, and love) (Harrington & Keenan, 2010). Ultimately, God is the source of the theological virtues, although the four cardinal virtues can be developed through human effort (Harrington & Keenan, 2010).

Another list of seven Christian virtues emerged in the 5th century, namely chastity (i.e., purity), temperance (i.e., self-control), charity (i.e., love), diligence (i.e., hard work), patience, kindness, and humility (Gregory & Rutledge, 2016). Among this list, love, patience, kindness, and humility are highly relevant for this workbook. Certainly, if virtues are principled, consistent moral behaviors that create an intentional life (Harrington & Keenan, 2002), applying these standards of living to our relationship with ourselves and others can help to ameliorate the shame and self-judgments that keep us stuck in life.

One important virtue that is not within either of these famous lists, though, is "detachment," briefly discussed in the last chapter. In the next section, I would like to revisit this virtue in the context of behaving with compassion. In other words, following Jesus with compassion requires relating differently to the inner world, letting go of our tendency to prioritize our thoughts and feelings above compassionate living.

"Detachment" as a Christian Virtue: Following Jesus with Compassion

Within Christianity, Jesus perfectly modeled detachment in his pursuit of God's will. Detachment has several characteristics, including the following (Lonsdale, 2005):

> [It is] an act of spiritual freedom. It is also the virtue of habitually choosing out of freedom not compulsion, fear, or routine. Therefore, it is a virtue that allows a person to review competing goods and choose that which most fulfils one's life ideals or values . . . Within the Christian tradition there have been a number of terms that spelled out applications of this Christlike detachment: abnegation, forgetfulness of self, humility, mortification, renouncement, renunciation, self-denial, self-sacrifice. (p. 234)

In the context of compassion and shame, detachment is the ability to let go of our shame and self-criticism in order to freely follow Jesus, purposefully choosing to love like he loves. In this process of surrendering our inner world to God (including our unilateral attempts to define who we are), we are shifting our focus from a preoccupation with our perceived shortcomings to displaying the heavenly Christian virtues of love, patience, kindness, and humility in our relationship with ourselves and others. This deliberate pivot, from a Christian perspective, is often called self-denial, consistent with Jesus' teaching on denying the self in order to follow him (Matthew 16:24). Before discussing a Christian view of moving from self to others, though, I would like to outline a method for exploring the theological virtues in your own life, drawing from Ignatian spirituality.

Ignatian Spirituality and the Daily Examen: Reflecting on the Theological Virtues

In Ignatian spirituality, a common saying involves "finding God in all things." In other words, God is active and present in our daily experiences. With the "daily examen," utilized twice per day, we set aside time to intentionally reflect on God's actions. Several steps are typically employed, including the following (adapted from Fleming, 2008; Ignatian Spirituality, n.d.):

- Recognize God's active, loving presence in your life in the here-and-now.
- Look back on your day with a sense of gratitude and thankfulness.
- Reflect on your thoughts, feelings, and behaviors, asking how God has revealed himself in these moments.
- Select one moment from your day, asking God to reveal the ways in which you have come up short; in turn, ask for God to love you and forgive you.
- Look to the next day with hope, putting your faith in God's providential care.

In the context of the Christian virtues (Ignatian Spirituality, n.d.), the following activity can help you reflect on your ability to exercise love, patience, kindness, and humility throughout your day.

The Daily Examen: An Exercise

Begin this exercise by finding a quiet place, sitting in a comfortable chair with your feet gently placed on the floor. Next, slowly move through each of the following steps (for ten minutes), reflecting on whether or not you were able to display faith, hope, love, patience, kindness, and humility in your relationships throughout the day, reminiscent of Jesus' example while on this planet (adapted from Fleming, 2008; Ignatian Spirituality, n.d.):

- Recognize God's active, loving presence in the here-and-now. In this very moment, God is offering you his love, patience, and kindness.
- Looking back on your day, thank God for extending his love, patience, and kindness to you from moment to moment.
- Reflect on your thoughts, feelings, and behaviors throughout the day, asking whether or not you were able to be loving, patient, kind, and humble towards yourself and others. Consider God's active involvement in these experiences.
- Select one particular moment from your day, asking God to reveal the ways in which you may have come up short in your efforts to be loving, patient, kind, and humble towards yourself or others; in turn, ask for God to love you and forgive you in response to these struggles.
- Look to the next day with hope, putting your faith in God's providential care and asking him to help you be more loving, patient, kind, and humble towards yourself and others.

When you have finished the exercise, try to reflect on the experience. What was it like to thank God for your day? Was it easy or difficult to do? In your time of reflection, were you able to identify successes in your efforts to live out the Christian virtues of love, patience, kindness, and humility? What, if anything, got in the way? Were you able to ask for God's love and forgiveness in response to your vulnerabilities? What was it like to place your hope and faith in God's providential care, trusting that he will help you in your attempts to be more loving, patient, kind, and humble towards yourself and others?

____

____

____

____

Moving from the Self to Others: Psychological and Christian Perspectives

In the *Mindful Path to Self-Compassion*, Christopher Germer (2009) noted that "taking ourselves more lightly" can be important when it comes to caring for ourselves, given "we have less 'self' to protect and promote in the world" (p. 110). In fact, within many of the world religions, we can pursue a "top-down" strategy, which involves looking up to God as a starting point, a "bottom-up" strategy, reflected in our beginning efforts to fully experience the life that unfolds around us, or a combination of the two (Germer, 2009). In either case, when we intentionally strive to cultivate spiritual health, there can be a natural tendency to shift our focus from ourselves to the world (including God) around us.

For Christians, self-denial has been perfectly modeled by Jesus, who lived a life of servanthood and self-sacrifice (Tan, 2006). To be sure, Jesus fully demonstrated his love for others with his atoning work on the cross (Philippians 2:1–8). Fast-forward over 1,000 years, and medieval and Protestant Christians have written extensively on the importance of self-denial in daily living.

Unfortunately, in the context of shame and self-judgments, we humans have a natural tendency to focus on, and protect, ourselves (Welsh & Knabb, 2009), struggling to keep our eyes on God in the process. Rather than depending on him as the source of life, we often want to be like God (Genesis 3:5; Bonhoeffer, 1955, 1959). In turn, we experience shame on an ongoing basis, which serves as a reminder of our separation from God and longing to depend on him (Bonhoeffer, 1955, 1959).

By turning our focus from ourselves to God, though, we have the opportunity to simultaneously deepen our relationship with him and ameliorate our shame and self-judgments. Medieval Christians referred to this way of living as self-forgetfulness, and the Puritans called this Christ-likeness self-denial. What follows is a review of self-denial and self-forgetfulness in the Christian tradition, with a special emphasis on the role that denying the self plays in compassionate living.

Protestant Spirituality and Self-Denial

Roughly 350 years ago, the Puritan author Jeremiah Burroughs (2015) wrote *Moses' Self-Denial*, which captures the importance of pivoting from being self-focused to God-focused. Using the biblical story of Moses' willingness to deny himself so as to follow God's will (Hebrews 11:24–28) as a catalyst towards a deeper exploration of self-denial in the Christian tradition, Burroughs made the case that our reputation, honors, wealth, and pleasures of the world are to be surrendered to God, "laying them down at Christ's feet" (Chapter 8, Section 1, para. 1). The way to let go of self-preoccupations, from Burroughs' perspective, is through the vehicle of faith.

In order to utilize faith in our efforts to deny the self, Burroughs recommended looking backwards to God's fulfilled promises in the Bible, as well as looking forwards to his promises in the future. In both efforts, we are attempting to bring God's actions into the immediacy of the moment, trusting that God will provide for us as we let go of our unilateral efforts to protect the self and provide for the self apart from his plan. In this process, we are relying on God's mercy and grace to see us through. Burroughs further explained:

> All things are under us while we are above our selves, and it is only faith that empties us of our selves, and raises us above our selves; Faith raises the soul to converse with high and glorious things, with the deep and eternal counsels of God, with the glorious mysteries of the Gospel, with communion with God and Jesus Christ, with the great things of the Kingdom of Christ, with the great things of Heaven and eternal life. Men, before faith comes into their souls, have poor low spirits, busied about mean and contemptible things, and therefore every offer of the world prevails with them, and every little danger of suffering any trouble scares them, and makes them yield to any thing; but when faith comes, there is another manner of spirit in a man.
>
> (Chapter 10, Section 1, para. 10)

Ultimately, Burroughs concluded that God offers us his comfort when we have faith in his providence and are able to let go of our self-preoccupations in order to look to him. In the final chapter of his work, Burroughs recommended three ways to cultivate a deeper, stronger faith so as to pivot from focusing on ourselves to fixing our eyes upon God (adapted from Burroughs, 2015):

- Remember that we are saved by faith in Christ, rather than relying on ourselves.
- Remember that God loves us like a father loves a child, even when we are facing pain and suffering.
- Remember that God offers us peace and comfort in the midst of trials and adversities; therefore, we can confidently turn to him when we are struggling.

For Burroughs, meditating on God's grace, promises, and goodness can help us to shift our focus from ourselves to him, especially when facing the inevitable challenges of daily living. Therefore, what follows is a form of *kataphatic* meditation to help you focus on God's grace, promises, and goodness, shifting your attention from self-critical thoughts towards your Lord and Savior. In turn, you will be focusing your attention on loving others, consistent with Jesus' command in the gospel of John (13:34).

Kataphatic Meditation: An Exercise

Each day this week, you will be meditating on God's grace, promises, goodness, and command to love others (adapted from Ball, 2016; Baxter, 2015; Beeke & Jones, 2012; Burroughs, 2015; Hall, 2016; Watson, 2012), working towards shifting from being self-focused to focusing on loving others because God will provide for your needs with his enduring, gracious goodness. In other words, you will be pivoting from yourself, to God, to others by meditating on several Bible verses. As one of the final steps in this meditative exercise, you will be making a commitment to love others (i.e., behaving with compassion), drawing from God as the source of grace, goodness, love, and compassion.

Try to find a quiet place, free from distractions, and meditate for ten minutes. Close your eyes and sit up straight as you meditate on the pre-selected Bible verses. Please consider using the corresponding audio recording, "Track 5," available at https://www.routledge.com/The-Compassion-Based-Workbook-for-Christian-Clients-Finding-Freedom-from/Knabb/p/book/9780815394365.

1. For the next ten minutes, you will be focusing on three short Bible verses that capture God's grace, promises, goodness, and command to love others: "My grace is sufficient for you" (2 Corinthians 12:9), "Never will I leave you" (Deuteronomy 31:6; Hebrews 13:5), and "Love one another" (John 13:34).

2. Say a short prayer to God, asking him for guidance during the next ten minutes.
3. Shift your focus from "earthly-mindedness" to "heavenly-mindedness," letting go of your self-preoccupations and self-criticisms by pivoting towards God's promises in the Bible. In this process, you are transitioning from focusing inward to outward, trusting that God will guide and sustain you along the way.
4. Repeat these three passages in Scripture with focused, sustained attention: "My grace is sufficient for you" (2 Corinthians 12:9), "Never will I leave you" (Deuteronomy 31:6; Hebrews 13:5), and "Love one another" (John 13:34).
5. Begin to move from your "brain" to your "heart," focusing on feeling God's grace and goodness.
6. Deeply feel the grace and goodness of God, compassionately extending this experience towards others.
7. As you conclude the meditation, make a commitment to act on this deeper awareness of God's grace and goodness by compassionately offering his love to others in a Christ-like manner.
8. Say a short prayer to God, thanking him for revealing his grace and goodness to you, as well as giving you the opportunity to extend this experience to others in a compassionate, Christ-like manner.

In the space that follows, please record your efforts over the next week.[1]

Day/Date	*Practice (Yes/No)*	*Comments*
Wednesday Date: __________	*Kataphatic* Meditation:	
Thursday Date: __________	*Kataphatic* Meditation:	
Friday Date: __________	*Kataphatic* Meditation:	
Saturday Date: __________	*Kataphatic* Meditation:	
Sunday Date: __________	*Kataphatic* Meditation:	
Monday Date: __________	*Kataphatic* Meditation:	
Tuesday Date: __________	*Kataphatic* Meditation:	

Medieval Spirituality and Self-Forgetfulness

In addition to Protestant spirituality, several medieval authors advocated for self-forgetfulness in Christian living. In doing so, we are striving to let go of our shame and our self-criticism, given our attention is on God. In the process, we are forgetting about our perceived shortcomings, since the goodness of God is sufficient. Just like losing track of time when we are immersed in an enjoyable activity, we tend to naturally let go of our self-preoccupations when we are looking towards him in a focused, sustained manner.

In *The Imitation of Christ*, Thomas Kempis offered a prayer to God so as to let go of earthly preoccupations by way of God's grace:

> Lord, I have great need of Your grace, of Your great singular grace, before I arrive where no creature will hinder me from perfect contemplation of You. As long as any transitory thing holds me or rules within me, I cannot fly freely to You.
>
> (Kempis, 2009, p. 116)

In a subsequent chapter (in an earlier translation of *The Imitation of Christ*), he took this need to pivot from earthly preoccupations to God to the next level, advocating for self-forgetfulness in daily living in the form of a response from God:

> My son, saith our Lord, thou shalt not have perfect liberty of mind, unless thou wholly forsake thyself. . .Hold well in thy mind this short word: Forsake all things and thou shalt find all things; forsake covetise and thou shalt find great rest. Print well in thy mind that I have said, for when thou hast fulfilled it, thou shalt well know that it is true.
>
> (Kempis, 1909, p. 155)

Here, we see that "liberty of mind" can come from letting go of our self-preoccupations, gently turning to God along the way.

In the 43rd chapter of *The Cloud of Unknowing*, the anonymous author advocated for placing our self-preoccupations beneath a "cloud of forgetting" in our time spent with God. In other words, in order to reach for God in love, we need to place everything—even our focus on ourselves—beneath a "cloud of forgetting" (Bangley, 2006). As the *Cloud* author revealed, "For a true lover not only cherishes his beloved more than himself but in a certain sense he becomes oblivious of himself on account of the one he loves" (Johnston, 1973, p. 83). Ultimately, medieval spirituality argued for an intentional pivot from ourselves to God, given that we are unable to cultivate a deeper relationship with him when we are overly self-preoccupied. When it comes to shame and self-judgments, we can get into the habit of spending our day constantly "looking in the mirror," so to speak, noticing all our imperfections. When we are doing so, however, we are unable to see that our closest friend is right by our side, inviting us to spend time with him as we walk along the roads of life together. Prior to medieval writers' efforts to stress the importance of being focused on God, the early desert Christians wrote on the topic.

Desert Spirituality and Self-Denial

Among the early Christians who moved to the deserts of Egypt, Palestine, and Syria, the task of self-denial was at the core of their efforts to deepen their intimacy with God (Burton-Christie, 1993). A particular strand of self-denial, from a desert perspective, involves surrendering the will to God, given that our own efforts to protect ourselves and assert our will can get in the way of a deeper union with him (Burton-Christie, 1993). One desert father, Abba Poemen, noted the following: "The will of man is a brass wall (Jeremiah 1:18) between him and God and a stone of stumbling. When a man renounces it, he is also saying to himself, 'By my God, I can leap over the wall' (Psalm 18:29)" (quoted in Burton-Christie, 1993, p. 219). By surrendering the self to God, desert Christians strived to remove the psychological barriers to true intimacy with their Creator. Essentially, these efforts capture their willingness to detach from the "false self" so as to find their "true self" in Christ (Pennington, 2000).

When considering shame and self-criticism, our unilateral attempts to define who we are can get in the way of a more intimate relationship with God, reminiscent of a strained marriage.

One spouse may be constantly saying he loves his wife, reassuring her that he cares for her and will never leave her. Yet, his wife may regularly believe she is flawed, struggling to receive his words, absorb them, and live her life in such a way as to consent to his enduring love. In a similar vein, we may struggle to receive God's love because of our preoccupation with self-criticism, focusing on our own self-judgments instead of God's unwavering promises in Scripture. The solution, of course, is to learn to focus on the Other, letting go of our tendency to rely on our own self-evaluations, which are inconsistent with the Other's understanding of who we are and our value in this crucial, life-giving relationship.

Another way of making sense of self-denial involves looking to Jesus' example of self-emptying in the New Testament (Philippians 2:7). In our efforts to emulate Jesus, we are called to deny ourselves so as to follow God's will. In the process, our self-preoccupations may begin to fade into the background, given we are increasingly passionate about loving God and others (Mark 12:30–31). One vehicle through which we can practice self-emptying is *apophatic* meditation, and more specifically centering prayer. As we spend time with God, in solitude and silence, we are preparing ourselves for a life of action, loving the world like Jesus does.

Kenosis, Centering Prayer, and Action

In the Apostle Paul's letter to the Philippians (2:1–8; italics added), he offered the following:

> Therefore if you have any encouragement from being united with Christ, if any comfort from his love, if any common sharing in the Spirit, if any tenderness and compassion, then make my joy complete by being like-minded, having the same love, being one in spirit and of one mind. Do nothing out of selfish ambition or vain conceit. Rather, in humility value others above yourselves, not looking to your own interests but each of you to the interests of the others. In your relationships with one another, have the same mindset as Christ Jesus: Who, being in very nature God, did not consider equality with God something to be used to his own advantage; rather, he *made himself nothing* by taking the very nature of a servant, being made in human likeness. And being found in appearance as a man, he humbled himself by becoming obedient to death—even death on a cross!

Here, we see that Paul clearly elucidated Jesus' willingness to surrender his will to God, humbling himself in order to serve. Instead of being motivated by "selfish ambition" or "vain conceit," we are tasked with modeling our lives after Christ, serving others with humility as the mechanism through which this happens.

Interestingly, the humility Paul pointed to in this biblical letter involves an active decision to follow God's will, rather than "passive inability or pathetic servility" (Hansen, 2009, p. 115). Jesus' humility, in fact, was all about compassionately responding to humanity's estrangement from God (Hansen, 2009). In Paul's instructions to "value others above yourselves," he was advocating for shifting from a preoccupation with the self to seeing the value in others (Hansen, 2009).

Referencing Paul's teaching on "self-emptying" in Philippians (the Greek word, *kenosis*), centering prayer author Cynthia Bourgeault (2004) suggested that the heart of *apophatic* meditation involves cultivating a "self-giving" posture, which enriches life in that "love [is] made full in the act of giving itself away" (p. 88). Throughout this workbook, you have opportunities to practice *apophatic* meditation, with a central feature of letting go of your own self-preoccupations so as to allow God to work through you, loving others with compassion, mercy, grace, and forgiveness along the way. Before moving on to the importance of balancing "being" and "doing" in the Christian life, I would like you to spend a few minutes journaling on your efforts to love like Jesus loves.

Loving Like Jesus: A Journaling Exercise

For the next ten minutes, try to write about what your life might be like if you were to radically love others like Jesus. In this newly attained reality, you have learned to shift your focus from shame and self-criticism to an awareness of God's active, loving presence. In other words, God's providential care extends to each of your daily interactions with others, and you are willing to offer God's love, compassion, mercy, grace, and forgiveness because you are wholeheartedly aware that he is moving in the here-and-now. As you journal, try to consider how you might behave with compassion, focusing on the concrete steps you will take to live out the most salient Christian virtues (e.g., love, patience, kindness, humility), resulting in a deeper compassion for others.

____

____

____

____

____

____

____

____

____

____

____

Balancing "Being" and "Doing": Psychological and Christian Perspectives

Now that you have been able to consider the role that Christian virtues play in loving others like Jesus loves, I would like you to explore the importance of balancing "being" and "doing" in the Christian life. Within mindfulness-based cognitive therapy, a contemporary approach to managing depression relapse prevention, two "modes of mind" are presented (Segal et al., 2012). With the "doing" mode, we are attempting to solve problems, pursue goals, and fix the situation in front of us; the "being" mode, however, involves accepting the present moment with non-judgment, letting go of the tendency to "close the gap" between how things currently are and how we wish they would be (Segal et al., 2012). Ultimately, we are focused on the past or the future in the "doing" mode, whereas the "being" mode encompasses staying planted in the here-and-now (Segal et al., 2012). When it comes to pursuing goals and solving problems, the "doing" mode is often ideal, with the "being" mode preferred when we are relating to difficult inner experiences that will not go away (Hayes et al., 2012).

In relating these two "modes of mind" to shame and self-criticism, we can often try to get rid of difficult inner experiences by employing the "doing" mode; yet, when we strive to somehow fix our thoughts and feelings, we may end up getting into a tug-of-war with them, leading to the tendency to be distracted on the sidelines of life. Because of this, shifting from the "doing" to the "being" mode during moments of shame and self-judgments can help us to allow these intrapsychic experiences to simply run their natural course as we pivot towards living out our values with compassion.

For Christians, the "being" mode is reminiscent of learning to sit at the feet of Jesus, like Mary in Luke's gospel (Luke 10:38–42; Knabb, 2016b). Within the Christian tradition, Mary has historically represented the contemplative life, whereas Martha captures the active life (Cutler, 2003). In other words, Mary's submissive, yielding posture reveals the importance of resting at the feet of Jesus, taking a break from action, basking in the love of God, and surrendering to God's will; on the other hand, Martha's activity reflects the need to serve through compassionate, charitable acts of love and kindness (Cutler, 2003). With Jesus, both contemplation and action seemed to be important, given he compassionately responded to those in need, and, at the same time, carved out time to spend with God in solitude (Cutler, 2003).

As a Christian who struggles with shame and negative self-evaluations, spending time sitting with Jesus can help you surrender your inner world to God, trusting that his providential care extends to your thoughts and feelings from moment to moment. Instead of trying to get rid of your shame, recognizing that it can help you reach for God in silence and solitude may allow you to find rest in him in your time of need. In these key moments, you are working towards trusting in God's view of who you are, rather than your own understanding (Proverbs 3:5). As you repeatedly yield to God's sovereign care, reminiscent of trusting a caregiver to be naturally responsive to your needs, you are slowly extending God's love, compassion, mercy, grace, and forgiveness to yourself, before pivoting towards applying this experience to others.

As the "other side of the coin," you are learning to live out a set of well-defined Christian virtues as you faithfully follow Jesus. Just prior to the story of Mary and Martha, Luke's gospel presents the story of the "Good Samaritan" (Luke 10: 25–37). In this famous narrative, a Samaritan compassionately responded to a man who was severely wounded, helping him to recover by meeting his needs (Carroll, 2012). With this biblical account, Jesus emphasized the importance of living out our faith, balancing this call to compassionate action with the need to attentively listen to Jesus as we patiently sit at his feet (Carroll, 2012).

In this workbook, you have learned a range of strategies for thinking and feeling with compassion, many of which involve resting in God's presence and accessing the "contentment" system (Gilbert, 2010). In addition, living out your faith by behaving with compassion (like Jesus) is especially important. Before concluding this chapter with a plan of action for doing so, I would like to offer three more discussions, including the relationship between a secure attachment to God and virtuous living, the importance of treating the body with compassion, and the role that Christian virtues can play in directly responding to compulsive, distracting thoughts.

A Secure Attachment to God and Virtuous Living

When we are securely attached to God, we have a positive view of our self-in-relationship-with-God, believe we are lovable in our relationship with God, and trust that God will be responsive to our needs when we need him the most (Clinton & Straub, 2010). In turn, when God functions as a secure base, we can confidently explore our world, returning to him for comfort and compassion (by accessing the "contentment" system [Gilbert, 2010]) when we are distressed or hurt (Mikulincer & Shaver, 2004). As revealed in the second chapter of the workbook, this "circle of security" can help us to confidently pursue our life goals, in that we have someone to help us in our time of need (Feeney & Collins, 2004). For Christians, of course, this "someone" is God, and our "life goals" include following Jesus based on a set of biblical virtues.

Along the roads of life, we are called to respond to a suffering world with compassion, just like the "Good Samaritan" in Luke's gospel. By living out a set of Christian virtues, including faith, hope, love, kindness, patience, and humility, we are learning to radically follow Jesus, emulating our Lord and Savior. After all, "We are God's handiwork, created in Christ Jesus to do good works, which God prepared in advance for us to do" (Ephesians 2:10).

When we are securely attached to God, we can have the confidence to venture out into the world, compassionately responding to those in need and faithfully returning to God—in solitude and silence—after a long, hard day. Rather than being preoccupied with an insecure attachment to God (potentially filled with self-doubt, self-criticism, and anxiety), we can rest in God's loving, compassionate arms, recognizing that he will see us through from moment to moment. In our moments of need, we can access our God-given "contentment" system (Gilbert, 2010), constantly oscillating between resting at Jesus' feet and serving him, reminiscent of Jesus' teachings in Luke's gospel. Certainly, though, we can get tired and worn down on the roads of life, meaning we need to find ways to behave with compassion towards ourselves, which will be reviewed in the next section.

Embodied: Treating the Body with Compassion

Along life's paths, we may encounter a range of obstacles, leading to the tendency to feel worn down and exhausted in our efforts to respond to a suffering world with compassion. When this is the case, we need to find ways to behave with compassion towards ourselves, given that our body is God's temple (1 Corinthians 6:19–20). In other words, we must take care of ourselves so we can faithfully follow Jesus wherever he asks us to go.

In *The Mindful Path to Self-Compassion*, Christopher Germer (2009) recommended using mindfulness to relate to the body with compassion, suggesting three easy-to-remember steps: stopping, observing, and returning. In other words, we need to begin this process by putting a halt to our tendency to move through life without noticing what is in front of us, followed by an intentional effort to realize what we are doing in the here-and-now. As the third step, we need to non-judgmentally return to the present moment when our mind has drifted to ruminations about the past, worries about the future, or any other distracting thought or feeling. The goal, ultimately, is to be more present to life, with this practice commonly extended to the body. Rather than allowing our mind to distract us from using our sensations to directly connect to our experiences, we can employ our five senses to fully experience the moment.

One way to do so is through an exercise called "mindful walking" (Germer, 2009; Kabat-Zinn, 2013). With this ten-minute exercise, we are using our senses to directly connect to the experience of walking, feeling our feet make contact with the ground, listening to the sounds around us, feeling the breeze on our face, and looking at the beautiful landscape that surrounds us. As we slowly walk about, the goal is to connect to the experience, rather than mentally travel to some other destination. Instead of getting lost in our thoughts or feelings, when we notice our attention has shifted to something else, we are to non-judgmentally and compassionately bring our focus back to the experience of walking.

For Christians, the human body is where God dwells, which means that we are called to be intentional about every one of our actions, recognizing that God is with us and guiding us (Morris, 1985). Certainly, this means that we are to avoid engaging in behaviors that do not bring glory to God; yet, on the other hand, this also means that life can be experienced on a deeper level when we realize even simple tasks (like going on a walk) are enriched because the Creator of life is with us (Morris, 1985).

In his letter to the Corinthians, Paul stated the following (1 Corinthians 6:19–20):

> Do you not know that your bodies are temples of the Holy Spirit, who is in you, whom you have received from God? You are not your own; you were bought at a price. Therefore honor God with your bodies.

The "you are not your own" phrase suggests that we are to move through life in such a way that honors God, given God dwells within us (Hays, 2011). Honoring the body means recognizing the things we should and should not do, with the former involving taking care of our bodies so as to bring glory to God, who lives and moves in us from minute to minute. What follows is a brief exercise for treating your body with compassion, bringing God along for the ten-minute journey.

Walking with God: An Exercise

In this exercise (adapted from Kabat-Zinn, 2013), you will be going on a walk with God, using your God-given senses to spend time with him. Rather than getting distracted by your thoughts and feelings, you will work on stopping, observing, and returning (Germer, 2009), recognizing that God is dwelling in you as you enjoy this precious time.

To begin, carve out ten minutes to go on a walk with God in your neighborhood. Try to find a location that is relatively free of distractions, offering you a quiet environment to spend time with him. Next, begin to walk, stopping every minute to notice your surroundings. Use your God-given senses to deepen your experience, recognizing that you are God's temple. In other words, he is with you as you directly interact with the world he created. Look around to notice the scenery, smelling the air as you slowly walk about. Once you have done this, use your sense of touch to feel your feet making contact with the ground. If you are on grass, you may want to take your shoes off to feel your feet make contact with the thin green blades created by God. Next, listen to the birds fly by, cars drive past you, or whatever else is making a sound in God's world.

In this process, your job is to use your bodily sensations to experience God's creation, recognizing that he is your trustworthy traveling companion. When your mind gets distracted with a thought, acknowledge you have lost your focus, before gently returning to God's creation. With gratitude and thankfulness, use your senses to enjoy God's gift to you—this world. When you have concluded the practice, say a brief prayer to God, thanking him for giving you your five senses, including the ability to directly interact with his creation. Most importantly, thank God for dwelling within you, recognizing that life comes alive when he is present.

Desert Spirituality, Tempting Thoughts, Virtues, and "Opposite Action"

Among the early desert Christians, Evagrius wrote about several tempting, compulsive thoughts (the Greek word, *logismoi*) that monks struggled with in solitude and silence (Harmless, 2008). These thoughts consisted of themes about gluttony, sex, greed, sadness, anger, boredom, vanity, and pride (Harmless, 2008). In response to these tempting, compulsive thoughts, we are called to cultivate a range of corresponding virtues: moderation for gluttony; love for sex; self-control for greed; patience and courage for sadness, anger, and boredom; and wisdom, understanding, and prudence for vanity and pride (Harmless, 2008).

In consideration of shame and self-judgments, love, patience, and courage are especially important, given we need to love both God and others in the Christian life, and exhibit patience and courage in the face of difficult inner experiences. Interestingly, a mindfulness-based therapy in the 21st century—dialectical behavior therapy (DBT)—advocates for engaging in behavior that is the opposite of our initial reaction to a situation (McKay, Wood, & Brantley, 2007) in order to be more intentional about pursuing what matters. For example, when we are struggling with a tempting, compulsive thought (and feeling) related to fear, we may withdraw to avoid the feared situation or person; doing the opposite action, though, involves moving towards the very situation or person that generates fear (McKay et al., 2007). With shame, we may criticize or punish ourselves, as well as withdraw, cover up, and shut down; the opposite behavior, though, involves doing what we can to ameliorate the situation and "make amends" (McKay et al., 2007). Drawing from Christianity, we may ask the famous question, "What would Jesus do?" In turn, we can make the choice to intentionally live out a set of Christian virtues, rather than reacting to the tempting thought or painful feeling by withdrawing, hiding, or shutting down.

In the next section, you will be fortifying your ability to respond to shame and self-criticism with Christian virtues, coming up with a list of the most salient principles of moral behavior to guide your actions. As you follow Jesus on the roads of life, you need a map to get you from here to there. By developing a proverbial map, you will be ensuring you have an intentional strategy for behaving with compassion, rather than responding to your shame and self-criticism by doing what comes naturally—hiding and covering up.

Behaving with Compassion: A Plan of Action

In this exercise, you will be identifying key biblical virtues to exercise throughout the week as you behave with compassion. In the space that follows, please write down the specific biblical virtues (e.g., faith, hope, love, kindness, patience, humility) you will be living out in your relationships, as well as the actual behaviors you will utilize to do so, and supporting passages in Scripture that can serve as a reminder when you get stuck (adapted from Knabb, 2016b; Stoddard & Afari, 2014). You will be recording this information in six relational domains so as to behave with compassion in your most important relationships.

	Intimate Partner	*Family*	*Friends*	*Church*	*Work*	*Community*
Biblical Virtues						
Specific Behaviors to Live Out the Virtues						
Bible Verses in Support of Biblical Virtues						

Once you have completed this exercise, the next step is to intentionally behave with compassion, applying these biblical virtues to the six relational domains in a consistent, Christ-like manner from minute to minute and day to day. Remember, these virtues are to be lived out in the present moment, rather than merely thought about in an abstract manner (Hayes et al., 2012; Knabb, 2016b). Try to imagine that Jesus is saying, "Follow me" (Matthew 4:19), in this moment, which requires that you act on these virtues in the here-and-now.

Behaving with Compassion: A Case Example

Madelyn, a 40-year-old married woman, presented to psychotherapy due to "extreme shyness." Growing up, she found it increasingly difficult to be around other people, fearing they were scrutinizing her every word and judging the way she looked. Over time, she started to criticize herself, believing she was unworthy of God's love because she was too "short and stupid."

Although she went to church regularly, she believed on a deeper level that she was incapable of following Jesus because of her level of intelligence and perceived physical imperfections.

In her young adult years, she married a Christian she had been dating in college for some time. Although he repeatedly told her she was pretty and "exactly what [he] wanted," she struggled to believe he was being truthful with her. Instead, she would dismiss his comments as "mere pity," increasingly isolating herself from her family and friends. Even with her children, she had a hard time displaying any type of confidence, downplaying their love for her as something "all children express to their mom."

When she presented for therapy, she reported both anxiety and self-criticism, sharing how she felt the need to "cover up and hide" on a daily basis. In her weekly sessions, her therapist began to help her connect to a set of biblical virtues for daily living, while also assisting her in practicing daily meditation. In combination, she was able to relate to her thoughts and feelings with a bit more distance and less judgment and shift towards following Jesus, who was always by her side.

She was especially drawn towards showing love and kindness towards others, and started volunteering in her church to serve children who had been physically abused. In this ministry, her job was to simply spend time with the kids, showing them the love of Christ. The more she was able to pour herself into this work, the less she was preoccupied with her perceived shortcomings. In fact, when she would feel especially down about these "flaws," she would engage in the opposite behavior, striving to follow Jesus in spite of her pain. Although she continued to experience the tendency to withdraw, she grew in her confidence over the years by focusing on living life with Jesus—compassionately, lovingly, kindly, patiently, and humbly.

Conclusion

In the sixth chapter, you worked on behaving with compassion and mercy towards yourself and others, attempting to live out a set of Christian virtues, reminiscent of Jesus' loving compassion.

Along the way, you practiced modified compassion-based exercises in the psychology literature that involved getting in touch with your values to practice compassion for yourself and others (Hayes et al., 2012; Tirch et al., 2014). In addition, you practiced shifting from being self-focused to being selfless in your interpersonal interactions, consistent with the contemporary compassion literature (Germer, 2009; Tirch et al., 2014), the faith integration literature (Welsh & Knabb, 2009), and medieval spirituality (Kempis' *The Imitation of Christ* and the *Cloud* author's instructions refer to this as self-forgetfulness).

In the next chapter, you will be focusing on attending and imagining with compassion, using a range of meditations to help you connect to God's love. From the Christian tradition, you will practice the Jesus Prayer and other breath prayers, Brother Lawrence's *The Practice of the Presence of God*, and several prayer methods from Ignatian spirituality. By attending with compassion—building on your efforts to think, feel, and behave with compassion—you will be moving towards deepening your ability to recognize God's presence as you extend his compassion towards yourself and others.

Note

1 This form is adapted from Segal et al. (2012).

References

Ball, J. (2016). *A treatise of divine meditation*. Crossville, TN: Puritan Publications.
Bangley, B. (Ed.). (2006). *The cloud of unknowing*. Brewster, MA: Paraclete Press.

Baxter, R. (2015). *The Saints' everlasting rest*. Louisville, KY: GLH Publishing.

Beeke, J., & Jones, M. (2012). *A Puritan theology: Doctrine for life*. Grand Rapids, MI: Reformation Heritage Books.

Bonhoeffer, D. (1955). *Ethics*. New York: Touchstone.

Bonhoeffer, D. (1959). *Creation and fall*. New York: Touchstone.

Bourgeault, C. (2004). *Centering prayer and inner awakening*. New York: Cowley Publications.

Burroughs, J. (2015). *Moses' self-denial* [Kindle edition]. Retrieved from Amazon.com

Burton-Christie, D. (1993). *The word in the desert: Scripture and the quest for holiness in early Christian monasticism*. New York: Oxford University Press.

Carroll, J. (2012). *Luke: A commentary*. Louisville, KY: Westminster John Knox Press.

Clinton, T., & Straub, J. (2010). *God attachment: Why you believe, act, and feel the way you do about God*. New York: Howard Books.

Cutler, D. (2003). *Western mysticism: Augustine, Gregory and Bernard on contemplation and the contemplative life*. New York: Dover Publications, Inc.

Feeney, B., & Collins, N. (2004). Interpersonal safe haven and secure base caregiving processes in adulthood. In W. Rholes & J. Simpson (Eds.), *Adult attachment: Theory, research, and clinical implications* (pp. 300–338). New York: The Guilford Press.

Fleming, D. (2008). *What is Ignatian spirituality?* Chicago, IL: Loyola Press.

Germer, C. (2009). *The mindful path to self-compassion: Freeing yourself from destructive thoughts and emotions*. New York: The Guilford Press.

Gilbert, P. (2010). *Compassion focused therapy: Distinctive features*. New York: Routledge.

Gregory, E., & Rutledge, P. (2016). *Exploring positive psychology: The science of happiness and well-being*. Santa Barbara, CA: Greenwood.

Hall, J. (2016). *The art of divine meditation* [Kindle version]. Retrieved from Amazon.com

Hansen, G. (2009). *The letter to the Philippians*. Grand Rapids, MI: William B. Eerdmans Publishing Company.

Harmless, W. (2008). *Mystics*. New York: Oxford University Press.

Harrington, D., & Keenan, J. (2002). *Jesus and virtue ethics: Building bridges between New Testament studies and moral theology*. Lanham, MD: Rowman & Littlefield Publishers, Inc.

Harrington, D., & Keenan, J. (2010). *Paul and virtue ethics: Building bridges between New Testament studies and moral theology*. Lanham, MD: Rowman & Littlefield Publishers, Inc.

Harris, R. (2009). *ACT made simple: An easy-to-read primer on acceptance and commitment therapy*. Oakland, CA: New Harbinger Publications, Inc.

Harris, R. (2013). *Getting unstuck with ACT: A clinician's guide to overcoming common obstacles to acceptance and commitment therapy*. Oakland, CA: New Harbinger Publications, Inc.

Hayes, S., Strosahl, K., & Wilson, K. (2012). *Acceptance and commitment therapy: The process and practice of mindful change* (2nd ed.). New York: The Guilford Press.

Hays, R. (2011). *First Corinthians*. Louisville, KY: Westminster John Knox Press.

Ignatian Spirituality. (n.d.). *The daily examen*. Retrieved February 5, 2018 from www.ignatianspirituality.com

Johnston, W. (Ed.). (1973). *The cloud of unknowing*. New York: Doubleday.

Kabat-Zinn, J. (2013). *Full catastrophe living: Using the wisdom of your body and mind to face stress, pain, and illness*. New York: Bantam Books.

Kempis, T. (1909). *The imitation of Christ* (W. Raynal, Trans.). New York: Duffield & Company.

Kempis, T. (2009). *The imitation of Christ* (H. Gardiner, Trans.). New York: Doubleday Religion.

Knabb, J. (2016a). *Acceptance and commitment therapy for Christian clients: A faith-based workbook*. New York: Routledge.

Knabb, J. (2016b). *Faith-based ACT for Christian clients: An integrative treatment approach*. New York: Routledge.

Kolts, R. (2016). *CFT made simple: A clinician's guide to practicing compassion-focused therapy*. Oakland, CA: New Harbinger Publications, Inc.

Linehan, M. (2015). *DBT skills training manual*. New York: The Guilford Press.

Lonsdale, D. (2005). Detachment. In P. Sheldrake (Ed.), *The new Westminster dictionary of Christian spirituality* (p. 234). Louisville, KY: Westminster John Knox Press.

McKay, M., Wood, J., & Brantley, J. (2007). *The dialectical behavior therapy skills workbook*. Oakland, CA: New Harbinger Publications, Inc.

Mikulincer, M., & Shaver, P. (2004). Security-based self-representations in adulthood: Contents and processes. In W. Rholes & J. Simpson (Eds.), *Adult attachment: Theory, research, and clinical implications* (pp. 159–195). New York: The Guilford Press.

Morris, L. (1985). *1 Corinthians*. Downers Grove, IL: InterVarsity Press.

Pennington, B. (2000). *True self/false self: Unmasking the spirit within*. New York: The Crossroad Publishing Company.

Segal, Z., Williams, M., & Teasdale, J. (2012). *Mindfulness-based cognitive therapy for depression* (2nd ed.). New York: The Guilford Press.

Stoddard, J., & Afari, N. (2014). *The big book of ACT metaphors: A practitioner's guide to experiential exercises & metaphors in acceptance & commitment therapy*. Oakland, CA: New Harbinger Publications, Inc.

Tan, S. (2006). *Full service: Moving from self-serve Christianity to total servanthood*. Grand Rapids, MI: Baker Books.

Tirch, D., Schoendorff, B., & Silberstein, L. (2014). *The ACT practitioner's guide to the science of compassion*. Oakland, CA: New Harbinger Publications, Inc.

Watson, T. (2012). *A treatise concerning meditation*. Charleston, SC: Waxkeep Publishing.

Welsh, R., & Knabb, J. (2009). Renunciation of the self in psychotherapy. *Mental Health, Religion & Culture, 12*(4), 401–414.

CHAPTER 7

Attending and Imagining with Compassion

Introduction

In the seventh and final chapter, you will work on attending and imagining with compassion and mercy towards yourself. The central goal is to help you relate differently to difficult inner experiences by inviting God into the process. To do this, you will be using your attention (by focusing on God for extended periods of time) and imagination (through visualization exercises) to cultivate a deeper awareness of God's active, loving presence. Along the way, you will strive to access the "contentment" system (Gilbert, 2010) by developing a deeper attachment bond with God (filled with safety and trust) and improving your God image (he is caring for you in the midst of your pain).

Attending with compassion involves a specific type of focused, sustained attention—recognizing that God is with you as you relate to your inner world with kindness and non-judgment. To attend this way, you will be learning to scan your body with God, breathe with God, recite prayers with God, and use the senses to deepen your experience of Scripture. Like Peter walking towards Jesus on the water (Matthew 14:22–33), you will be working towards keeping your eyes on your Lord and Savior, especially when you feel like you are sinking in shame and self-judgments, crying out to him, "Lord, save me!" To imagine with compassion, you will be visualizing spending time with God, practicing seeing yourself relating to him in a healthy, life-sustaining manner.

Exercise-wise, you will utilize a modified version of the "giving and taking meditation" (van den Brink & Koster, 2015), focusing on the breath as a way to breathe in and out the mercy of Christ. Within the Christian tradition, this is called "breath prayer," and involves selecting a short phrase in Scripture to align with your breathing cycle. With this phrase, you will be practicing calling out to God with the in-breath, followed by petitioning God with a request with the out-breath. One of the most famous versions, drawn from Orthodox spirituality, is the Jesus Prayer: "Lord Jesus Christ, Son of God, have mercy on me." Furthermore, the body scan, utilized to cultivate self-compassion (Desmond, 2016), will be modified for you as a Christian; in this practice, you will spend 45 minutes slowly scanning your body, breathing God's presence into each region. As another practice to attend with compassion, in Ignatian spirituality, the "prayer of the senses" is commonly employed, helping Christians to experience Jesus in the gospels with our five God-given senses. With the "prayer of the senses" (drawn from the second week of *Spiritual Exercises*), you will be focusing on seeing, hearing, touching, and smelling to deepen your experience of a biblical story. In this biblical account, you will be cultivating compassion and mercy for yourself. To practice imagining with compassion, you will be engaging in visualization exercises so as to actually see yourself being loved and protected by God (e.g., picturing you are the younger son in the Parable of the Lost Son), and drawing from Ignatian spirituality to better understand the "mystery of the incarnation." Throughout the chapter, exercises, writing assignments, a guided meditation (with an audio file), and examples from the Bible are offered in order to help you attend and imagine with compassion on a deeper level.

The Importance of the Breath: Psychological and Christian Perspectives

In mindfulness meditation, breathing is an anchor to the present moment. When we learn to follow the breathing cycle with openness and non-judgment, we are cultivating focused, sustained attention, ameliorating the tendency for the mind to be scattered and dispersed throughout the day (Nhat Hanh, 1987). In this process, the idea is to simply watch the natural rhythm of our breathing, rather than trying to force it in any way. Stated differently, since our autonomic nervous system controls our breathing for us—through no effort of our own—we can learn to gently observe the entire breath cycle from moment to moment. In addition, when we slow down our breathing, we can begin to develop "calm mind" by getting into a "soothing breathing rhythm" (Gilbert, 2010). For many people, slowing down in life by watching the natural breath cycle can be an important way to attend with compassion.

In the Christian tradition, God gave Adam the "breath of life" (Genesis 2:7), which means that we are reliant upon God for the life he has given us (Hartley, 2012). In this passage of Scripture, "breath" is typically translated as "spirit" (McGrath, 2011). The famous Puritan writer Matthew Henry (1991) explained this second chapter of the Bible as follows:

> God is not only the former but the Father of spirits. Let the soul which God has breathed into us breathe after him; and let it be for him, since it is from him. Into his hands let us commit our spirits, for from his hands we had them.
>
> (p. 8)

From a Christian perspective, our breath captures God's providential care, given he generously offers us life in the here-and-now. In other words, we do not need to control our breathing in any way; rather, God guides our breath as we walk along the roads of life with him. If this is the case, by noticing our breathing, we can recognize that God is caring for us with the gift of life. With each in-breath and out-breath, we realize our utter dependence on God for survival, and can cultivate a sense of gratitude for God's life-sustaining role in daily living (Hoekema, 1986).

In relating our God-given breathing to the development of self-compassion, the very act of connecting to the breath cycle can help us to recognize God's love, compassion, mercy, grace, and forgiveness. As we learn to thank him for giving us life, we can simultaneously maintain an awareness of his providential care. Over and over again throughout our day, we can imagine that he is lovingly, compassionately, mercifully, and graciously breathing into us the "breath of life," reminiscent of Adam's first breath in the Garden of Eden. As a corollary concept, the compassion literature presents a method for breathing that can help us to cultivate compassion. Next, I will briefly review this technique, followed by a modified version for Christians with shame and self-judgments.

"Giving and Taking": A Compassion-Based Approach

With "giving and taking" meditation (also referred to as "compassionate breathing"), we imagine actually breathing in suffering and breathing out well-being (van den Brink & Koster, 2015). Thus, we may start the practice by breathing in physical pain, focusing on the area that brings us discomfort. Then, we shift towards breathing out well-being, imagining we are breathing in the dark and breathing out the light (Germer, 2009). In this practice, the goal is to relate to our most difficult inner experiences with compassion, rather than trying to avoid (or fight against) our inner pain

(Germer, 2009). For Christians, this practice can be modified so as to invite God into our pain (i.e., "taking") with the in-breath because he is the Suffering Servant (Isaiah 53), empathizes with our weaknesses (Hebrews 4:15), and is the source of love, compassion, mercy, and grace. In turn, we can hand him our struggles (i.e., "giving") with the out-breath so he can carry our burdens for us (Psalm 55:22; 1 Peter 5:7).

Breathing with Jesus: An Exercise

In the beginning of John's gospel, we read the following: "In [Jesus] was life, and that life was the light of all mankind. The light shines in the darkness, and the darkness has not overcome it" (John 1:4–5). In this passage, the gospel writer noted that Jesus is "the life-bringer and light-bearer," meaning that he is the source of both (Morris, 1995). Ultimately, Jesus offers us physical, spiritual, and eternal life, with his generous gift of life being "the light of men" (Gangel, 2000). Just like the light of the sun brings forth life in the physical world, Jesus is the source of a specific type of human life—eternal life—with his life functioning as a "light of all humankind" (Gundry, 2010).

In this exercise, I would like you to practice breathing in Jesus as the "life-bringer and light-bearer" (Morris, 1995), imagining that you are "taking" in his active, loving presence, then exhaling as you visualize "giving" him your psychological burdens (e.g., shame) so he can carry them for you. In other words, by breathing in Jesus' presence as the life-giving light, you are learning to rely on his compassionate care in the midst of your pain, with nowhere else to be and nothing else to do. As you access the "contentment" system (Gilbert, 2010), you are practicing gently resting in his presence, over and over again. Try to imagine Jesus holding your emotional pain—symbolized in the form of his life-giving light—without attempting to fix your feelings or suppress them in any way. Because Jesus is present, you can just be with him in your state of distress. Breathe in his presence (i.e., "taking"), then breathe out your pain (i.e., "giving"), as you envision he is holding you (including your pain) in his loving arms.

When you are ready, find a quiet environment that is free of distractions, sitting in a comfortable chair in an upright position. Close your eyes and place your feet on the floor in front of you. Now, begin to breathe in Jesus' presence, symbolized in the form of his life-giving light, recognizing that he is all you need in the midst of your enduring pain. He is the source of your physical, psychological, spiritual, and eternal life; thus, you can find comfort in his presence as he holds you in your distressed state. Try to imagine that Jesus is actively responding to your affective struggles from moment to moment. However, instead of fighting against the emotional pain (e.g., shame), just notice it, then attend to Jesus' presence. Because Jesus is with you, there is nothing you need to be doing, other than focusing on him.

If you can, try to carry on with this activity for about ten minutes, breathing in Jesus' presence ("taking," symbolized in the form of his life-giving light), then breathing out all of your efforts to fight against the pain ("giving" him your pain as you rest in his loving arms). As you exhale, imagine letting go of your tendency to avoid, wall off, suppress, or fix your emotional struggles. Instead, try to envision that Jesus is embracing your pain. He is all you need in this very moment.

When you have finished the exercise, journal for a few minutes, writing about the experience. You may want to reflect on your ability to allow Jesus to permeate your inner world, even as you struggle with emotional pain. Were you able to allow Jesus to be with you? Were you able to let your pain simply be, with Jesus by your side? What, if anything, got in the way of your ability to do so? Were you able to give him your unilateral efforts to fix the situation? What, if anything, was difficult about this process?

In addition to "giving and taking" meditations, the "body scan" can be a way to attend to your pain with compassion. In this exercise, you will be inviting Jesus into your physiological experience, scanning your body over a 45-minute period of time as you breathe in his presence.

The Body Scan: Attending to the Body

The "body scan" exercise is a popular strategy in the mindfulness literature to connect to our body in a non-judgmental way and cultivate acceptance towards painful experiences (Kabat-Zinn, 1990). Often, we can get into the unintentional habit of being lost in our thoughts, without an awareness of the amazing functions of our God-given body. In addition, we may become especially critical and shaming towards our body, including our physical appearance, without ever feeling comfortable in our own skin (Kabat-Zinn, 1990).

With the "body scan" (Kabat-Zinn, 1990), we are spending 45 minutes lying on our back in a comfortable position. In a quiet environment, we scan the entire body, moving from region to region as we inhale and exhale. For example, we may start with our left foot, then slowly scan the left leg, before moving to the right leg and right foot. Next, we might focus on our abdomen, before moving towards our arms, chest, neck, and so on. Within the context of the natural breathing cycle, we imagine inhaling to the particular region we are focused on, then exhaling from this same area. Over time, we are learning to attend to each region of the body in a non-judgmental way. When a thought or feeling comes up, we notice the experience with a calm curiosity, then shift our attention back to the particular region we are attending to. Ultimately, we are learning to just "be," rather than trying to fix or avoid unpleasant inner experiences (Kabat-Zinn, 1990).

The Body Scan for Christians: Breathing in God's Love, Mercy, and Grace

For Christians, the human body is God's dwelling place (1 Corinthians 6:19). Because of this, we can learn to accept our physiological experiences, recognizing that God is present. Rather than engaging in the "body scan" on our own, though, God is with us. Thus, we can learn to breathe in his love, compassion, mercy, and grace from moment to moment and bodily region to bodily region. In doing so, we are developing self-compassion for our body, as well as acceptance as we learn to sit patiently at Jesus' feet (Luke 10:38–42).

The Body Scan for Christians: An Exercise

In this exercise (adapted from Kabat-Zinn, 1990), please set aside 45 minutes. Find a quiet environment, free from distractions. Lay down with your back to the floor and eyes closed. Begin to notice your breathing, recognizing that God is generously caring for you as you effortlessly breathe in and out during this time. Spend a couple of minutes just noticing your breathing cycle, including God's life-sustaining role. As you breathe, imagine that you are inhaling God's unlimited love, compassion, mercy, and grace, recognizing that he is loving you from second to second, even as you may be struggling with psychological pain. In turn, exhale your emotional pain, handing it to God so he can do with it what he pleases. Imagine that he is holding it for you, compassionately embracing you in this moment. When your mind begins to get distracted, just notice that your focus has shifted, before gently and non-judgmentally returning to your breathing.

Next, shift your focus to your left foot, imagining you are breathing God's love, compassion, mercy, and grace into this region of your body. Recognize that God has given you a foot, including the miracle of movement in this bodily area. He has even created your bones and skin, and knows what you need in this very moment.

Now, breathe out any pain you may be having, handing it over to God. Rather than trying to avoid your physical pain, though, imagine that God is holding it for you. Even if the pain remains, he is carrying this experience for you, and has your best intentions in mind. In other words, his providential care extends to even the smallest bones in your left foot, as well as the aches and pains you may be feeling. When you notice that your mind has drifted, gently return to your left foot, breathing in God's love, compassion, mercy, and grace, then breathing out the entire experience by surrendering it to him.

Continue with this exercise for 45 minutes, scanning each part of your body. As you do so, invite God into the experience by breathing in his love, then breathing out as you hand him your aches and pains. Practice non-judgment and acceptance in this time, recognizing that God is in control of the situation. He has given you this body, and is carrying you through this 45-minute event.

Once you have finished, thank God for giving you this life, which includes the inevitable aches and pains of daily living. Acknowledge that he has generously given you this body, allowing you to move about on the roads of life with him by your side. Although you may continue to struggle with physical ailments, each breath you take symbolizes his life-sustaining providence.

The Jesus Prayer Within the Bible

In addition to a Christian version of the "body scan," the Jesus Prayer—"Lord Jesus Christ, Son of God, have mercy on me"—can be a way to experience God's presence through the vehicle of your God-given breathing cycle. In the New Testament, variations of the Greek word, *eleos*, are used over a dozen types to capture people asking Jesus for mercy (e.g., Matthew 17:15; Luke 18:38). For example, in Matthew's gospel (17:15, italics added), we read the following passage:

> When they came to the crowd, a man approached Jesus and knelt before him. "Lord, have *mercy* on my son," he said. "He has seizures and is suffering greatly. He often falls into the fire or into the water."

Jesus responded to the man's request by healing the boy (Matthew 17:18), revealing Jesus' responsiveness to the suffering that was in front of him. In your own life, Jesus is ready to compassionately respond to your pain, reminiscent of his consistent, loving action in Scripture.

The Jesus Prayer Within Orthodox Spirituality: A Brief History

To review from the first chapter, Christians began to move to the deserts of Egypt, Palestine, and Syria in the first few hundred years after Jesus' life in order to get away from the materialism that dominated their respective societies. Upon moving to the desert, they attempted to face their inner temptations and cultivate a deeper, more intimate relationship with God (Burton-Christie, 1993), resembling Jesus' 40 days in the wilderness (Matthew 4:1–11).

Over time, they recited Scripture to focus their attention on God, pivoting from the tempting, compulsive thoughts they often struggled with in the desert terrain (Laird, 2011). Eventually, the Jesus Prayer, an *apophatic* form of meditation, developed: "Lord Jesus Christ, Son of God, have mercy on me" (Laird, 2011). When reciting the Jesus Prayer, we are striving to meet a variety of foundational goals (adapted from Johnson, 2010; Ware, 2000):

- We are focusing our attention on God (the Greek word, *proseuch*).
- We are remembering God (the Greek phrase, *mneme theou*).
- We are watching the inner world with vigilance and awareness (the Greek word, *nepsis*).
- We are cultivating a peaceful inner state (the Greek word, *hesychia*).
- We are relating differently to negative thoughts by repeatedly pivoting towards God.

In the context of shame and self-judgments, the Jesus Prayer can help us to focus on God, remember God, and notice our self-critical thoughts with increased awareness. As we repeatedly shift towards God, we are learning to let go of our preoccupation with shame, given we are pivoting from ourselves to God over and over again. In this process, we are attempting to develop a sustained inner peace, in that God is with us in both formal and informal practice.

In a recent study, I found that the Jesus Prayer can be helpful in reducing stress and improving the ability to surrender to God over a two-week period of time (Knabb & Vazquez, 2018). Although the Jesus Prayer has been used among Christians as a spiritual strategy for hundreds of years, the practice can also be used as a psychological intervention in the 21st century. As mentioned previously, I also found success in using the Jesus Prayer in an eight-week program for Christians with daily worry (Knabb et al., 2017). What follows is an exercise to help you formally practice the Jesus Prayer, learning to shift your focus to him when you experience shame and negative self-evaluations.

The Jesus Prayer: An Exercise[1]

To prepare for this ten-minute exercise, please find a quiet environment that is free from distractions. Sit in a comfortable chair, with your hands in your lap and feet on the floor. Sit up straight and close your eyes. Please consider using the corresponding audio recording, "Track 6," available at https://www.routledge.com/The-Compassion-Based-Workbook-for-Christian-Clients-Finding-Freedom-from/Knabb/p/book/9780815394365.

Now, start to notice that you are breathing. God is giving you your breath as a generous gift from moment to moment. With each passing second, you do not need to do anything, other than rest in God's care.

After a minute, start to slowly and gently recite the Jesus Prayer in your mind: "Lord Jesus Christ, Son of God, have mercy on me." Try to breathe in with the first half, "Lord Jesus Christ, Son of God," acknowledging that Jesus is the Lord of your inner world in this very moment. Then, attempt to breathe out with the second half, "have mercy on me," exhaling so as to let go of your own efforts to define who you are by criticizing yourself. Over and over, inhale and exhale, aligning the prayer with your breathing cycle in a compassionate manner. Recognize that Jesus is offering you his mercy during this ten-minute practice.

As the practice concludes, thank Jesus for this time, acknowledging that his love, compassion, mercy, grace, and forgiveness are all you need. He is your author; therefore, you can let go of your own efforts to define your worth and value. Ask him to continue to be with you throughout your day, turning to him by practicing the Jesus Prayer whenever you are experiencing shame and self-judgments.

In the space that follows, please record your efforts over the next week.[2]

Day/Date	*Practice (Yes/No)*	*Comments*
Wednesday Date: ________	*Apophatic* Meditation:	
Thursday Date: ________	*Apophatic* Meditation:	
Friday Date: ________	*Apophatic* Meditation:	
Saturday Date: ________	*Apophatic* Meditation:	
Sunday Date: ________	*Apophatic* Meditation:	
Monday Date: ________	*Apophatic* Meditation:	
Tuesday Date: ________	*Apophatic* Meditation:	

Beyond the Jesus Prayer, there are other formal prayers that you can practice within the Christian tradition, referred to as "breath prayers." Although the Jesus Prayer is typically considered the most popular version, once you know the ingredients, you can come up with your own "breath prayers" based on Scripture.

Breath Prayers in the Christian Tradition

In the Christian tradition, breath prayers are a way to align our breathing with a prayer to God. With the in-breath, we call upon God by name, then petition him with a heartfelt request with the out-breath (Calhoun, 2015). Although the Jesus Prayer is the most famous breath prayer, once we understand the two steps, we can come up with our own so as to converse with God during formal or informal practice.

Possible breath prayers for shame (inspired by Scripture) include the following:

- Forgiving God, have compassion on me (Nehemiah 9:17).
- Living God, care for me (Jeremiah 10:10).
- Faithful God, love me (Deuteronomy 7:9).
- Ever-present God, be with me (Isaiah 7:14).
- Peaceful God, protect me (Judges 6:24).
- Lord Jesus, save me (Matthew 14:22–23).

Designing Your Own Breath Prayers: An Exercise

In this exercise, you will have the opportunity to come up with your own breath prayers. Remember, the first part consists of God's name, followed by some sort of request to God. If possible, try to link each breath prayer to a passage in the Bible, consistent with my examples. Although you can come up with more than six, try to start with half a dozen breath prayers, using them throughout the day by aligning them with your in-breath and out-breath. If possible, try to keep them short, given you want to be able to experience them on a deeper level and quickly remember them in your time of need.

Passage in the Bible	Name for God (First Part of the Breath Prayer)	Petition to God (Second Part of the Breath Prayer)

One of the most important parts of the breath prayer is our ability to cry out to God when we need him the most, consistent with Peter's experience with Jesus in Matthew's gospel.

"Lord, Save Me": Crying Out to God in the Midst of Pain

Like Peter walking towards Jesus on the water (Matthew 14:22–33), you may have moments of confidence as you get out of your proverbial boat. Yet, at other times, you may feel like you are sinking, struggling to keep your eyes on God. By cultivating focused, sustained attention, you will be working on steadily walking towards Jesus, especially when you are in pain. Returning to the story of Peter and Jesus in Matthew's gospel, when Peter started to sink, Jesus "immediately reached out his hand and caught him," suggesting he is ready to respond to your needs during moments of shame and self-doubt.

In the next exercise, you will be learning to recognize God's presence throughout your day, keeping your eyes on him when you begin to sink in your shame and self-doubt. Following this practice, you will have the opportunity to deepen your understanding of Scripture by using your God-given senses to be with Jesus in the midst of your shame. In both practices, my hope is that you will continue to keep your eyes on God, developing focused, sustained attention so as to steadily walk towards him whenever the storms of life distract you from this life-giving relationship.

The Practice of the Presence of God with Brother Lawrence

Brother Lawrence, a Carmelite monk who lived in the 1600s, was a cook and sandal maker (Lawrence, 2015). In his humble life, he wrote about the importance of recognizing God's presence from moment to moment:

> We must continually apply ourselves so that all our actions, without exception, become a kind of brief conversation with God, not in a contrived manner but coming from the purity and simplicity of our hearts.
>
> (Lawrence, 2015, p. 38)

Throughout the day, we have countless opportunities to talk to God, reminiscent of having a pleasant conversation with a friend as we travel across the country on a winding road in a comfortable car. In fact, one such way to do so involves inviting God into our daily activities—even the tasks that seem unimportant, as Brother Lawrence revealed:

> We must perform all our actions carefully and deliberately, not impulsively or hurriedly, for such would characterize a distracted mind. We must work gently and lovingly with God, asking him to accept our work.
>
> (Lawrence, 2015, p. 38)

When starting this lifelong process, Brother Lawrence advocated for the use of a short phrase in order to repeatedly remember God's presence in the activities of the day:

> It would be appropriate for beginners to formulate a few words interiorly, such as: "My God, I am completely yours," or "God of love, I love you with all my heart," or "Lord, fashion me according to your heart," or any other words love spontaneously produces.
>
> (Lawrence, 2015, p. 44)

In the next exercise, you will have the opportunity to attend with compassion by inviting God into a daily activity. Remember, you can focus your attention on God's active, loving presence within even the most trivial tasks. In doing so, you are simultaneously cultivating compassion for yourself and others and bringing the world to life, given the Creator of the universe is right by your side from second to second and minute to minute.

Practicing God's Presence: An Exercise

In this next exercise, I would like you to select an activity that you engage in daily, such as brushing your teeth or washing the dishes. When completing this task, strive to focus your attention on God's active, loving presence, silently repeating Brother Lawrence's phrase, "My God, I am completely yours." As you carry out the required chore, recognize that God is offering you his love, compassion, mercy, grace, and forgiveness in this very moment. What is more, God is pleased when you carry out even the most insignificant tasks by giving glory to him (1 Corinthians 10:31; Colossians 3:17).

When you are finished, try to reflect on the activity by answering the following questions:

What was it like to complete the chore with your attention focused on God? Were you able to experience the activity differently, given God was with you? In completing the task, how well were you able to receive God's love, compassion, mercy, grace, and forgiveness? What, if anything, might have gotten in the way? How can you extend this practice to other activities so you are deepening your relationship with God throughout your day, drawing from his infinite love, compassion, mercy, grace, and forgiveness from moment to moment?

Ignatian Spirituality and the "Prayer of the Senses"[3]

Within Ignatian spirituality, the *Spiritual Exercises* (a collection of prayers, meditations, and exercises written by Ignatius Loyola) can assist you in developing a more intimate union with God (Ignatian Spirituality, n.d.). Specifically, the "prayer of the senses" (presented in the second week of *Spiritual Exercises*) can help you to use all five senses—sight, sound, taste, touch, and smell—to embed yourself in a biblical story (Hansen, 2012). By feeling your way into Scripture, you will be positioning yourself to have an important talk with Jesus, conversing within him so as to experience him in a new, more compassionate manner. In other words, in this prayer, you will be learning to receive his love, compassion, mercy, grace, and forgiveness in order to relate differently to shame and self-criticism.

There are at least four important ingredients within the "prayer of the senses," including (a) selecting a gospel story to meditate on for a predetermined amount of time; (b) asking God to guide the exercise by inviting him into the experience and presenting him with several salient questions; (c) employing the five senses to embed yourself in the biblical story, leading to a conversation with Jesus that involves actually asking him the aforementioned questions; and (d) patiently waiting for Jesus to reply to your questions, listening as he responds to your needs (Hansen, 2012).

In the next exercise, you will have the opportunity to talk with Jesus, inserting yourself into a famous gospel story and using your senses to bring the biblical account to life. As you experience the narrative on a new level, remember to imagine that you are face-to-face with your Lord and Savior; thus, you have the opportunity to personally ask him questions, and patiently wait for his reply.

The "Prayer of the Senses": An Exercise[4]

To start this ten-minute exercise, slowly read the following section in Scripture (John 8:1–11).

> Jesus returned to the Mount of Olives, but early the next morning he was back again at the Temple. A crowd soon gathered, and he sat down and taught them. As he was speaking, the teachers of religious law and the Pharisees brought a woman who had been caught in the act of adultery. They put her in front of the crowd. "Teacher," they said to Jesus, "this woman was caught in the act of adultery. The law of Moses says to stone her. What do you say?" They were trying to trap him into saying something they could use against him, but Jesus stooped down and wrote in the dust with his finger. They kept demanding an answer, so he stood up again and said, "All right, but let the one who has never sinned throw the first stone!" Then he stooped down again and wrote in the dust. When the accusers heard this, they slipped away one by one, beginning with the oldest, until only Jesus was left in the middle of the crowd with the woman. Then Jesus stood up again and said to the woman, "Where are your accusers? Didn't even one of them condemn you?" "No, Lord," she said. And Jesus said, "Neither do I. Go and sin no more."

As you read this section of John's gospel, try to imagine a situation that involved feeling tremendous shame, reminiscent of the "woman caught in adultery." Try to remember this particular feeling of shame, along with the corresponding judgment from others. Imagine what you might have needed in this painful moment, as you felt isolated and alone.

Next, spend a few moments with God, asking him to reveal two questions that you would like to ask Jesus towards the end of the "prayer of the senses." Write your two questions below in preparation for the rest of the exercise:

1. ____
____
2. ____
____

Once you have written down your questions, return to the story of the "woman caught in adultery." Imagine that you are this person who has been brought before Jesus. Use your senses to bring this scene to life. Consider the smell in the air, the heat of the sun on your face, the dust under your feet, and the cool temperature at the Temple. Listen to the crowd surrounding you, including their murmuring judgments. Take a look around, watching the scene quickly unfold.

Try to imagine that you are standing in front of Jesus, with the hostile crowd circling you. Feel the shame, given you are seemingly isolated and alone. In the midst of this pain, Jesus stands up, proclaiming, "Let the one who has never sinned throw the first stone!" As you watch Jesus confidently assert himself before the crowd, you suddenly feel much less alone, given he is not condemning you. Next, you watch him lean down to draw something in the dirt in front of you. As you are observing Jesus writing, the crowd slowly begins to disappear. In fact, the murmurs and accusations fade away as people head in another direction. While the sun is shining on your face, you look towards Jesus, making eye contact with him for the first time.

As he speaks to you, he tells you he does not condemn you for your past behaviors. In this moment, your shame is lifted as you recognize he is loving you with his perfect compassion, mercy, grace, and forgiveness. The Temple is quiet, and you are alone with your Lord and Savior.

Now, ask Jesus the questions you previously wrote down, waiting patiently for his loving response. Savor this time with him, basking in his compassionate attentiveness. In this very moment, there is nowhere else to be and nothing else to do, other than listening for his merciful reply.

Upon completing the exercise, write down your thoughts about the "prayer of the senses." What was it like to embed yourself in this famous biblical story, culminating in your questions to Jesus? How did Jesus reply? What did he say to you? What might have gotten in the way of utilizing your God-given senses to experience Jesus' compassionate, merciful reply? How can you continue to receive Jesus' love when experiencing shame, remembering his famous reply: "Didn't even one of them condemn you. . .Neither do I."

____
____
____
____
____
____

Beyond using our senses to spend time with Jesus in a famous biblical story, we can find ways to visualize God's active, loving presence in daily living. In this next section, you will have the opportunity to visualize spending time with God, and imagine that his outstretched arms are welcoming you home.

Visualizing with Compassion: Psychological and Christian Perspectives

Using visualizations and our imagination can be a way to cultivate self- and other-compassion (Germer, 2009). For example, rather than automatically believing your judgmental thoughts about yourself, you can imagine that they are like cars slowly driving by on the street. Instead of seeing yourself as the cars, you can visualize that you are sitting in the living room of your home, safely observing the cars passing by through your front window. Because you are just watching the cars on a peaceful Sunday afternoon, there is nothing you need to do, other than simply notice all of the different colors, shapes, sizes, and so on. In this time, just imagine that your self-critical thoughts are written on the side of each car as it moves in and out of your field of vision.

From a Christian perspective, we can develop compassion for ourselves and others when we are aware of God's active, loving presence from moment to moment. Within Orthodox spirituality, this intrapsychic experience is called *hesychia*, capturing a calm inner stillness. In this state of silence, we are at peace with our thoughts, which have settled because we are focused on God. In the context of shame and self-criticism, we are content to simply rest in God's presence, accessing the "contentment" system (Gilbert, 2010) in our time with him.

In the next exercise, I would like you to turn to the first book of the Bible for inspiration, imagining what it might have been like to be with Noah on the ark, trusting in God's providential care as the flood waters surrounded you.

Floating on the Ark with Compassion: An Exercise[5]

To begin this exercise, imagine that God has selected you to board the famous ark with Noah (Genesis 6:22–8:22). Upon closing the large door to the wooden vessel, you look out at God's creation, knowing that the rain will eventually flood the land and destroy both your town and home. Yet, you also know that you will be safe in spite of the chaos outside, given that God is infinitely good, wise, and powerful. In fact, his providential care is guiding this entire process, and you are safely resting in his loving hands.

As you get used to your new home on the ark—at least for the coming days and weeks—you recognize there are a variety of distractions. You smell the stench of dirty animals, and can hear the odd sounds of creatures lined up and down the boat. Outside the ship, you see the rain tumbling down, and hear its loud impact when hitting the ground. Whether the distractions come from inside or outside the large wooden vessel, you are still able to feel loved in knowing that God is guiding the process. Certainly, because you are being held in the palm of his hand, there is nowhere else you need to be and nothing else you need to do. In this moment, your task is to simply feel safe and loved on Noah's ark.

When a self-critical thought arises, similar to the distractions around you on Noah's gigantic wooden boat, see if you can just notice it, then return to an awareness of God's loving, protective care. Because God is with you on the ark, guiding each and every step, you can just rest in his presence, without getting overwhelmed by the animals inside or rain outside.

As you notice the busyness of the day—the destructive storm outside and unfamiliar creatures inside—you are able to gently return to an awareness of God's presence, knowing that he has chosen you to take the next step forward to rebuild humanity. Because of this awareness of God's providence, you are able to be still and quiet, resting in his presence. Based on the notion that God is guiding the ark, you are able to remain focused on him, rather than the distractions around you.

In this very moment, God is caring for you, and you have "found favor in the eyes of the Lord" (Genesis 6:8), just like Noah. You may even want to repeat this phrase to capture the safety, comfort, and protection that God is giving you as you float on the flood waters, surrounded by chaos inside and outside the boat: "I have found favor in the eyes of the Lord." Because of Jesus' redemptive work on the cross, you have been reconciled with God (Colossians 1:19–20). As a result, God has invited you into his loving arms, reminiscent of a father welcoming home a lost son (Luke 15:11–32).

Next, try to reflect on the experience, journaling some of your thoughts about the visualization exercise. Some possible questions to get you started include the following:

1. What might Noah have experienced on the wooden ark, with chaos both inside and outside the boat? How did he maintain his trust in God, despite the uncertainty he experienced?
2. In your own experience of shame and self-doubt, how can you look to God for guidance, consistent with safely residing in Noah's floating boat while God controls each unfolding moment around you?

The Lost Son: An Exercise

In this next exercise, I would like you to imagine that you are like the younger son in the Parable of the Lost Son (Luke 15:11–32). You have asked your father for your inheritance and have traveled around the world to spend this newly acquired money. After a period of time, though, you realize you are down to your last dollar and can no longer support your lifestyle.

In the midst of your shame, you recognize that you must travel home to ask for your father's forgiveness. In making this decision, your shame only grows, given you recognize you have fallen well short of your father's expectations. As the day to trek home approaches, you are highly critical of yourself, convinced you are unworthy of your father's love.

Walking up the driveway of your father's home, you see him standing on the porch. Upon making eye contact, you see him start to run to you, with compassion in his eyes. In fact, his arms are outstretched, and he embraces you as he meets you on the familiar driveway.

Now, spend a few minutes imagining what this experience might be like with God, visualizing God embracing you as you ask him for forgiveness. Instead of condemning you, God is holding you and kissing you, telling you all about the celebration he is planning for you because you are safely home in his loving arms. Try to just sit in this awareness, imagining that God is overjoyed with compassion for you, given you have finally traveled home.

To conclude the exercise, reflect on this experience, journaling your thoughts and feelings about the visualization task. Questions to consider:

1. What might the younger son have experienced as he was being held by his father?
2. In your own experience of shame and self-doubt, how can you allow yourself to be embraced by God, feeling his compassion as you travel home after a period of wandering?
3. How can you remember to visualize the ending of the Parable of the Lost Son (the father's compassionate, accepting embrace of an ashamed son) so as to access the "contentment" system (Gilbert, 2010) when you are experiencing shame and self-criticism?

The "Mystery of the Incarnation": An Exercise

To conclude this workbook, I would like to offer one last exercise, building on your experience of being embraced and kissed by God in the midst of your shame. Within Ignatian spirituality, the second week of the *Spiritual Exercises* offers an exercise (Ignatian Spirituality, n.d.) for imagining how God viewed the world before the incarnation. In particular, God observed how horribly we were treating each other, as humans. As a result, he sent his Son in order to offer us redemption in the midst of our estrangement from him and each other.

In this exercise, try to imagine what God might have seen as he looked to our planet prior to sending his Son. Visualize all of the violence and turmoil between humans, even in your own life. Really try to get a sense of what God might have seen in preparation for the incarnation.

In the midst of what he saw, God offered his Son as a compassionate reply to our interpersonal estrangement from him and each other. Although we were separated from him, he chose to reconcile us by way of his atoning work on the cross. Try to really visualize God sending his Son to fulfill this purpose, in response to the suffering, pain, and violence he observed.

To conclude this exercise, pray to God, asking how you can more faithfully follow him in the midst of your struggles, and ask for his love, compassion, mercy, grace, and forgiveness in spite of your enduring shortcomings. Because he responded to humankind via the incarnation and atonement, you can have confidence that you are being guided by his providential care from moment to moment.

Conclusion

In the seventh and final chapter, you worked on attending and imagining with compassion and mercy towards yourself. The goal was to help you relate differently to difficult inner experiences by inviting God into the process, using visualizations and imagery to connect to your "contentment" system (Gilbert, 2010) during moments of shame and self-doubt. To do this, you learned to scan your body with God, breathe with God, recite prayers with God, and use the senses to deepen your experience of a famous passage in Scripture. Like Peter walking towards Jesus on the water (Matthew 14:22–33), you practiced keeping your eyes on your Lord and Savior during moments of self-doubt.

To bring this workbook to a close, you have practiced thinking, feeling, behaving, and attending and imagining with compassion, working towards accessing your God-given "contentment" system (Gilbert, 2010), deepening your attachment bond with God, and improving your image of him in the process. My hope is that your eyes have shifted from focusing on yourself to God, similar to exchanging a mirror for a window. In other words, rather than holding up a mirror, which solely reveals your self-reflection, my desire is that you are now looking through a window towards God, who shines his proverbial sun rays of hope and love through the transparent glass pane from moment to moment.

Ultimately, my wish is that this time has been well spent, given that God created you in his image (Genesis 1:27) and is constantly pursuing you; in fact, whenever you wander away, he celebrates when you come back to him (Luke 15). Therefore, at the center of your experience of shame and self-criticism, God's arms are outstretched, patiently awaiting your return to him.

To summarize our time together, I would like to end this workbook with the following passage in Scripture (Psalm 131), which captures the importance of accessing your God-given "contentment" system (Gilbert, 2010) in your time of need. To be sure, rather than working towards unilaterally growing, expanding, or inflating your sense of self in response to shame (possibly heading in the opposite direction to God in the process), God is offering you his perfect comfort, safety, and tranquility in this very instance (Dunn & Rogerson, 2003).

> My heart is not proud, Lord, my eyes are not haughty; I do not concern myself with great matters or things too wonderful for me. But I have calmed and quieted myself, I am like a weaned child with its mother; like a weaned child I am content. Israel, put your hope in the Lord both now and forevermore.

As the psalmist revealed, God offers us soothing comfort from moment to moment, reminiscent of the safety of a mother's arms. In our daily efforts to reach for God, he calms and quiets our shame and self-criticism when we put our hope in *him*, not our own understanding of who we are or personal attempts to arbitrarily assign self-value.

Notes

1 This exercise is adapted from Knabb and Vazquez (2018) and Talbot (2013).
2 This form is adapted from Segal et al. (2012).
3 This section is adapted from Knabb and Frederick (2017).
4 This exercise is adapted from Hansen (2012) and Knabb and Frederick (2017).
5 This exercise is adapted from Knabb (2016) and influenced by Saint-Jure and Colombiere (1980).

References

Burton-Christie, D. (1993). *The word in the desert: Scripture and the quest for holiness in early Christian monasticism*. New York: Oxford University Press.

Calhoun, A. (2015). *Spiritual disciplines handbook: Practices that transform us*. Downers Grove, IL: InterVarsity Press.

Desmond, T. (2016). *Self-compassion in psychotherapy: Mindfulness-based practices for healing and transformation*. New York: W. W. Norton & Company, Inc.

Dunn, J., & Rogerson, J. (2003). *Eerdmans commentary on the Bible*. Grand Rapids, MI: William B. Eerdmans Publishing Company.

Gangel, K. (2000). *Holman New Testament commentary: John*. Nashville, TN: B&H Publishing Group.

Germer, C. (2009). *The mindful path to self-compassion: Freeing yourself from destructive thoughts and emotions*. New York: The Guilford Press.

Gilbert, P. (2010). *Compassion focused therapy: Distinctive features*. New York: Routledge.

Gundry, R. (2010). *Commentary on John*. Grand Rapids, MI: Baker Academic.

Hansen, G. (2012). *Kneeling with giants: Learning to pray with history's best teachers*. Downers Grove, IL: InterVarsity Press.

Hartley, J. (2012). *Genesis*. Grand Rapids, MI: Baker Books.

Henry, M. (1991). *Matthew Henry's commentary on the whole Bible*. Peabody, MA: Hendrickson Publishers, LLC.

Hoekema, A. (1986). *Created in God's image*. Grand Rapids, MI: Wm. B. Eerdmans Publishing Co.

Ignatian Spirituality. (n.d.). *The spiritual exercises*. Retrieved January 22, 2018 from www.ignatianspirituality.com
Johnson, C. (2010). *The globalization of hesychasm and the Jesus prayer: Contesting contemplation*. New York: Continuum.
Kabat-Zinn, J. (1990). *Full catastrophe living: Using the wisdom of your body and mind to face stress, pain, and illness*. New York: Bantam Dell.
Knabb, J. (2016). *Acceptance and commitment therapy for Christian clients: A faith-based workbook*. New York: Routledge.
Knabb, J., & Frederick, T. (2017). *Contemplative prayer for Christians with chronic worry: An eight-week program*. New York: Routledge.
Knabb, J., Frederick, T., & Cumming, G. (2017). Surrendering to God's providence: A three-part study on providence-focused therapy for recurrent worry (PFT-RW). *Psychology of Religion and Spirituality, 9*(2), 180–196.
Knabb, J., & Vazquez, V. (2018). A randomized controlled trial of a 2-week Internet-based contemplative prayer program for Christians with daily stress. *Spirituality in Clinical Practice, 5*(1), 37–53.
Laird, M. (2011). *A sunlit absence: Silence, awareness, and contemplation*. New York: Oxford University Press.
Lawrence, B. (2015). *The practice of the presence of God* (S. Sciurba, Trans.). Washington, DC: ICS Publications.
McGrath, A. (2011). *Christian theology: An introduction*. Oxford: Blackwell Publishers Ltd.
Morris, L. (1995). *The gospel according to John*. Grand Rapids, MI: Wm. B. Eerdmans Publishing Co.
Nhat Hanh, T. (1987). *The miracle of mindfulness: An introduction to the practice of meditation*. Boston, MA: Beacon Press.
Saint-Jure, J., & Colombiere, C. (1980). *Trustful surrender to divine providence: The secret to peace and happiness*. Charlotte, NC: TAN Books.
Segal, Z., Williams, M., & Teasdale, J. (2012). *Mindfulness-based cognitive therapy for depression* (2nd ed.). New York: The Guilford Press.
Talbot, J. (2013). *The Jesus prayer: A cry for mercy, a path of renewal*. Downers Grove, IL: InterVarsity Press.
van den Brink, E., & Koster, F. (2015). *Mindfulness-based compassionate living: A new training programme to deepen mindfulness with heartfulness*. New York: Routledge.
Ware, K. (2000). *The inner kingdom*. Crestwood, NY: St. Vladimir's Seminary Press.

INDEX

For Product Safety Concerns and Information please contact our EU representative GPSR@taylorandfrancis.com
Taylor & Francis Verlag GmbH, Kaufingerstraße 24, 80331 München, Germany

www.ingramcontent.com/pod-product-compliance
Lightning Source LLC
LaVergne TN
LVHW080810011026
849160LV00015B/1588

9780815394365